PRAISE FOR *100 Days in Vietnam*

"For all of us coming of age in the class of 1969, the Vietnam War was always looming. After receiving a draft notice post-graduation, Joe Tallon scratched and clawed his way through Army training, ultimately finding himself in Vietnam by 1972. His resiliency and strength to overcome shine through in this poignant survival story told in tandem by father and son."

—**Mike Krzyzewski**, Head Coach, Duke University, West Point Class of 1969

"Joseph Tallon's story, told through his wartime letters, recollections, and the words of his son, is a moving account of an American family's experience with war, loss, and remembrance. *100 Days in Vietnam* offers readers both a rare window on the final days of our painful national odyssey in Vietnam and a remarkable record of an individual's determined quest to honor a fallen comrade."

—**Ken Burns**, Filmmaker and Director of *The Vietnam War, The Civil War,* and many other films

"Father and son Army veterans Joseph and Matthew sing a soulful duet of remembrance and revelation in this evocative narrative of love and war, suffering and struggle, resilience and healing. *100 Days in Vietnam*, a cross-generational memoir, offers us rare insights into the deep bonds of friendship, the ravages and gifts of survival, and the complex meanings of a true patriotism."

—**Sara Lawrence-Lightfoot**, Emily Hargroves Fisher Research Professor of Education, Harvard University, and Author of *Balm in Gilead: Journey of a Healer* and *Exit: The Endings That Set Us Free*, among other books

"*100 Days in Vietnam* is a remarkable firsthand account of one man's experience of war. Framed by stories of his own father and son, it is a moving tribute to the traditions of honor, respect, affection, and sacrifice shared by three generations of a single family. In gifting this story to the public, Matthew Tallon has taken a little piece of history, made it personal, and brought it home."

—**Christina Thompson, PhD**, Editor of Harvard Review, and Author of *Sea People: The Puzzle of Polynesia*

"A father–son team tells a great story about Vietnam combat service in the Army's air force. Joseph Tallon's time was spent as a Mohawk pilot flying recon missions into North Vietnam. His story is sandwiched between daily letters exchanged with his wife back home. His tour of duty ends with an engine shot out by enemy fire and a crash landing and fire that killed his observer and severely burned Tallon. Highly recommend this book!"

> —**Joseph L. Galloway**, Co-Author of *We Were Soldiers Once . . . And Young, We Are Soldiers Still*, and *They Were Soldiers: The Sacrifices and Contributions of Our Vietnam Veterans*

"Superbly written, rife with humility, heart, and a relentless sense of hope and longing, *100 Days in Vietnam* is a tale of love, war, recovery, remembrance, and the pursuit to honor those who don't always get recognized in the after-action reports, the homecoming parades, or the headlines featuring hometown heroes. Former Army pilot Joseph F. Tallon's day-to-day musings and letters home are at times reminiscent of Joseph Heller's *Catch-22*. Joe Tallon does a great job capturing both the mundane and those life-altering moments when mayhem and tragedy strikes. His eldest son, Matthew A. Tallon, a gifted writer and former Army officer, opens and closes the story with prose so beautifully rendered you are compelled to keep reading. Matt writes lovingly of his grandfather, a WWII veteran, whose death is the catalyst that starts the journey to bring this book into the world. With empathy and compassion, both father and son weave a story you will not soon forget."

> —**Kathleen M. Rodgers**, 2020 MWSA Founder's Award Winner, Author of *The Flying Cutterbucks*

"In this beautifully rendered portrait of a great hero fighting the tragic Vietnam War, and then explaining what he had to cope with afterward, Matthew Tallon provides deep insights into the lives of those who fight our wars when ordered to, and what they suffer when it's over."

> —**George C. Daughan**, Author of *Revolution on the Hudson* and *Lexington and Concord*

"A book about an American journey of one of the few who served and sacrificed. A must-read to understand the personal feelings of the soldier and those who loved him and in many ways shared in that sacrifice. Every time you see someone who has worn the cloth of this nation, remember the freedoms you enjoy are not free. Joe Tallon was a special American soldier. Semper Fi."

> —**James E. Livingston**, Major General, USMC (Retired), Medal of Honor Recipient

"Every now and again, we have the opportunity to set the wrongs of life right. *100 Days in Vietnam* tells the story of Lt. Col. Joseph Tallon's quest to right the wrongs. It is a story of devotion between brothers, between husband and wife, and between father and son. If only we were all so willing to sacrifice in order to lift up others."

—**Karen Spears Zacharias**, Author of *After the Flag has Been Folded*

"In 1972, it was a privilege to share a rare moment with Lt. Joseph Tallon. This must-read book brought back a flood of memories and profound perspectives. Our forgotten warriors deserve respect and honor for their dedication, sacrifice, and service to our nation. I'm proud to be associated with these patriots!"

—**Laurel Lea Schaefer**, Miss America 1972

"From the Greatest Generation to the Vietnam War and beyond, the warrior ethos is the thread that bonds and shows itself as we look back through the lens of battle staff rides like the one Matt describes in his introduction and further illuminates so poignantly . . . always remembered and never forgotten."

—**Stephen E. Farmen**, Major General, US Army (Retired)

"So powerful is the story of one person fighting not only for his life but for all America. This is a most vivid and gut-wrenching actual report of one man's struggle for not only his life but the lives of so many he never met or knew. How can we as Americans ever forget those who placed our country above themselves? I know there were protesters and marchers, but the fact of his focus on mission tells the story of a hero who sacrificed everything to the limits of life. I look forward to this publication being shared with those of us who went and served America, as well as with our next generation, who today are preparing to be tomorrow's warriors."

—**George Patton (Pat) Waters**, Grandson of General George S. Patton, Jr.

"Starting with a childhood on Charleston's Bull Street and culminating with a Purple Heart quest in Summerville some sixty-six years later, Joe's story is steeped in the South Carolina Lowcountry. Whether he's surviving a plane crash on the last day of the American ground war, meeting Miss America in the China Beach hospital, getting the attentive support of Betty Ford at a White House visit, or surviving a horrible storm off Morris Island on a shrimp boat with his cousin Bubba, Joe's serendipitous adventures would bring a smile to the face of any Forrest Gump fan. The beautiful love story with his wife sustains him on a long, winding road of recovery. Joe's story is a magnificent one told quite well in concert by father and son."

—**Joseph P. Riley, Jr**, Former Mayor of Charleston (1975–2016), Professor of American Government and Public Policy at The Citadel

"*100 Days in Vietnam* grounds the story of Joe Tallon's military service not only in the act of heroism and survival that defined his career, but also in the common soldier's everyday sacrifice and humanity. Joe's quest to honor his fallen compatriot, as told by his son, Matt, mirrors America's continued efforts to fully honor this generation of soldiers and their families."

—**Ronald J. Mariano**, Speaker of the House, Commonwealth of Massachusetts

"The Vietnam era was a historical anomaly, most notably because that war occurred in the sad era when too few Americans had the decency to thank those who fought in their place. Generations of warfighters before and now two generations of warfighters since Vietnam were welcomed home by the ticker tape and yellow ribbons of a grateful nation, an honor deserved by but denied to most Vietnam vets. *100 Days in Vietnam* is a compelling reminder of why such displays of gratitude are common sense and should be commonplace when fellow citizens stand in the gap like they did in Southeast Asia. At its core, this page-turner is a love story. It's a story of how three generations of Tallons loved their country enough to deny themselves for others—before, during, and after combat. It's a story of how a family loved each other through the perils of war again and again and again. It's a story of how an aviator loved his battle buddy so much that he refused to give up until his wingman received the recognition he was due. Most importantly, it's a story that should be devoured by anyone willing to be inspired and ready to make a difference. Readers will love this story!"

—**Dondi E. Costin**, PhD, Major General, US Air Force (Retired), President, Charleston Southern University

"Joe Tallon is a rare breed. Patriot, leader, soldier, husband, father, and grandfather whose love and service for his nation is amplified through *100 Days in Vietnam*, a masterfully written firsthand account of a turbulent time in American history. Lieutenant Colonel Tallon's tenacious pursuit of a Purple Heart for his fallen comrade, Daniel Richards, is a reminder of the heart and soul of the American soldier exemplifying brotherhood and service. Every student of leadership must read this book!"

—**Rick Brewer**, PhD, MBA, President and CEO and Professor of Management at Louisiana College

"*100 Days of Vietnam* is a distinguished tale of Joe Tallon, a Lowcountry war hero, illuminating his distinctive Vietnam experience, adversities that followed, and endeavors of remembrance for the fallen. Joe's riveting journey as a soldier and veteran exudes valor and displays the true meaning of sacrifice and love for country, family, and fellow warfighter."

—**R. Keith Summey**, Mayor of North Charleston (1994–present)

"Whether in uniform or civilian clothes, I've never seen Joe Tallon when he didn't appear to be standing at attention. He was a proud American soldier through and through. This book, *100 Days in Vietnam*, is a riveting read that includes uncanny detail about his experiences as an Army pilot. The love letters he exchanges with his wife, Martha Anne, add human texture to an otherwise chaotic existence. It's in those same letters, though, that Charlestonians will appreciate his memories of fishing in Colonial Lake and eating shrimp at the Sand Bar restaurant on Folly Beach. There are moments of turmoil, danger, angst, heroism, and homesickness as Tallon counts the days to his return to his new bride. It's a compelling story told in a first-person narrative sure to grab your attention and maybe even make you stand a little taller as an American."

—**Warren Peper**, Television and Print Media Award-Winning Journalist

"*100 Days in Vietnam* is not just the story of a young officer's service at the conclusion of the Vietnam War; it is also a testament to the primacy of character in one's life. Having commanded First Lieutenant Matt Tallon (Joe's son) while serving in Germany, I have a unique appreciation for this book. Matt was an exceptional officer and perhaps the hardest-working soldier I have had the privilege of leading. It is clear to me now that Joe's love and sense of service were ingrained in his son. Deeply personal and surprisingly candid, *100 Days in Vietnam* is a valuable addition to literature on the Vietnam War and an honest account of the American experience."

—**Mark D. Wolf**, Lieutenant Colonel, US Army, Instructor, Command and General Staff Course, Fort Leavenworth, Kansas

"I have always been interested in the US involvement in Vietnam and the brave souls that were required to go fight in that war. The timeline of your stories were amazing. This book was an excellent read. Thank you both for sharing your experiences through your stories."

—**Thomas Rouse, Jr.**, Command Sergeant Major, US Army (Retired)

"*100 Days in Vietnam* is an honest recollection of an unpopular war that divided the country, from the point of view of a truly humble, quiet, professional, and compassionate leader. As I read this book, it reminded me of my love for my fellow soldiers during my own twenty-two-year career and combat deployment. The admiration and desire to honor a brother in arms can only truly be understood by one who has walked in those same boots and has shared the sights, sounds, smells, heat, cold, and discomforts while putting the mission before your own life in some cases. Sadly, America checked out on our Vietnam veterans even before they returned from mandatory deployments and turned its back on these warriors who did only what was asked and required of them. This recollection of then Lieutenant Joe Tallon and SPC-5 Daniel Richards brings some much-needed awareness to current generations of the sacrifices and losses experienced by a generation of young Americans who made incredible personal sacrifices for our country, but more so for the men and women to their left and right who shared their common suffering while they were simultaneously scorned by the citizens they served for. *John 15:13* captures the true spirit of this book, and for Joe, it is a truth that he has carried for forty-nine years."

—**Charles Shank**, First Sergeant, US Army (Retired)

"I was inspired when I read the book, *100 Days in Vietnam*, which is a story of heroism and sacrifice of brave Americans during the Vietnam War. Lieutenant Joe Tallon was ejected from his airplane and miraculously survived as his OV-1 Mohawk crashed. Unfortunately, Specialist-5 Daniel Richards did not survive the wreckage. Following the tragedy, Joe worked tirelessly to ensure that Specialist Richards received the Purple Heart posthumously. This book, written by Joe and his Army veteran son, Matt, highlights the dedication and sacrifice that our service members endure for freedom. Joe Tallon, along with other brave soldiers, has unselfishly served his country with honor and distinction. This dynamic book is a must-read for every person who has served in the armed forces."

—**Jairy Hunter**, President Emeritus and Professor of Business at Charleston Southern University

"It's gripping, sad yet happy, ripe with irony, and overall a testament to the human spirit."

—**Jeff Walker**, Book Reviews at HolyCitySinner.com

"The book is nevertheless a powerful reminder of sacrifices made by members of the much maligned baby boomer generation whose wartime experiences are often lost in the 'long shadows' of their parents' 'greatest generation.'"

"From the lush South Carolina Lowcountry to the jungles of Vietnam and beyond, this veteran and son of a veteran salutes Matthew A. Tallon and his father, Lt. Col. (retired) Joseph F. Tallon, for their missions accomplished."

—**Lynn Seldon**, Army Veteran, Author of *Virginia's Ring*, Co-Author of *100 Things to Do in Charleston Before You Die* and *Our Vanishing Americana: A South Carolina Portrait*

100 Days in Vietnam:
A Memoir of Love, War, and Survival

by Lt. Col. Joseph F. Tallon, US Army (Ret.)
with Matthew A. Tallon

ISBN 978-1-64663-255-8

Published by

◣ köehlerbooks™

3705 Shore Drive
Virginia Beach, VA 23455
800-435-4811
www.koehlerbooks.com

100

A MEMOIR OF

DAYS IN

LOVE, WAR, AND SURVIVAL

VIETNAM

LT. COL. JOSEPH F. TALLON, US ARMY (RET.)
with MATTHEW A. TALLON

FOREWORD BY LT. GEN. H. R. MCMASTER

VIRGINIA BEACH
CAPE CHARLES

TABLE OF CONTENTS

FOREWORD

JOE TALLON IS an extraordinary man, and he tells an extraordinary story. He is an extraordinary man because he encountered and overcame extraordinary hardships. This is an extraordinary story because it overcomes the stigma associated with acknowledging traumatic stress while also demonstrating the value of approaching physical and psychological trauma with a mild measure of stoicism. And it is an extraordinary story because it also provides a window into American society and its relationship with America's Army during the Vietnam War and its aftermath.

Above all, *100 Days in Vietnam* is a story of determination and will. Joe Tallon overcame physical injury in his youth; navigated through bureaucracy to accomplish his goal to become an officer and army pilot; recuperated from serious wounds in combat; overcame an unsympathetic command to continue serving after the post-Vietnam reductions in the Army; recovered from setbacks as an entrepreneur; and persevered to ensure that a fallen comrade was honored for his service and sacrifice. *100 Days in Vietnam* is a story of selflessness and self sacrifice, qualities that have been and remain essential to the strength of our nation and our Army.

Joe Tallon's story is important because it will help readers appreciate the importance of the warrior ethos, the covenant between fellow soldiers comprised of values such as honor, duty, courage, loyalty, and self-sacrifice. His story is also important because readers will understand that the warrior ethos also depends on our military's connection with our society. When we are valued by others, we value ourselves. The way American society turned away from its warriors during the Vietnam War not only dishonored individual servicemen and women, but also weakened our military profession. It is the warrior ethos that permits servicemen and women to see themselves as part of a community that sustains itself through a covenant that binds them to one another and to the society they serve.

Although the American public and the warriors who fight in their name enjoy mutual trust that was absent in the Vietnam and post-Vietnam periods, the warrior ethos is at risk today because fewer and fewer Americans are connected to a very small professional military. As Joe Tallon's story reveals, the military's separation from the society it serves is consequential because warriors depend on respect for what they do to maintain their self-respect. Today, popular culture waters down society's respect for warriors. Warriors are most often portrayed as fragile, traumatized human beings. Hollywood tells us little about the warrior's calling or commitment to his or her fellow warriors or what compels him or her to act courageously, endure hardships, take risks, or make sacrifices. Joe Tallon, with the assistance of his son and fellow soldier, Matthew Tallon, tell us much about these things.

Lieutenant General H.R. McMaster
United States Army (Retired)

INTRODUCTION

BY MATTHEW A. TALLON

I HAD TIME.

I was twenty-five years old, an Army first lieutenant. The busload of fellow officers and I rode downhill from the French town of Vierville-sur-Mer to the beachfront, then to the Dog Green sector of Omaha Beach. We stood in a gaggle near the surf, listening to the guide. The sky was overcast but didn't look like rain, and the waves rolling in were small, allowing us to hear our guide easily over the surf. The smell of exposed seaweed and algae-covered rocks hung in the air.

The guide led us over the sand to the Easy Green sector. There, an old man with a scraggly gray beard stood stoop-necked next to two younger men, his arm resting on one of their shoulders for support. On his head was a black ball cap with gold-braid lettering. *World War II Veteran*, it read.

One of our officers chatted him up. He was standing with his two sons on the exact spot on the beach where he came ashore at H hour plus three, or three hours after the invasion began, on June 6, 1944. He was a young private first class then and talked with reverence about his sergeant's ingenuity at keeping his team alive while he and his fellow soldiers hopscotched around dead bodies as they ran back and forth for supplies at the landing craft. Our executive officer asked him what he did during that first hour he was on the beach.

"I shook," he replied, his eyes wet with tears.

Suddenly, it felt like we'd barged into a silent cathedral and interrupted this old man and his sons at an altar in prayer. Sensing our intrusion, our battalion commander moved us along. I wished my own grandfather were there with me to retrace his steps on the Normandy beaches. I fought back my own tears, not wanting to appear soft in front of my officer peers.

My grandfather, Harry, was a twenty-year-old gunner in the Navy when he approached the shores at Normandy. I knew he had been there, but I knew nothing about his experience. What had this beach looked like to him? Did he shake as well when he saw it? Did he get to the beach, or did he stay on one of the naval ships offshore?

Our group made its way up the slight incline of the beach in the same direction that the assaulting Allied forces moved on D-Day. We reached the long parallel pile of smooth rocks called the shingle, what remained of the only defilade that would have separated troops from the relentless German machine gun fire. Many of us laid prone on our bellies alongside it to get a better sense of the perspective our fighting forebears would have had six decades earlier.

I thought about the German bolt-action Mauser rifle that my grandfather brought back from Normandy and wondered how he came to have it.

Our guide led us up a winding trail through Les Moulins Draw to the top of the large ridgeline over land that would have been littered with buried mines and barbed wire. Americans assaulting the ridgeline on June 6, 1944, would have found enemy bunkers and trench lines to engage at the top. When we came over the rise, we found instead a large, beautifully manicured, lush green lawn, containing the most striking military cemetery I had ever seen.

Our unit leadership brought with us a large floral wreath with a banner across it emblazoned with our 28th Transportation Battalion name and colors. We laid it at the prominent central monument that housed bells that rang at that moment, playing the Star-Spangled Banner. We stood silently at attention. A group of French armor officers in uniform passing by stopped and saluted. The anthem was followed by Taps as we looked out across a field of thousands of white crosses and occasional Stars of David. Again, I wished my grandfather were there with me.

After the wreath laying ceremony, we were on our own to explore the cemetery. I stopped at Theodore Roosevelt Jr.'s grave, one among the many. As I walked, I let my fingertips graze the tops of the stone markers, aware that buried under each marker was a man, likely close to my age when he had been killed. I made my way to the edge of a high bluff overlooking the beach. In the distance, along the edge of the rolling channel surf, I spotted two horses and riders crossing the Easy Red sector of Omaha Beach. The riders seemed unhurried and let their horses playfully splash in the edge of the surf.

I envisioned how different the scene would have been there on Omaha Beach sixty years earlier. I stood near where Germans would have rained fire down on the attacking force. My grandfather had been there, had survived this brutal assault. But I knew nothing of his experience. Right then, I resolved to find out, to talk to my grandfather and document his D-Day memories.

I had time.

Just two years later, in the summer of 2006, I finished a one-year stint in Korea near the demilitarized zone. I resigned my commission as an Army officer and re-entered civilian life as a public high school teacher in Durham, North Carolina. Late that summer, I drove back home to Summerville, South Carolina for a visit. My grandfather, suffering from congestive heart failure, wanted to talk to me. I'd spent many days of my teenage years in his home—a single-story, brick ranch house on a tidal stream called Turkey Creek. We'd watched countless baseball games together on his cable television—both the Chicago Cubs and Atlanta Braves—while at the same time playing rummy on a small table next to his chair.

Harry handed me a bundle of manila folders and envelopes tied together with a piece of twine.

"These here are my documents from my time in the Navy and World War II. I figure you're 'bout the only person who might be interested in this stuff." He fingered through the papers, pulling one out every so often to show me.

"This here's my certificate from when I crossed the equator for the first time. And this here's the thank you letter my momma received from President Roosevelt for having four a-her boys in the service at one time during the war."

Under the pile of folders was an old three-ring binder. He told me he had added a few items to his funeral service since we last went over things. It had been a good five years or more since he had showed me some of this stuff. I'd been overseas with the Army for those years, and I didn't remember all the old items. He had all the songs carefully curated, the sheet music and the corresponding names of the people who he wanted to sing.

"Now you take a look here at these other pages and tell me if you've got questions."

"Do you want me to go through this now?" I asked. The idea of his death seemed so remote and abstract.

"Well, yeah, I definitely ain't getting any younger!"

I opened the binder and slowly turned the pages. There were numerous poems and motivational writings of unknown origins. Many had been cut out of newspapers and magazines, the paper brittle and yellow. Some looked like they'd been cut out of books. He loved to go to garage sales on the weekends, so I imagined some of them came that way. Several of the passages were in his distinctive scrawling handwriting that most couldn't read.

"Some of these have names on them and some don't. What does that mean?" I asked.

"I wrote on there who's supposed to read each of these at the service. For the ones that ain't got a name, I want you to read it."

"What's this piece right here?"

"Those are notes for the sermon. I've got some specific Bible verses I want the preacher to use. You make sure he gets this beforehand."

I started to mentally add up how much time it would take to do all of these readings and songs, and it seemed like a solid ninety-minute or two-hour ceremony was required to cover all that ground. He then produced a list with the names of the pallbearers and a stack of bulletins from previous funerals he'd attended. He wanted me to draw inspiration from that stack when designing his funeral program.

"It's important that you read this statement at the end of the service. I don't have any outstanding debts, so you shouldn't have nobody come up to you with an IOU signed by Harry Tallon. You tell 'em if anybody thinks that Harry owes 'em any money, they need to see your daddy after the service. Joe will take care of any debt claims."

We were sitting at the dining room table, and he was in the only chair that had armrests. He clutched them, bracing against them to push himself up, and I noticed just how slow and shaky he was getting up.

"Now come on back here. I want you to see where I keep this stuff. I don't want nobody but you messin' with it."

His eighty-three-year-old body had aged considerably in the years I was living overseas. I followed him back into the smaller guest bedroom down the hall. On the walls were a myriad of framed certificates and photographs. One frame contained his honorary South Carolina high school diploma awarded many years after he dropped out of school in the ninth grade to leave his family's farm and make a living in Charleston. As a part of the fiftieth anniversary commemorations of the war, the state awarded a lot of surviving World War II veterans with high school diplomas, since the high school educations of many had been interrupted by the war. The two twin beds in the room were covered with stacks of framed photographs and certificates as well. I knew my mom was working with both him and my Granny Bertha on gathering materials to display at their upcoming sixty-fifth wedding anniversary celebration that January. I picked up a framed photo of him wearing a nice suit standing with Granny and another man in a suit.

"That's Mr. Newton from Piggly Wiggly. That was took when they gave me the award recognition for my sales numbers. Bertha got a real nice mink stole, and they gave me this here ring."

He slid a gold ring off his finger and passed it to me. I held it with reverence between my thumb and forefinger as he proceeded to point out the diamond in the center and showed me the tag label saved in a box with my name on it. I told him it was a nice ring, but my words seemed inadequate. The label showed the ring was destined to be mine. He'd placed tags or labels on just about everything in the house, and he made a point to show me a number of them as I dutifully watched. He was a traveling salesman for his forty-year career after the war, so he was used to keeping meticulous records. He didn't want any of us in the family fighting over his stuff when he was gone.

Not wanting to dwell any longer on having to divide a dead man's property, I looked up at the wall and changed the subject. I pointed at a signed photo of Vietnam-era Army General William Westmoreland

and asked where he got it. Apparently, it was a thank-you gift. My grandfather had found an envelope addressed to Westmoreland at the post office just laying on the counter, cut open and inside of which was a book royalty check for five hundred dollars. He mailed the check to the general and some weeks later a signed photograph came in the mail with a brief thank-you note from Westmoreland himself.

My attention then shifted to a framed shadowbox on the wall with his military service medals and fabric epaulets of his enlisted naval ranks. My dad had that made for him, and I could tell that my grandfather really liked it. He already had an adhesive sticker on the bottom right corner with the name of my father, Joe, on it.

My grandfather had two main reflections about his old age. The first was that he would have taken a lot better care of himself had he known he was going to live that long. The second was his oft-repeated phrase, "Life is like a roll of toilet paper. It moves faster and faster the closer you get to the end."

I didn't realize just how fast things were moving for him. Over the next two years, while I was starting a new career as a high school history teacher in North Carolina, he was shuttling to the hospital every other month to get excess fluid drained or to deal with some other complication from congestive heart failure. I kept thinking that I was going to have time to sit down with him during the summer break and finally document his experiences from the war, especially those on D-Day.

On a late August night in 2008, while I was driving a moving truck through Connecticut, I got the call. Harry was dead. I had run out of time.

When my dad came to me less than a year after Harry's death and handed me a stack of yellow legal pad pages with handwritten remembrances from his service in Vietnam, I vowed not to let the opportunity pass me by as it had with my grandfather. We were going to do something with these memories.

I quickly realized how little I knew about my dad's wartime experiences and his life as a young man. I knew he had survived, just barely, ejecting from his plane after being shot down. I had seen the roadmap of burn scars on his body, and I had watched his eyes swell as he touched a name on the Vietnam Veterans Memorial wall on a childhood trip to Washington DC.

"I survived. He didn't," was all he told me at the time.

But I didn't know that my dad wrote letters to my mom almost every single day he was in Vietnam. Contained in those letters was not only a passionate love story, but also a chronicle of the insecurities of a young lieutenant whose place in the unit and purpose in the entire war effort was very uncertain. I dug deeper. We pulled back the emotional and mental scabs and reconstructed his time in Vietnam, and the childhood experiences that shaped him. What I found in my dad's past was not only my own origin story but also the classic struggle so many young men of the baby boom generation went through to prove themselves to their parents, who cast such long shadows as members of the reputed *greatest generation*.

What follows are his recollections of his 104 days in Vietnam coupled with primary source documents, such as the aforementioned trove of handwritten letters sent from Joe to Martha Anne and audio cassette recordings they exchanged as a means of wartime communication. Other primary sources, such as the unit yearbook and additional artifacts, are supplemented with contemporary newspaper reports to situate Joe's 1972 experiences into the greater historical context.

Using his uncanny remembrance of details, along with these other sources, which were minimally copyedited for clarity, my father and I recreated his experience into the first two parts of this narrative, *The Deployment* and *The Recovery*, told in a first person, journal-entry style. The third part, *The Quest* is my account of his tireless efforts to bring long-overdue recognition to the observer lost in the Vietnam plane crash that changed my father's life—Specialist 5th Class Daniel Richards.

PART I

★ ★ ★

THE DEPLOYMENT

CHAPTER ONE

GOODBYE

Monday, May 8, 1972

I HAD ON my tan-colored tropical-weight uniform. Dry cleaned. Not starched. Like all my uniforms, this one was custom-made by the Schwartz Uniform Company out of Baltimore. I am a young, newly minted lieutenant and want to look the part.

Yesterday, twenty-five members of both my family and my wife's family gathered inside the first floor of the Charleston Municipal Airport to witness my departure. The late afternoon flight time gave Martha Anne and me time for a long goodbye at our apartment. I can still feel her warm kisses on my lips. On Sunday, we had a big dinner with family before we took off on a drive to spend some time alone and talk. We parked at the Stono River landing, looking out on the salt marsh. We knew it might be a long time before I come home.

A trip to the airport is a rarity for my family, but everyone seemed to know the unwritten dress code. Passengers getting ready to board the plane were dressed up—men in coats and ties and women in dresses and heels. Even my Uncle Willard, married to my mom's older sister Grace, was wearing his Sunday best, though I know he is more at home in a pair of khaki workpants or a hunting jacket than a shirt and tie. We were fishing and hunting buddies while I was growing up. He's a crack shot with any weapon he puts his hands on.

Uncle Willard put his hand on my shoulder. "My tax dollars are paying for all of your bullets," he said. "Don't waste any of 'em."

My cousin Liz handed me a copy of the New Testament. The Bible was about as big as the palm of my hand.

"We inscribed it," she said. I took it in my hands and opened the black leather cover. *Good luck and Godspeed. Liz, Chuck, and Bev* was written in blue ink on the first page.

"Thanks, Liz," I said. "I'll take this with me wherever I go." And I knew I would.

As my boarding time approached, my family and I walked as an ensemble down the wide covered sidewalk to the gate. A four-foot-high cyclone fence separated the sidewalk from the tarmac where the plane sat. There was no security present—just a sign on the chain link fence that read *Ticketed passengers only beyond this point.* Looking out from the fence on the far side of the runway, I could see the planes and hangars of the Charleston Air Force Base.

My mother was not present. After saying goodbye to my father so many times during World War II, she told me that she could not watch me leave for war. During that war, she went nine full months without any word from my father, but she hoped it would be easier to stay in touch with me. The night before last I stood with her in the kitchen, a wad of tear-dampened Kleenex in her apron pocket.

"Write to me," she said. I told her I would.

At the airport, my dad, a talker by disposition and trade, was unusually quiet. He was in his work clothes—short-sleeved, white dress shirt; thin, black necktie; dress slacks; and polished shoes—the trademark outfit of a traveling salesman. He took Monday afternoon off from his job with Piggly Wiggly selling Greenbax stamps to be there. Leaning in, he shook my hand while at the same time depositing a set of brass knuckles in my pocket. Looking me directly in the eyes, he said quietly, "Use these if the fighting gets in real close."

My dad was drafted in early 1943 while working on the Charleston dry docks. Since he was already in a job supporting the war effort, he hadn't expected to get drafted, but they made him a member of the Naval Armed Guard, whose mission was to protect our merchant ships from attack. After nearly a year, he worked his way up from seaman to gunner's mate third class as part of a crew that manned a five inch, .38-caliber deck gun. In the spring of 1944, his ship returned to dock at Baltimore, and while there, he received word his wife and one-year-old daughter in Charleston were sick with the flu. His ship left Baltimore harbor before he could get back to it after rushing to see them, and he was thrown into the brig and reduced in rank from gunner's mate back down to seaman. However, he learned weeks later that the ship he was supposed to be on was torpedoed off the coast of Scotland and all on board were lost, among them his training buddies. As I was saying goodbye, I wondered if he was thinking about that with me leaving for Vietnam: the strangeness of war. Was it fate or just randomness?

"I'm going to go over there and win that war," I said to my assembled family. "All I have to do is get there, and I will show them how the Tallons fight."

My dad pulled a white handkerchief out of his pocket and wiped the sweat on his forehead. My older sister Lindler stood next to him. She's already been married eleven years and her dark curls have shocks of white hair mixed in. She's actually only twenty-eight, just three years older than I am. She graduated high school on a Friday night as class valedictorian and got married on Sunday afternoon two days later. Lindler's advice to me was simple: "If you get captured, tell them everything they want to know. Don't try to be a hero."

I wasn't sure that was the best advice, but she's always trying to tell me and Roy, our little brother, what to do. Roy, reed thin and tan to the bone from endless days surfing, stood near Lindler wearing a bright floral-print shirt, his hands shoved deep in the pockets of his Bermuda shorts. Normally quite talkative and telling jokes, he was very quiet.

Martha Anne's mother, Mattie Leigh, hugged me, and said they would be praying for me, and I knew they would. Her father, Joe Francese, told me that he would look out for Martha Anne, and I was sure of that as well. I kept glancing at Martha Anne. She was quiet.

I thought about when I first saw her at her parents' small house in North Charleston. She was folding laundry, a vision with her dark hair tied up in a blue kerchief. I guess the Army tried to warn me before getting married. We scheduled our wedding in Charleston for the weekend of July Fourth. At the time, I was stationed at Fort Rucker in Alabama and needed the Army's permission, since it required me to travel beyond 250 miles of my post. I submitted a pass request in

June, and to my surprise, was summoned to see the training school commander—Lieutenant Colonel Jerry G. Patton. I reported to his office in the flight operations center and snapped off a crisp salute before getting to the point. With all the confidence I could muster, I declared, "Sir, I'm requesting a pass this weekend to go get married."

In a deep, gravelly voice, he replied, "Son, if the Army wanted you to have a wife, they would issue you one." That was a line I'd heard before. He chewed on the stump of a cigar in the corner of his mouth as he spoke, and at that moment, I thought that he might just be the son of legendary General George Patton.

I fired back. "Sir, three hundred people have been invited. I'm going to the wedding whether you sign it or not." Three hundred was an exaggeration, but I thought it sounded impressive. Usually catching an attitude with someone who outranks you isn't a good idea, but it had worked for me in the past, and I hoped it would work this time.

He chuckled under his breath. "I wanted to see how serious you were about getting married, and that this wasn't some weekend fling."

"No, sir. We've been engaged for thirteen months, and we dated for eighteen months before that. I promised her mother that we would wait until she graduated from college to get married. She graduated last month, and we're gonna get married this weekend."

Lieutenant Colonel Patton signed the pass and handed it back to me. I thanked him, saluted, and hurried out.

That day seems long ago. We never did get to go on a honeymoon. I so wished that instead of boarding a plane bound for war that Martha Anne and I were on our way to Hawaii together. I put my arms around her. She pressed her hands flat against my chest and looked me hard in the eyes. "I love you so much," she said. "I'll be waiting for you."

I promised her I would write every day. "No matter what you might hear while I'm gone, I am coming back," I said. "And I am a man of my word."

Of course, I had no way of guaranteeing anything.

One last squeeze of Martha Anne's hand, and I walked through the fence gate and across the seventy-five yards of concrete to the stairwell leading into the aircraft. I looked up and saw a stewardess posted at the top of the stairs to greet us. In the line of passengers boarding the civilian flight, I spotted a few other military men, not surprising given that Charleston has both a naval and an air force base. I wondered if anyone else in uniform on my flight has orders to Vietnam. Nixon's de-escalation of the ground war, which he calls *Vietnamization*, is at a level that I think there is a possibility I might instead be diverted to Alaska, Korea, or even Germany to fly Mohawk missions there. We have been hearing quite a bit about the ground war being over. But on the eighth day of May 1972, it seemed the Vietnam War was just beginning for my family.

I turned back at the top of the stairs to see the people I love lined up on the sidewalk outside the fence waving at me. I raised my hand once more in their direction and ducked my head to enter the side of the plane.

CHAPTER TWO

STANDBY

Tuesday, May 9, 1972

COMING FROM THE early-May heat of Charleston, the first thing I noticed about San Francisco as I deplaned and boarded the military bus to nearby Travis Air Force Base is how cool and dry it is. We are housed in an open-bay barracks room with about forty others in bunks. It's not fully packed, so there are a lot of open bunks. I walked over to the passenger terminal in the morning, at lunch, and again in the afternoon to see if my name is on the passenger manifest list. In between, I have access to the bowling alley and the movie theater on base. I have quickly settled into the monotony of checking for my name on the passenger manifests. This routine is my reason for being. Whether I am brimming with confidence or false hope, I cannot say, but I am hopeful at any hour I'll receive new orders sending me to any place but Vietnam. Everyone here is talking about the increased bombing and the mining of the harbors in North Vietnam that was just authorized by the president. Apparently in the last twenty-four hours, we dropped time-delay mines into Haiphong harbor and other ports in the north that are set to go live this Thursday. Also, reports today indicate that our first admiral was killed when his helicopter crashed in the Gulf of Tonkin—Rear Admiral Rembrandt C. Robinson. All of this feels like escalation more than *Vietnamization* to me.

★ ★ ★

The path that brought me to this moment mostly has been in my control—one decision leading to the next, and then the next landing me squarely where I am now. I thought back earlier today to that moment when I was a senior at the Baptist College at Charleston in fall of '68. Back then, I could not resolve being a man of God and a soldier for my country and possibly find myself in a place where I might kill someone, so I made an appointment with my favorite professor, Dr. J. Walter Carpenter. When I arrived, he did not look up but instead motioned toward a single spindly chair, the only chair in the room other than the one he sat upon behind a massive wooden desk. He was preparing a test for his students on an A.B. Dick blue stencil, writing questions out in longhand on mimeograph paper. He seemed to be in no hurry, which only added to my agitation.

On his desk was the familiar blue Harper Study Bible that he used in the Old Testament course I took with him my freshman year. In addition to being the department chair, he was also a veteran minister of thirty years, so I considered him an authority on the Bible. The walls of his office were lined floor to ceiling with books. I scanned the titles—the very kind of reading one might expect of the chair of the religion department at a Baptist college, and the very kind that reassured me he was the right man to whom I should pose my question. I was in the throes of a crisis of conscience— patience was not my strong suit. But I did my best to wait wordlessly, occupying myself by studying his head, which sported a thinning web of wispy, silver hairs that arranged themselves as haphazardly on his head as his books and papers were arranged on his desk.

When he finally looked up at me from behind large, black horn-rimmed glasses, I blurted out, "How can I justify going into the military and killing people when the Bible tells me not to kill?"

Dr. Carpenter raised an eyebrow above his glasses. "You know many of the Old Testament warriors. You know their stories, and that they killed many men. Often, their wars were blessed by God, and He even ordered the Israelites to do killing in His name. David was God's anointed one, and he was a warrior who killed over 10,000."

"But how does that square with the Ten Commandments?"

"The Commandments state *thou shall not murder*. When you're serving in the military and defending your countrymen and your fellow soldiers, this type of killing is not murder. You would be doing your duty as a citizen."

When I left his office after less than a half hour, I was more at ease than I had been in a long time. Maybe he just reaffirmed for me the answer I wanted to hear, but I left content with his explanation.

When I first entered college, I thought I would major in math and become either a teacher or an engineer, but over time, I became more and more enamored with the idea of joining the Air Force, determined that I wanted to fly transportation missions on C-141s. This goal served a dual purpose—these C-141 missions could keep me at a distance from combat and keep me stationed in my hometown at the Charleston Air Force Base. With this thought in mind, I mentally mapped out my future—a decade with the Air Force, then transition to a civilian job flying passenger planes. So, early in January of '69, I went to see the Air Force recruiter to volunteer to be a pilot.

This meeting with the recruiter was not my first with the military. I had considered signing up during my senior year of high school when some of my close friends nearly convinced me to join the Marine Corps. But my mother's pleas that I get a college education won the day. My father had dropped out of high school, and the elusive dream of a college education was passed down to me. So instead I opted for a college deferment.

Even with a college degree nearly in hand, volunteering to be a pilot felt a bit like designating myself to be the starting pitcher on my Dixie Youth baseball team. With young men getting snatched in the draft for ground infantry duty in the Marines or the Army, the Air Force recruiter had his pick of young, able-bodied men, and he knew it. The recruiter claimed to be impressed with my aptitude scores, especially the math, but that did nothing to move me to the front of the Air Force line.

After graduation in May 1969 from Baptist College with nothing but a nod of reassurance from the Air Force recruiter, I started working for the Fletcher Paint Company making $5.50 an hour. Most of my fellow painters were drunk half the time and profoundly lazy the other half, which made a sober and motivated worker like me a candidate for speedy advancement to crew foreman that summer.

One late-June evening after a long day of painting, I walked into my parents' house and saw a plain, white business envelope on the kitchen table. In the upper left-hand corner were the words *Selective Service Center*. The letter inside, signed by President Richard Nixon, stated at the top: *You are hereby ordered for induction into the Armed Forces of the United States, and to report at Fort Jackson on July 14, 1969 at 0700.* The induction medical examination was just another step in the path that put me here in San Francisco studying passenger manifests, scanning for my name, waiting to find out the course my life would take next.

★ ★ ★

On the evening of my second full day waiting at Travis Air Force Base, my name appeared on the manifest. At dawn, the plane lifted off the runway and climbed steadily over San Francisco. I could see streetlights turning off as the city awoke to a new day. In the east, the sun rose directly at our backs while we flew in the opposite direction over the dark skies of the Pacific, heading toward Vietnam.

CHAPTER THREE

LEAVING
FOR SAIGON

Wednesday, May 10, 1972

I HAD A clear view of the fuselage from the cockpit door to the rear. The American Airlines plane body was stripped bare of all nonessentials. Bulkheads and luggage compartments had been removed, and the only serviceable bathroom was the latrine in the rear of the plane. I was one among some 200 servicemen jammed in there like cordwood. We refueled in Hawaii and Guam, but neither stop was anything to write home about. In Hawaii, we were allowed off the plane for about three hours, but we couldn't leave a certain holding area of the terminal.

During the flight, I reflected more about the nearly three-year odyssey that led to me heading off to fight in Vietnam. It seemed like I'd been fighting someone all along the way. During basic training at Fort Leonard Wood, I was the only Southerner in my company and everyone else in our company was from Chicago or the suburbs of the city. They thought of themselves as tough city guys and thought I talked funny, so we got into it quite often. I wasn't going to be intimidated, no matter what. One time I was down on my hands and knees scrubbing the floor in the barracks as punishment for a previous fight, when some other recruit tried to stick a broom handle in my ass. I didn't appreciate that at all, so a pretty serious fight erupted. I ended up bashing his head against the wall until blood came out of his ears. I never did see that recruit again.

Officer Candidate School (OCS) was no picnic either. They were always looking for ways to break us down. The cadre was relentless. There was this one guy who lost it while leading us in physical training (PT) one morning. He was on the stand leading the formation in jumping jacks, and he forgot the cadence he needed to make us stop. I guess no one reminded him, so we just kept going and going until people were falling out from exhaustion. Later that day, all his stuff in the barracks was packed, and he was gone.

OCS was in Fort Belvoir, Virginia, in the dead of winter, and they made us go on these night runs. One night when there was a ton of snow and ice on the ground, it was my rotation to lead the run. Of course, they made us run it in our Corcoran combat boots. I slipped and fell countless times going up and down hills and ended up having to get my foot wrapped for an Achilles injury that put me on crutches for three weeks. They wanted to put it in a cast and bump me to a later class, but I wouldn't let them. I just told them to wrap it up. Then, as we were getting close to the end of OCS, we did some field training exercises. On one daylight maneuver, we set up an ambush along a road to attack one of the other training companies. They left their vehicles and charged up the hill at us, and the rest of my squad pulled back from the ambush line. I was out on a point and didn't hear them withdraw, so I kept shooting at the aggressors coming up the hill. I was just firing blanks, so those guys were refusing to go down as they were supposed to. One of them charged right up and hit me in the mouth with the butt of his rifle. He hit me so hard that my bottom teeth stuck through the skin below my bottom lip. I was spitting blood as they grabbed me to take me down the hill as their prisoner.

When we got to their vehicles at the road, they were distracted long enough for me to grab a rifle. I swung the muzzle end of it as hard as I could at the neck of the guy who hit me. I missed a little high and opened up a gash on his face from his ear all the way down to the corner of his mouth. The flash suppressor on the barrel was particularly sharp. As soon as he started bleeding all over the place, his friends pushed me down and proceeded to kick the shit out of me. When the instructor got back to find us both bleeding, he just said, "All right, we've got some real combat here. Real blood!" When he called in the medics, we had to ride to the clinic together in the back of the same truck. OCS was brutal.

When I graduated from OCS, I was thirteenth out of a class of more than one hundred officers, so I had a bit of a choice about what branch I joined. That's when Major Canfield convinced me to join intel so I could fly the Mohawk, which he sold to me as the fastest plane in the Army inventory. Of course, he didn't tell me during the sales pitch that I had to first get qualified on helicopters down at Fort Wolters in Texas and at Fort Rucker in Alabama before I could take the transition course to advance into my fixed wing training. What I experienced at Fort Wolters is the main reason I don't want anything to do with helicopters when I get to Vietnam. We trained with a large number of South Vietnamese pilots in Texas who just played follow-the-leader while flying and the leader didn't always know what he was doing. It was just a free-for-all and we had to keep our heads on a swivel. The helicopters already felt like a crash looking for a place to happen without those kinds of distractions. I cannot imagine what it would be like to actually have to fly helicopters in Vietnam where they're shooting at me as well.

★ ★ ★

In the row behind me on the plane to Vietnam, I overheard a couple of guys talking about a newspaper article. Just in the past couple of days over 2,000 Miami University students marched in Oxford, Ohio, protesting the latest response to the Easter offensive by the Nixon administration. Before OCS, I'd never seen any anti-war demonstrations, except on television. It's just not like that in Charleston, where we call those folks *hippies and potheads*. In early May of '70, when I was in OCS at Fort Belvoir, the instructors had us on an alert to respond to protests, so we actually conducted some rehearsals. Then one day we got the call and two battalions of OCS candidates all loaded onto buses to go clear Highway 1. When they dropped us off, we assembled on a side street before lining up in a giant V formation to head down Highway 1. There were buildings on either side of the street, which felt like a pretty big city to me. I had no idea where we were, since we just got dropped off in buses, but I figured out later we were in College Park, Maryland. We wore our green fatigues and carried our long M-14 rifles with heavy wooden stocks and bayonets fixed and pointing forward. We had a second rank of men standing in the gap between our shoulders. The cadre issued us no ammunition.

National Guard troops had just killed those four students at Kent State. We did have one of our training, advising, and counseling (TAC) officers—a lieutenant—walking a few feet behind our double ranks, and he had a soldier with a loaded rifle next to him. He was the one allowed to shoot if a weapon was brandished in the crowd. The weather was overcast and drizzly, and I remember my eyes and nostrils burning from the cloud of CS gas still in the air. The tear gas seemed to linger like a low-level fog. We had gas masks on our belts, but we weren't given the order to put them on.

Just as we had practiced on Belvoir, we stomped and dragged our feet to a cadence. The left foot and toe pointed forward made a *whoop* sound at each stomp, and then we dragged our right foot forward with a *swoosh* sound until we were standing upright again. That's how we proceeded down Highway 1, with a methodical *whoop-swoosh* that caused the crowd to continually back up. As we cleared our sector of street, police in riot gear posted themselves at doorways along the sidewalks to make sure no one got behind our lines. I also heard a tow truck come up and hook up to one of the burned-out vehicles that clearly couldn't move.

Most of the protestors looked like students. Some of them could have been townspeople, too. I didn't know and didn't care. We just did exactly as we were told, since none of us wanted to be kicked out of OCS. I do remember thinking how I was just one year removed from college myself, and I was on the other side of the line trying to clear these college students off the street. When I started the formation that day, I had no ill will toward the protestors at all, but then as we cleared the street, I saw things being thrown at my classmates in our formation. Tomatoes and bags of liquid that I think were filled with urine. Then suddenly out of the corner of my eye, I saw something flying right at my face. I ducked my head down but still got hit hard by a flying cucumber. It pushed my helmet down onto my ears and actually gave me a headache. After that, I was upset. It was good we weren't issued live rounds because I would have been tempted to fire. Once we cleared our sector on Highway 1, they loaded us back on the buses and took us back to Belvoir and the regular hell that was OCS training.

★ ★ ★

The flight was long. People were trying to sleep. I wasn't comfortable enough to sleep, so I pulled out a book that I picked up at Fort Hollabird in Maryland. All of us in the military intelligence basic course had to take the Southeast Asian Orientation course since I guess they figured we'd all make it over there at some point. I never thought I would have to go until I boarded this flight. One of the books they gave out was *How to Stay Alive in Vietnam: What it takes to Survive in this Different Kind of War* by Colonel Robert B. Rigg. I never read it in Maryland, but I brought it along for this long flight. I opened the first chapter called *Zap Me Not* and started to read. It was about playing dead:

> *A U.S. Army Special Forces sergeant told of his 1965 experience in a battle at Song Be, capital of mountainous Phuoc Long province 75 miles northeast of Saigon. Still deaf from concussion of grenades, the sergeant told his story by jotting it down on a pad while recovering from his wounds at Clark Air Force Base Hospital in the Philippine Islands.*
>
> *"I was in a foxhole with a machine gun, trying to fix it, when my buddy yelled the Viet Cong were throwing grenades. I heard one thud and my friend was blown on top of me. I looked down to see a grenade sputtering at my feet. I tried to jump out of the hole but didn't make it. My legs went numb. I crawled back to the next trench and loaded magazines for two other sergeants. I tried to get back to my room for my rifle and ammunition—once inside I started looking around. Then there was an explosion. It knocked me down, cut my neck, and I was deaf."*
>
> *He was finally carried into the mess hall which was now an aid station. But the place was overrun by Viet Cong. Unable to defend himself, he played dead while a Viet Cong soldier used his body as a support to steady his rifle aim. Each time the VC fired a bullet grazed his arm . . . This American had to play dead. But he was really "playing alert."*

★ ★ ★

Stewardesses sold alcoholic drinks for a dollar as fast as they could tote them down the aisles while, at the same time, the majority of the passengers acted like they were racing to get in that last cigarette before walking to the gallows. The air became a putrid mix of body odor, beer belches, and Lucky Strike plumes, a haze as thick as the LA skyline.

As a non-drinker and a non-smoker, I found the brief stops on Hawaii and Guam did little to relieve my nose and lungs. By the end of the twenty-five-hour trip, I could hardly wait to get off that plane to breathe fresh air.

Approaching the airfield at Tan Son Nhut Air Force Base outside Saigon at 2100 hours, I could see illumination rounds dropping in the night sky. The attached mini parachutes slowed their descent for thirty to forty-five seconds, enough to light up the base's security perimeter as they burned off. I felt the landing gear drop into position. A jolt of adrenalin coursed through me in anticipation of getting off that flight and into the night air. The drag slowed the plane as it aligned itself, reduced thrust, and touched down on the runway.

The passenger door opened. Rather than a burst of fresh air, however, the smell that hit me was like a dumpster behind a Chinese restaurant. The stench of rotting food and oppressive humidity enveloped me. I heard the rumbling of artillery and the distinctive thump, thump, thump of mortar fire. I had arrived. I was in Vietnam.

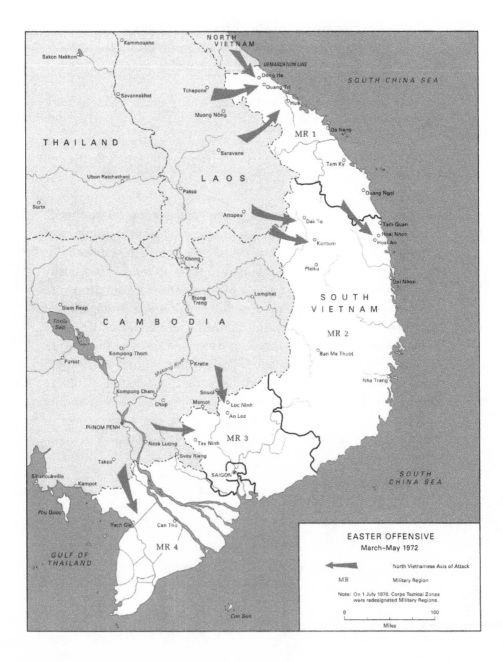

CHAPTER FOUR

IN COUNTRY

Wednesday, May 10, 1972
DAY 1:

Before Deadline: 5 Ships Leave Mined Harbor

SAIGON (AP)—Five merchant ships, including four flying the Soviet flag, pulled out of Haiphong harbor before the deadline set by President Nixon for safe passage through the mined entrance, the U.S. 7th Fleet announced today. The mines dropped by U.S. planes Tuesday across the entrances to Haiphong and six other North Vietnamese ports were set to arm themselves at 7 p.m. Saigon time today, or 7 a.m. EDT. After that they can be exploded by ships passing over or near them. Intense U.S. air and naval bombardment continued

(cont.)

against military targets in North Vietnam for the third successive day . . . Informants said U.S. fighter-bombers flew 300 strikes against the Hanoi-Haiphong military complex and other areas of North Vietnam Wednesday, and pilots reported shooting down 10 MIG interceptors, the biggest one-day bag of the war. Another 200 air strikes were flown against North Vietnam today, the sources said. Navy Lt. Randy Cunningham, pilot of an F4 Phantom from the carrier Constellation, and his co-pilot Lt. (j.g.) William Driscoll of Framingham, Mass., shot down three of the MIGs, raising their total kills to five since Jan. 19 and qualifying them as the first aces of the Vietnam War.

Antiwar Protests Spreading

(United Press International)—Thousands of antiwar demonstrators battled police, barricaded streets and besieged government and campus buildings Wednesday in the third night of angry protests against U.S. harbor minings and air bombings in North Vietnam . . . Nearly 1,000 persons have been arrested in protests across the nation since President Nixon announced in a televised address to the nation Monday night that he had ordered the mining of North Vietnam ports and bombing of supply routes. The announcement resulted in the most widespread and turbulent protests since May 1970, when four Kent State University students were slain by National Guardsmen.

Thursday, May 11, 1972
DAY 2:

I was dead tired when we arrived last night. Trying to sleep sitting up in a transport plane full of talking, snoring, farting GIs in a cigarette smoker wasn't easy. Twenty-three hours of that makes this plywood temporary barracks seem downright inviting. Not only did I sleep in a bed for six hours straight, but this morning I took my first shower since leaving Travis Air Base. Feels good to be clean.

They call this place the *Repo Depot.* Its official name is Camp Alpha, but *Repo Depot* is more fun to say. We're all under this tin roof doing the same thing—a whole lot of nothing. We are like spare parts waiting to be plugged into a unit with a hole to fill. My only required task is to check the ready board each morning at 0700 to see if I am scheduled for a unit assignment. Already did that. Nothing was posted.

Where you get assigned in Vietnam can determine how long you will survive in combat. I just talked to some seasoned pilots. They told me the Army desperately needs helicopter gunship pilots. The casualty rate for pilots flying Cobra gunship missions is very high. The Easter offensive earlier this spring has especially taken a toll on the Cobra crews. The last thing I want to do in this war is man a helicopter, but I am, unfortunately, qualified. When Major Canfield convinced me at the end of OCS to fly for the Army, he pointed out that the Army has more aircraft than all the other branches of the military combined, but a lot of that total is the tremendous number of helicopters. To get my training on fixed-wing Mohawks, I had to take the Army's transition course on choppers. I knew enough going into that transition course to know that rotary wing is not my thing, but actually experiencing it more than cemented that impression.

In the winter of 1970, I was stationed at Fort Wolters just outside of Mineral Wells, Texas. The sign over the entrance read *US Army Primary Helicopter Center.* They were really pumping through the trainees—both Americans and South Vietnamese. Our primary training helicopter was the TH-55 made by the Howard Hughes Company. With a less than 100-horsepower engine, it didn't have much power, but the controls were very responsive and nimble. This meant that even minor adjustments on the controls while flying could have immediate and dramatic effects—no matter the speed. It had three main blades and one tail rotor, and the rotor blade system was turned by five fan belts that we affectionately called *rubber bands*. For pilots, the TH-55 had a small, sealed Plexiglas cockpit covered with a bubble canopy manufactured by the Mattel Toy Company that made it look like a dragonfly. While it was not a forgiving training platform, it was certainly low cost, and this was the main benefit for churning out so many rotary-wing pilots.

Given my present tropical context, it seems odd that I associate helicopters with snow. But when I started my training in Texas in early December that year, snow had already started to fall, which was bad news for us trainees. Because we needed flexibility in our hands, feet, and head to control the helicopters, we couldn't bundle up while flying. With the bitter cold that time of year, we flew with the cockpit heaters on full blast. The rudimentary heating system in the TH-55 consisted of a jacket cover over the exhaust manifold, which warmed the air as it passed over the scorching hot exhaust pipe and flowed into the cockpit.

During my first week of training in the helicopters, five pilots died. We were told that the pilots crashed because they had heart attacks while flying. Although you can quite literally have the shit scared out of you while in a helicopter, it was hard for us to believe that twenty-two to twenty-five-year-old trainees who had recently passed the thorough Class I flight physicals suddenly were having cardiac arrests. By the second week, three more in our class were dead, and the speculation spread that it was due to carbon monoxide poisoning. The protective jackets around the exhaust piping that were supposed to the keep the air around it from getting contaminated were instead developing minor cracks from the vibration of the helicopters. So, the warm air pumped into the cockpit had traces of carbon monoxide from the exhaust.

The Army's impromptu solution to deal with the problem was to fit the cockpits with a two-by-two-inch white square carbon monoxide indicator. If it turned black, we were instructed to land immediately. After two more weeks of flying with the new indicators, three more pilot trainees died. Waiting to see black on the indicator was way too late. This led to the Army's second impromptu solution: we were ordered to take the doors off the helicopters and fly without the heaters.

After twenty minutes of flying with an open canopy in frigid December temperatures, we couldn't bend our fingers or toes, a dangerous condition since the hypersensitive controls required a deft touch. The final solution was to cut our flying time. As a consequence, no one in my class had enough flight hours to meet the requirements for solo flight. I did eventually complete my rotary-wing training sessions, but I never lost the belief that a helicopter is a crash looking for a place to happen. Here in Vietnam, we have a lot more than carbon monoxide to worry about bringing down our helicopters, but I sincerely hope I left behind the helicopters with the Texas snow.

Friday, May 12, 1972
DAY 3:

I reported to the assignment board at 0700. My name was not there. The waiting game is dragging me down. Minutes pass like hours. If each day in country feels like these first two, I'm going to spend a lifetime in Vietnam before I get to go home.

It has not rained since I arrived. It's hot and humid, a lot like Charleston. I miss Martha Anne so much it hurts.

Dean Meeks showed up at my barracks this morning. My family got word to him that I am here in Tan Son Nhut. He is not blood kin but is related to me through marriage to one of my cousins. I met him once in Charleston, and he graduated from the Citadel in '69, the same year I graduated from the Baptist College. Dean suggested we go to the officer's club for dinner tonight. Even though we aren't close, it is still nice to see a family member on the other side of the world.

I told him I haven't been assigned a weapon. His response surprised me. "Man, I haven't heard a shot fired in anger since I've been in country. We keep 'em locked up in the arms room anyway."

I can't figure what good a weapon does you if it's locked up when you need it.

He told me about his job in G-3 Operations at US Military Assistance Command, Vietnam (MACV) headquarters, how he rubs elbows with generals all day long. "But I'm getting real short," he said. "Less than three weeks now. Nineteen days and a wake-up to be exact."

Dean came back to the *Repo Depot* this evening. He wanted to catch the new movie on post, *The Sting*, starring Paul Newman and

Robert Redford, and I did too. The movie showed in an old airplane hangar with 300 others in uniform. Afterward, we took a short walk across the base to the officer's club where we had dinner, and Dean filled me in on what it's been like to work in the G-3 Operations with all the high brass. Like this morning, he kept touching on two themes: one, he has never been shot at, and two, his time in Vietnam is getting really short.

Just as we finished our meal, a commotion started in the bar and spilled into the restaurant. We joined the growing crowd like it was a schoolyard fight. In the center was Randy Cunningham, who just became the Vietnam War's first flying ace. To gain the title of ace, a pilot has to down at least five confirmed enemy planes, and Cunningham shot down three MiGs yesterday. Tan Son Nhut is a major air base, and the nearly 200 officers in the club—many of them pilots—vigorously shook beer cans and showered him right there on the floor. A couple guys turned over a table, then a couple more. Soon all the tables were flipped. Dean and I asked one of the Air Force pilots the reason for flipping the tables. He said a single table is overturned to signify a kill when that pilot returns to the club. Because Cunningham is an ace, the officers honored him by overturning all the tables.

His nickname is *Duke*. He looked too tall to be a pilot, but he's got that icy calm and cool about him. I got a chance to ask him how close he was to the MiGs when he shot them down. He said he never saw the first two before firing but picked them up on the target acquisition radar before he ever made visual contact. I wanted to ask him more about the dogfight, but an entire group of officers was elbowing in to get his attention. I can't believe I met a real F-4 fighter ace. Wish I had his job.

Saturday, May 13, 1972
DAY 4:

It's Saturday and my hurry-up-and-wait is finally over. My name was on the ready board with a dozen other aviators at 0700. We had to meet the 1st Aviation Brigade commander in his office at 0800 hours. The Brigade is a monstrous 20,000-man command that controls all of the Army aviation assets in Vietnam, so I quickly got my uniform ready to see the general before all thirteen of us lined up in front of Major General McClendon's desk. This is the same General McClendon who was the base commander at Fort Wolters when I was in helicopter training. I did not want him to make the association of me with helicopters, so I set the commander's mind straight when I introduced myself. "Sir, my name is Lieutenant Joe Tallon. I'm a Mohawk pilot, and I'm here to fly Mohawks."

"Tallon. I had a Colonel Bill Tallon who worked for me at MACV headquarters—is that your dad?"

"No, sir. He's my cousin." He was actually a very distant cousin, but the general didn't need to know that.

"Damn fine officer! He was my operations officer on a previous tour. In his third floor office, he had an exit door labeled *Airborne Only* that had no steps." The general laughed, and I laughed with him. He told me there's only one Mohawk unit left in Vietnam, the 131st up north, and he mentioned he was going up there early next week to visit some units.

"Be at my helipad at 0700 Monday," he told me. "I'll give you a lift."

★ ★ ★

I think I spoke too soon about the lack of rain. Yesterday afternoon, the wind and torrential rains blew through here. It felt like Hurricane Gracie. Today, the sky is blue and only a few puffy white clouds linger overhead. I decided to take advantage of the good weather and got into a basketball game on the outdoor courts. We've got nothing but time to kill while we wait. I know I've been assigned to the 1st Aviation Brigade in I Corps, but once I get to Da Nang, I'll either be assigned to the 131st Aviation Company or the 64th Helicopter Company. I pray to God it's the Mohawks. Maybe the general will help me in that regard.

★ ★ ★

Dean and I met outside my barracks near the taxi stand for my first trip to Saigon. I packed no civilian clothes for Vietnam, so I was in uniform. Dean was too. Neither of us had a weapon. I wasn't sure I actually wanted to make the eight-mile trip into the heart of the city. I heard stories back in the States of Viet Cong (VC) attacks in Saigon—horrifying attacks using children to deliver bombs.

The taxi that stopped for us looked like a motorcycle with two rear wheels and a canvas-draped passenger compartment thrown on the back. It would supposedly hold four people, but I doubted it would hold Dean and me. We managed to jam ourselves in by facing one another with our legs angled in opposite directions.

During the eight-mile drive to Saigon, the driver only obeyed one rule of the road—the largest vehicle had the right of way. Roadside stands constructed of shipping crates and folding tables held clear liter bottles of gasoline to serve as gas refill stations. Little mopeds resembling gasoline-powered bicycles swerved in and out of the traffic making high-pitched squeals. As we entered Saigon, the traffic got heavier and the city sounded like a lumberjack challenge with moped chainsaws buzzing around every corner. We kept a conversation going, but for me it was difficult. My eyes kept darting, looking out at the masses of people on the sidewalks and streets, wondering which one might be carrying a grenade or a live charge. Dean seemed oblivious to it all and just kept talking.

We hit the restaurant first. The scant light inside was made dimmer by excessive cigarette smoke. Dean has been there many times, so he knew exactly what to order. I told him to order for me. The cook prepared the food in a wok within sight of our table—the sizzle and smell of stir-fry vegetables and fish sauce cut through the cigarette smoke. I got my first taste of Vietnamese food, and it was pretty good, but I was happy when we finished and got out of that smoke-filled air.

From there, we headed to a nightclub. Dean warned me about local teenage *cowboys*, notorious for speeding by on their mopeds and snatching anything of value right off a serviceman—watches, sunglasses, whatever they can grab. I slipped my watch off my wrist and tucked it deep into my pocket.

A Vietnamese cover band was playing "Joy to the World" by Three Dog Night when we entered. Their playlist was mostly American Top 40 songs. They butchered them up pretty well, but it still felt good to hear familiar songs. There was another show going on adjacent to the band—some kind of exotic act from Korea consisting of men biting, chewing, and swallowing highball glasses.

On smaller stages throughout the club were imported Asian women of all varieties engaged in striptease. I guess Dean thought this would impress me. It didn't. I didn't tell him it was actually the first time I have ever been to a strip club. Nor did I tell him I didn't think much of him enjoying striptease while married to my cousin. And no amount of swallowed glass or bare breasts kept my mind off the possibility of a VC bombing.

Sunday, May 14, 1972
DAY 5:

Today was a slow day of waiting around the Repo Depot. I watched a group of Vietnamese women sweeping the street and another group loading a trash truck. Dressed in black silk, the women over here seem to do most of the work. I saw one older woman today stooped over a metal washtub on the side of a busy street doing her laundry while foot and motor traffic whizzed by.

Sitting around the barracks this afternoon, I thought about my summers with Uncle John Wyatt on the farm. At eleven years old back in '58, one of my jobs was holding the milk cow while it fed by the roadside. One old cow was brown with white splotches and gave milk twice a day—morning and night. In between those milkings, she did quite a bit of feeding. The unmolested grass along the shoulder of the road and along the ditch bank was prime eating. We had a twenty-five-foot chain tied around the horns on the cow's head to keep her from wandering into the two-lane country road and getting hit by a passing car. I held her by the chain, but I also had to watch what she was eating. We didn't want her to eat bitterweed or yellow-top flowers, which tarnished the taste of the milk. Instead I made sure she ate clover or tall Bermuda grass. Sometimes I was by myself the whole time for three or four hours of feeding, and sometimes my cousin Steve was out there with me. Every day or every other day somebody would be out there by the roadside letting that old milk cow feed. When we brought her back to the pitcher pump behind the house after feeding, it took a #3 washtub to fill her up with water.

★ ★ ★

This evening, I pulled out the small pocket Bible my cousin Liz gave me at the airport. It has the words *New Testament* printed in gold lettering on the cover, and the pages are so thin that it feels I might tear them as I turn them. When I was thirteen years old, I read the entire Bible from cover to cover starting with the Old Testament. This New Testament also includes the book of Psalms, so I spent most of my time tonight reading the poems. It helped put my mind at ease.

I end most every day writing to Martha Anne, and I don't feel complete until I've written to her. It's the best part of my day knowing that the very paper I am writing on will be in her hands and that my handwritten words will be seen by her eyes. I hope I'm able to keep it going.

Dear Martha Anne,

I didn't realize it was Sunday until nearly 1 p.m. It really shocked me. I had heard that there was no difference between weekdays and weekends but I thought I would have recognized Sunday. I hope God will forgive me for such an error. It really caught me by surprise when I found out it was Sunday.

It is raining again today here at Camp Alpha. It looks like I may spend the war here. I have a briefing at 4 p.m., telling me where to go and how to get there. I'm putting 50 piasters in this letter so you can show everyone Vietnamese money. It is worth about $0.10. When you get in country, they take all your money and turn it into M.P.C. (Military Payment Certificates). These are supposed to keep greenback dollars out of the country.

I love you very much and already am planning our R&R. Would you be terribly disappointed if I get an early return to the States & miss the R&R? It is really great to see about twice as many people leaving as there are coming into this place. I just hope that the rate of troops departing increases instead of decreasing.

Much love as I can send,
Joe

Monday, May 15, 1972
DAY 6:

This morning, for the first time in Vietnam, I put on my flight suit and helmet. As promised, General McClendon had me join him in his chopper. Looking down from above once we got clear of the Saigon city area, I was expecting to see jungle. But instead there were vast stretches of open rice paddies with only occasional spatters of palm tree stands. The general told me the area around Saigon is intensely agricultural and that in this climate, the paddies can produce two or three crops a year, which means that they are continually in plant or harvest cycle. The only places I saw thick foliage were the banana and rubber tree plantations. As a lieutenant, my place was to do more listening than talking in the company of the general, even as I hoped to remind him of the Tallon connection so that he might favor my preference for flying Mohawks. He turned back for Saigon before we made it to the I Corps area.

★ ★ ★

A couple hours after we landed back at Tan Son Nhut, I was on a C-130 transport to Da Nang Air Force Base and (thank you, Colonel Bill Tallon!) on my way to the last Mohawk unit in Vietnam. Da Nang has earned the name *Rocket City* because of all the rocket attacks it receives. Soldiers here say *a mortar will put a hole in your hut but a rocket will put your hut in a hole.*

When my C-130 taxied to a stop, I jumped out with my duffle bag and an oversized flight helmet custom-made for my large head, and I immediately scanned the airfield for the closest bunkers. It is hot as blue blazes here, and as I stood there scanning, I felt like the soles of my boots were melting to the tarmac.

The airfield operations sergeant placed a call to the 131st to let them know that they had an incoming lieutenant who needed to be picked up. My father always placed an emphasis on making quality first impressions. I waited a full five hours. What showed up was a three-quarter-ton truck driven by a lone sergeant from the aircraft maintenance section. I rode in the back with a load of spare repair parts. Hardly a quality first impression.

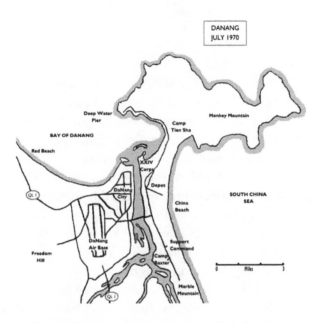

Map by Terry Cochran, www.boomernet.com, published with permission

In Vietnam, we measure distances in kilometers that everyone likes to call *klicks*. Depending on the route, it is ten to twelve klicks from the base in Da Nang to the Marble Mountain Army Airfield, my new home in Vietnam. The truck was heavy and slow, never breaking more than forty kilometers per hour. Like in Saigon, pesky mopeds swerved in and out of the Da Nang traffic, buzzing like flies around our lumbering vehicle. In those clogged, narrow streets, I was not at all comfortable with the fact that neither one of us was armed.

The dwellings in Da Nang are one-story, small, box-shaped houses jammed in side by side. It's easy to tell which ones have rocket damage. Mortars have left holes the size of basketballs in the rooftops, whereas the rockets have reduced houses to rubble. Homes of greater consequence have eight-foot-tall concrete block walls protecting them with broken glass bottles cemented to the top to discourage intruders. The sergeant pointed out the dangerous areas of Da Nang, particularly the critical I Corps bridge over the Han River, which he says is under constant threat. We had to cross it to get over to China Beach and Marble Mountain. He also cautioned me about Blood Square, named so for all the bombing attacks.

Once at the airfield, my eyes were immediately drawn to the two large limestone mountains that seem to rise from the relatively flat terrain like twin camel humps. One is much larger than the other, but both of them are peppered with green vegetation so thick that it is difficult to see the deep folds and curving lines in the limestone. I am told that the Marbles are considered sacred by the Vietnamese people. They are an imposing presence at the end of our runways, but our access to them is strictly limited.

I spent the afternoon moving in with my new roommates, Pat McGarvey and George Davis. Both are first lieutenants like me. Our hooch is made up of scrounged furniture. We have two air conditioners, three bedrooms, and a common party room with a black light and florescent pictures on the walls. The beach is not that far. This war wouldn't be so bad if I could have my wife with me.

Wallace Shot, Badly Wounded, Spinal Damage Feared

LAUREL, Md. (UPI)—Gov. George C. Wallace, who won the support of millions of Americans with his plea to "send them a message," was shot at close range by a young white man Monday as he campaigned for votes in Maryland's presidential primary. Rushed to a hospital by ambulance and helicopter, Wallace was on the operating table about five hours as a team of surgeons removed one bullet from his chest but decided to "wait a few days" on another lodged near his spine.

Tuesday, May 16, 1972
DAY 7:

The airfield is connected by a maze of sandbags and gravel roads within the perimeter that allows us to drive the two klicks to the China Beach hospital and recreation area without leaving the wire. The crystal blue water and lush vegetation make me think this could be a premier resort area if not for this war. But miles of spiraled rolls of concertina wire and tall wooden guard towers, not to mention the subterranean minefields, mess up the vision. The airfield runways, built by the Marines in 1965, are paved in asphalt, whereas the taxiways are made out of metal landing mats called *PSP* that are somewhat portable. Large piles of sandbags mark underground bunkers.

The first combat troops came here to Vietnam seven years ago on March 8 and 9. More than 3,500 Marines from the 9th Marine Expeditionary Brigade landed without resistance on Red Beach and were given the mission of securing an American base in Da Nang so the South Vietnamese military could be freed to conduct operations. By August that year, the Marines completed the construction of the airfield at Marble Mountain for use by their own helicopter units. The Army took control of the airfield from the Marines exactly a year ago. Running parallel to the ocean, one end of the runway points south to the Marble Mountains and the other stretches north toward Da Nang and a peak higher than the Marbles known as *Monkey Mountain*. Because of its prominence, Monkey Mountain serves as an excellent landmark for the base when flying in daylight, but pilots in the unit warn me it can be deadly when flying at night in bad weather. Depending on the wind, we can take off in either direction.

I met my Commanding Officer (CO). I don't think much of him. His name is Major Davis, and he greeted me coldly and quickly, as if pronouncing my last name was two syllables more effort than he wanted to expend. His time is getting short, and his replacement is already on the ground in the form of Major Roger Smith. Shortly before I arrived, Major Davis had flown him around the immediate area in a Mohawk to show him the installation's surroundings. This standard orientation flight was an opportunity for Major Davis to show his replacement what shape his unit was in before turning over command. Instead, Davis was embarrassed when he discovered green sandbags on the corrugated tin roof of his hooch organized to form the letters F.T.A. Translation: *Fuck the Army*. To an Army filled primarily with draftees who don't want to be here, these initials are as familiar as J.F.K. Major Davis is so angry he's launched an investigation to punish those responsible.

I had my first flight in Vietnam today and, interestingly, it was with Major Davis. He rode with me on my check ride as I demonstrated some basic maneuvers and landings in the Mohawk. It was a smooth flight, and I kept my interaction brief and professional. We are going back up again tomorrow afternoon to finish my orientation. It sounds like most pilots are only getting about forty to fifty hours of flight time per month, so I'm not sure how much time I'll actually see in the air.

I went to the PX today and bought a case of cokes, a bathing suit, some Tide laundry detergent, a pitcher for Kool-Aid, and some orange juice. Transportation is really a problem over here, so for the most part I end up walking nearly everywhere I go.

A rumor is circulating that they have cancelled all drops for aviators, meaning it is back to a full twelve-month tour. Maybe I'll be fortunate, and they'll declare a cease-fire before my full year is done.

Wednesday, May 17, 1972
DAY 8:

I am getting to know the other two lieutenants in my hooch. I shared a room with my little brother Roy for years, so having a couple roommates over here is nothing new.

Lieutenant Pat McGarvey likes to spend most of his spare time sunbathing on the roof. Laying down directly on top of our hooch is not an option because the corrugated tin roofing gets so hot it would sear a set of grill lines on his hide. Lucky for him, the marines constructed a rooftop wooden platform for a machine gun firing position. There is no longer a gun mount on the platform, so it has been repurposed as a tanning bed. McGarvey says he was inspired by Joe Namath's *Cosmo* magazine spread. He has an athletic build, and with his dark hair and mustache, looks a bit like Burt Reynolds. I try to avoid the roof when he is laid up there in the nude tanning every inch of his body.

My other roommate, Lieutenant George Davis from West Virginia, has proven to be quite a good cook. His family sends him packages of dried red beans in the mail, which George soaks in water for a full day. He gets onions and bacon from the mess hall and tosses it all in an electric pot to let it cook all day. It's better food than we get at the mess hall, so I tolerate the smell. George also plays the guitar pretty well. He plays popular songs while we sing along. He re-wrote the chorus to John Denver's "Take Me Home, Country Roads" to "Take Me Home Quang Tri Roads." The Quang Tri province is just north of the Quang Nam province, which is where Da Nang is—my new home away from home.

Today, I went to the XXIV Corps finance office to straighten out my pay. To get there, George Davis and I had to drive through downtown Da Nang, which is off limits to us other than to pass through. Leadership discourages us from carrying weapons around Marble Mountain, but I always make a point to sign out more firepower from the arms room than just my sidearm when I leave post. I don't think repeated trips through that city are good for my health, according to what I've heard. Remembering Dean's warning, I'm always on the lookout for cowboys who are ready to snatch anything that hangs off an American, whether dangling from their neck, perched on their head or slung around their wrist.

Thursday, May 18, 1972
DAY 9:

We were postponed yesterday, so I had my second check ride with Major Davis today. We spent most of our time doing single engine work and practicing emergency procedures. The check ride aircraft is a Mohawk stripped of its surveillance equipment and not in very good condition. The unit has a variety of Grumman OV-1 Mohawks from C to Super C to the D model. The OV-1C is being used for infrared (IR) missions, and its cameras are built into the belly of the aircraft. The Super C can be modified to fly either an IR or a side-looking airborne radar (SLAR) mission. The OV-1D is exclusively used for SLAR, and when the plane is set up for that kind of mission, a boom runs almost the entire length of the aircraft. To take off with the SLAR equipment attached before running off the end of our short runway, I must back up as far as possible into the overrun of the airstrip. The 131st only has fourteen Mohawks total of all configurations, and at least two and sometimes up to four are tasked away to an operating base in Thailand.

Last night we had a mortar attack, but they landed far enough away from my hooch that they didn't even wake me up. But that wasn't even the biggest surprise of the day. This morning, a former classmate, Mike McClendon, showed up! I thought he'd been sent to Germany, but it seems he drew a short straw, too. Mike was in my training class the last few months at Fort Huachuca in Arizona. We flew Mohawk familiarization missions to learn better how to employ the imagery and SLAR equipment. Flying with Mike was like pulling down the locking arm on a roller coaster: you were reasonably sure that you were going to survive, but you knew that you didn't have any control during what promised to be one hell of a ride. Mike was from New Jersey, and he said flying a plane was easy compared to driving the Jersey Turnpike because in the air, no other vehicles got in his way.

Training class at Fort Rucker standing in front of a Mohawk. I am second from the left in the front row, kneeling, and Mike McClendon is next to me kneeling, third from the left.

I've been assigned as his sponsor, which is a laugh. I've only got a week here under my belt and now I'm a guide. He asked about the Marble Mountains that loom over our base like a pair of runaway orphans from the nearby Annamite Range, and I gave him the tour of our general operations area—even found him a better room than I have.

During our training missions at Huachuca, Mike and I alternated between the pilot and observer roles to gain an understanding of both. The OV-1 Mohawk aircraft consists of two side-by-side seats in a cramped cockpit area that resembles a bug-eyed bird from the outside. On the inside, the control panel, foot pedals, and steering stick keep my six-foot-three-inch frame in a perpetual state of discomfort. The cockpit is designed to hold a much shorter man. Just like back at Huachuca, I'm one of the tallest pilots here in the unit at Marble Mountain. The seat on the left is for the pilot, and the seat on the right is for the observer.

Taking off one sweltering ninety-degree Arizona evening, Mike and I were headed south for a training mission along the Mexican border. I was assigned as the navigator for that flight, which meant I spent much of the flight time spinning around to adjust settings on the navigational Doppler behind me. Just five miles south of the 5,000-foot-high main runway at Fort Huachuca, we were required to climb above 8,000 feet in altitude to clear the Huachuca Mountains. Normally, this was not a problem for the OV-1 Mohawk, which could gain altitude at the rate of 3,450 feet per minute. The plane was relatively light, and it could really stand up on its tail and climb if we poured the throttle to it. On this particular takeoff, we were not climbing fast at all, and Mike responded by increasing the thrust. First, the engines were at 70 percent, then 80, 90, and finally 100 percent. Five miles south of the runway, we had only climbed 800 feet, and the Huachuca Mountains were looming straight ahead. Mike steered into a canyon to give us more time to gain altitude before clearing the crest of the Huachucas. Meanwhile, we steadily reviewed a mental checklist to figure out what was slowing our ascent.

"The gear's up on my side," I said, making a visual check to my right.

"It's up on my side, too," Mike answered.

"You checked the flaps?"

"I've already set the flaps."

A strained silence permeated the cockpit as Mike flipped multiple control switches. I glanced out at the turboprop engine on the right wing working at full throttle and then back forward at the canyon wall ahead. The plane shuddered under the strain of the engines at 100 percent thrust. We continued to climb but way too slowly. The canyon walls closed in on both sides of the plane, and it became apparent to me that we were not climbing fast enough to clear the ridge line ahead of us. I saw a small ground squirrel running along the canyon ledge, and I thought what a good idea it was for that squirrel to get out of our impact area. I wished that I too were running alongside that squirrel as it safely scurried over the fast-approaching ridgeline. Suddenly, there was a jolt, and I rocked back in my flight seat with my head pressed against the rest. We started to rapidly climb.

"What the hell was that?"

"The speed brakes," Mike answered. "I just pulled them in."

"Are you serious?"

"Guess I left them out on my ground check."

We both laughed nervously, and I wondered how Mike could have been so stupid to leave the speed brakes extended.

Dusk was settling in and we were safely over the Huachuca Mountains, so as navigator on the mission, I had to spin around in my seat and plug multiple coordinates into the Doppler system. While I was doing that, Mike put the plane into a steep turn. During our classroom training, the instructors told us never to put the plane in a steep bank when our observer was turned in his seat entering coordinates. Apparently, Mike thought it was a good idea to test their warning, and when I turned back around, I was instantly struck by the vertigo. It felt as if a sledgehammer hit me in the stomach.

"What are you doing?" I asked Mike.

"I wanted to see if that turn would really make you sick."

I just mumbled incoherently, my insides roiling.

"Guess they were right, huh?"

I groaned and rubbed my temples. By this point in the flight, it was getting dark, and I was having trouble gaining my equilibrium again. Looking out for the horizon wasn't helping me gain my bearings. It was like the pain of seasickness where you just want to throw up for a moment's relief. I stared at the lunch bag (slang for our cockpit vomit bags because that is where you lost your lunch) by my side and just prayed that I wouldn't throw up in the cockpit, even though it might provide some relief from the nausea. I couldn't stand the idea of giving Mike the pleasure. Mike continued to fly in an erratic manner, and I was totally consumed in a green, stomach-churning world of nausea for the next twenty minutes.

During that period of agony, I wasn't able to turn around in my chair and stare at the navigation system. My brain was jumbled, and I was trying to regain my equilibrium by staring forward into the ever-darkening horizon.

"Mike, where the hell are we?"

"I don't know. You're the navigator on this mission."

With my nausea finally subsiding a bit, I turned around to look at the Doppler, and it appeared that we were flying fifty miles into Mexico. We could see some distant lights of a city to the north.

"This ain't good," I said.

"What's the matter?"

"That is the Nogales, Mexico border crossing, and looking at this compass, we are to the south," I explained.

"No way."

"See those lights out there at one o'clock?"

"Yeah, I do," Mike confirmed.

"That's Nogales. I think we've invaded Mexico."

Mike and I eluded detection by the Mexicans and by the instructors back at Huachuca. Without incident, we made it back into American territory and completed our mission that night by hitting the required landmark points and snapping some surveillance photographs with the belly camera.

I can't believe I actually set him up today in a better hooch than mine.

Saturday, May 20, 1972
DAY 11:

China Beach is only two blocks from the end of the runway here, but our hooch is on the opposite side, making the beach a good mile away instead. It's still easy to access. Two lieutenants invited me to join them for an afternoon recreational day at the beach. It made me think of my hometown Folly Beach on the Atlantic. I spent many summers

Joe and Roy with Skip

there growing up. This was my first crack at the Pacific Ocean, though technically they call it the South China Sea. The waves were at least six feet high. My brother Roy would go crazy here on his surfboard, which he calls Little Red Hen. He used to ride longboards, but he recently got a nice, squatty red short board that he's really had fun riding. I let my body be my surfboard and floated on my back, allowing the waves to push me where they would. The only thing Roy loves more than his surfboard is Skip, his ridiculous little Chihuahua. Daddy brought him home in his pocket one day as a puppy barely bigger than a small rat. On Skip's first night with us, Roy put water in an ashtray for him. In the morning, we found Skip all curled up and asleep inside it. Roy, Skip and the Little Red Hen are inseparable.

The sand at China Beach feels much coarser than back home, and it rubbed my feet pretty raw while playing volleyball. I saw games of touch football, Frisbee and volleyball, along with plenty of beer drinking. It didn't really feel like we were in a war zone at all this afternoon.

I saw some pilots from the 131st gathered around a three-quarter-ton truck sunk up to its axles. One pilot was in the driver's seat shifting rapidly between drive and reverse trying to rock the truck enough to get it out of the sand. The others were cheering him on. The loud grinding sound followed by the chuckles of the surrounding pilots told the story. The transmission was destroyed. I approached just as the driver dismounted and one of the other pilots turned to me and said, "Joe, this is going to be your problem now." Some of the other pilots laughed.

"Why? I'm not the motor officer," I said.

"Well, you will be next week."

Everyone seemed to know about my new responsibility except for me. I saw no humor in it whatsoever, but I tried to appear cool as we all piled into Jeeps headed back to Marble Mountain. I am so upset that I want to punch some of those guys.

Dear Martha Anne,

I received my first letter from you today. It was really a great relief. I had given up on getting any mail until you returned from Mary Theresa's graduation.

I'm not very happy with my job over here. It looks like I'll be doing very little flying. I don't know anything about a motor pool but that is where I got stuck. For the first time since I've been in the Army, I feel completely useless.

I'm putting a little surprise in this letter for you. It is a shell off of the beach here at Marble Mountain. How about that? A shell from the opposite side of the world. I recalled many of our beach walks when I went to the beach last Saturday. I certainly would like to see you. When I come home this time, we are going to be very selfish. That means we spend most of our time together alone.

I love you,
Joe

Monday, May 22, 1972
DAY 13:

At dusk, I met at the airfield for a night check ride with a warrant officer. It was dark by the time we completed the preflight checklist. When I took over the controls in the air, I asked him what he wanted me to do. He told me to take it through its paces so that's what I did. There's a difference between painting by the numbers and being an artist. A lot of pilots can fly a plane by the numbers, whereas I consider myself more an artist with a feel for the plane. I trust the plane's capabilities and my abilities wholeheartedly.

Shortly after taking over the controls, I put the plane in a shallow dive to build up forward air speed. Then, I pulled the nose of the Mohawk up while rolling the left wing up to execute an aileron roll. The execution of the roll was crisp, and we didn't lose any altitude as the plane completed the roll and snapped back around to level in an instant. The warrant officer was not impressed and gave me an UNSAT on my check ride, for unsatisfactory. He thought that I was showboating in the aircraft and putting him and the plane at risk. I told him that's the way I learned to fly back at Fort Rucker. That is how we got a feel for the aircraft. I surprised him with the roll, and he didn't like it. Even though I technically outranked the warrant officer, there wasn't a damn thing I could say to change the UNSAT.

If that warrant officer had seen us back at Fort Wolters training on helicopters, he would have really been upset. I took more chances in those little TH-55 trainers than I would ever take in a Mohawk. During our routine training cycle, we typically spent half the day studying in the classroom and half the day flying with instructor pilots. But whenever we got the opportunity to fly solo, we tried to make the training fun by turning the mundane into competitive games. In one game, we used our rotor-wash to roll dried cow patties down the runway like little Frisbees. Turning them up on their side, a deft-handed pilot at the controls could get one to roll 300 to 400 feet. I got to the point where I could really roll a turd.

Inside the fragile wire and Plexiglas bubble of the TH-55, I pretended I was flying a large, majestic B-52. My favorite spot to fly over was Possum Kingdom Lake, twenty miles west of Fort Wolters. From above, the lake looked like a large, uncoiled snake with tentacles jutting out in every direction. Sprinkled around the shoreline were designated landing areas marked with painted tires for the trainees. These areas were various sizes and located in different types of terrain.

Once on a solo flight over the lake, I began my descent from an altitude of 2,000 feet by pretending that I was doing a B-52 bombing approach. I thought I was on a gradual descent across the surface of the lake, but when I crossed the shoreline, I noticed the mesquite bushes whizzing by and realized just how fast I was still traveling. In my descent calculations, I had neglected to shave off enough forward air speed. Safe landing speed was thirty knots, and I was at seventy. It was too late to pull up. So, I leveled the skids, turned the auto rotation down, and cut the power to the blades. I hit the ground hard and skidded at least 100 yards across the landing area before coming to a halt.

Although the landing was far from graceful, I embraced the saying that *any landing you can walk away from is a successful one.* I got out and walked around my aircraft and saw more mud than damage. Before returning to Dempsey Field, I flew out over the lake and hovered at the surface of the water to clean the mud off my skids and the bottom of the helicopter. Back at the base, no one was the wiser.

Nixon, Brezhnev Talk Privately

MOSCOW (UPI)—President Nixon talked privately for almost two hours with Communist Party Secretary Leonid I. Brezhnev Monday on his arrival for eight days of Soviet-American summit negotiations. Nixon expressed hope the summit might bring peace throughout the world . . . Nixon is the first U.S. President to visit Moscow and the first chief executive to journey to the Soviet Union since President Franklin D. Roosevelt's wartime strategy meetings with Josef Stalin at Yalta.

U.S. Planes Renew Bombing in North

SAIGON (AP)—American fighter-bombers returned to the Hanoi and Haiphong areas of North Vietnam on Monday as ground fighting on the southern front continued inconclusively. U.S. military sources said Air Force and Navy jets flew about 600 strikes Sunday and Monday against military targets from the demilitarized zone north toward the Chinese mainland in President Nixon's campaign to choke off war materials destined for the fronts in the South . . . The U.S. Command has

(cont.)

reported 90 aircraft, including 39 helicopters lost since the start of the North Vietnamese offensive more than seven weeks ago. Sixty-five Americans have been killed, 23 wounded and 85 are missing, including 26 airmen downed in the North.

Tuesday, May 23, 1972
DAY 14:

I was asked to report to the commander's office at 0900 hours. In short order, our new CO has already impressed the pilots of the 131st in ways that his predecessor did not. Major Roger Smith is a West Point graduate and a former Mohawk instructor pilot at Fort Rucker, and his confident style of leadership is a welcome contrast. I strode into his office this morning and snapped off a sharp salute. "Sir, Lieutenant Tallon reporting as ordered."

He asked me to sit down, and I felt beads of sweat streaming down the small of my back as I tried to maintain eye contact and sit up straight. Major Smith kept small talk to a minimum before diving into the list of issues that had plagued the unit's motor pool. "Three captains in succession served as the motor officer before you, and all of them were relieved.

Nineteen out of forty-eight vehicles are currently on deadline. It is your responsibility to get them mission ready."

He gave me a direct set of orders and measurable mission objectives. In no way did I ever envision my Vietnam War consisting of vehicle maintenance in a motor pool. But Major Smith's direct manner was motivating. After explaining for a few whirlwind minutes the importance of the motor pool, Major Smith stopped long enough to ask me for my feedback.

The head's up about the assignment over the weekend at the beach had given me time to think and prepare. I knew I had only one card to play.

"Sir, I can't take this job unless I'm the motor pool commander, and my word is law." I hoped that my words came out evenly and in a confident tone.

He responded quickly, "Yeah, you do what it takes to get these vehicles off the deadline report, and I'll support you. I'm gonna get you a real motor sergeant down there, too."

At that point, I didn't even know where our unit motor pool was located, but I left the CO's office with a real sense of purpose about my mission. Smith doesn't know me, but he seems to be placing his trust in my ability to get the job done.

There is no mystery as to why nearly half of the vehicles are on the deadline report, which means they are currently unusable. Officers drive them on all manner of personal errands. Almost all our officers are pilots, so their disregard toward wheeled vehicle maintenance contrasts greatly with their serious regard for aircraft maintenance. To them, the ground vehicles are expendable. The three-quarter-ton trucks and deuce-and-a-halfs are often taken to China Beach and abused in the soft sand. What I witnessed the other day at the beach was not unusual. Also, 131st officers are notorious about driving the Jeeps to see the *Sergeant Major*. This is code for the whorehouse near the base that is run by an old Vietnamese madam so authoritarian that she has earned herself the nickname.

After landing their Mohawks, many pilots are too lazy to walk from the flight line a half mile back to their hooch in the sweltering heat, so Jeeps are used as shuttles. Also in total disregard for the safety of the vehicles, members of our unit have left vehicles parked outside the protective revetments of the motor pool, which means that they often sustain damage from mortar attacks.

Wednesday, May 24, 1972
DAY 15:

It has been a remarkably busy two days. Yesterday afternoon, I met the men down in the motor pool for the first time. I quickly saw the impact of the high number of deadline vehicles on the low motivation of the men working there. To follow up on the motor officer assignment, I was also tasked this morning to be the unit's voting officer. With this being an election year, we are helping our soldiers to mail voter registration paperwork back to their home states. I didn't feel well at all today. I had congestion and a cough that was causing me pain in my chest. I went over to see the doctor at the clinic here, and he gave me some pills and grounded me from flying for two days.

Thursday, May 25, 1972
DAY 16:

Dear Martha Anne,

I remained in bed most of today, but I'm happy to say I feel much better tonight. I even went to see a movie at the club. It was *On a Clear Day You Can See Forever* with Barbara Streisand. There were a lot of roses in the movie and a rose garden. It reminded me how much roses have been a part of our life. It was in a rose garden when I first asked you to marry me. It was in a different rose garden that I placed an engagement ring on your finger and so many times since have said I love you with roses and meant it every bit. I just wish I could send you roses now.

Love always,
Joe

Friday, May 26, 1972
DAY 17:

We keep hearing rumors that *Round Ranger* will be shipped out to Saigon. I feel certain that someone in the unit is going to kill him before he gets transferred—likely to be a fellow officer. His actual name isn't Round Ranger but Roger Thiel, and he holds captain rank. But he's more than earned the moniker by his unnerving habit of carrying a battle-ax around with him. If someone fails to show up at one of his parties, the offending no-show is likely to find the door to his hooch chopped down by Round Roger and his battle-ax. He's chunky, with short crew-cut hair and a pair of beady eyes that flicker like faulty light bulbs. The community latrine has sustained periodic damage as his ax has taken signature chunks out of the stall doors, toilet tops, and sink bowls. Most of us are military intelligence branch officers, but for some reason, Thiel is the only infantry officer in the whole unit trained as a Mohawk pilot. Maybe he isn't getting enough combat action as a pilot and uses the violent swings of his ax to feed his need for aggression. Maybe he is just insane. I'm keeping my distance and my sidearm loaded near my bed in case one of his nocturnal Paul Bunyan sessions carves its way into my hooch.

Dear Martha Anne,

I sometimes wonder why the Army spent all the money they did in training me to fly and collect intelligence. Here I am in an aviation unit doing very little flying and working my wits out in a motor pool which I know nothing about. I feel wasted and frustrated like I have never felt before in my life. I want to do a good job but I just don't even know how to start.

I have one man who was sent to our company from another unit. He is constantly AWOL. I talked to him this morning and explained how serious this offense was in a combat zone but it had little effect on him. He worked until lunch and then went AWOL again.

I'm sure that in a few weeks things will look better because right now they could hardly look worse. I thought I was here to fly but it looks like I'll be spending only 30-40 hours a month flying and the rest will be additional duties.

I wish you could be here or I could be there. I just want us to be together again. I love you so very much.

Love always,
Your lover Joe

Offensive Missiles Frozen: Nixon Signs Arms Curb Pact

MOSCOW (AP)—President Nixon and Soviet leader Leonid I. Brezhnev have signed a summit agreement of historic scope, aimed at curbing the superpowers' nuclear arms race and slowing a spiral of potential death and destruction born with the atomic age 27 years ago . . . It gave the President the concrete results he said he sought in the summit talks and it gave him a foreign policy success to carry home to an election year.

Communist Tanks Attack Kontum

SAIGON (UPI)—Tank-led Communist troops attacked the Central Highlands city of Kontum for the second straight day Saturday despite heavy attacks by American warplanes. Field reports said American missile-firing helicopters knocked out two Communist tanks less than one-half mile from the northern edge of the city. B52s pounded suspected North Vietnamese troop concentrations within two miles of the city, dropping 300 tons of high explosive in raids Friday and early Saturday.

Saturday, May 27, 1972
DAY 18:

Today I received a package from my father, which included seed
packets for both okra and butter beans. He grew up on a farm and
knows how important it is to me to grow my own vegetables. I'm
planning to start a little garden in the large sand and dirt-filled fifty-
five-gallon drum barrels that serve as protective revetments around
our living quarters. A warrant officer just a few hooches down from
me has a couple of watermelon plants thriving in the revetments. I
can't wait to get my okra and butter beans in the ground to see if I
can grow my own fresh vegetables because I'm already tired of the
powdered eggs and powdered milk at our mess hall.

I've been thinking about my father a lot lately. I cannot believe
he was away from my mother for so long during World War II. How
did they do it? They had very little chance to communicate with one
another during those three long years. At least I can write and receive
letters and attempt the occasional call on the Military Affiliate Radio
System (MARS) line. Even so, I haven't been here twenty days yet,
and I don't know how I'm going to make it without Martha Anne for
a whole year. My father was on ships in both the Pacific and Atlantic
for several months at a time with only sporadic mail delivery.

When he finally came home after the war, he worked as a traveling
salesman, which put him on the road a lot. I was about twelve when
he began working sales for the Greenbax stamp company. In 1959, he
purchased a brand-new Ford Fairlane—the first new car the family ever
owned. He put between 60,000 and 70,000 miles a year on that Ford.
Each night when he stayed out on the road, he placed a collect call to
my mother. We picked up the phone and the operator typically said, "A
collect call from Harry Tallon in some small town, South Carolina. Will
you accept the charges?" My mom always said no. We weren't going
to waste the money to actually talk. It was just a code to let us know
he reached the hotel safely in the town he planned to stay that night.

Normally he stayed out on the road on Monday through
Wednesday nights, three weeks each month and stayed one week
locally in Charleston. If a local customer needed another book of
Greenbax stamps while he was away, I did the delivery with my mother
in the car. She did all the bookkeeping anyway since you couldn't read

my father's handwriting. If an out-of-town customer ran out of stamps, we took a booklet of stamps down to the Greyhound bus station. On our behalf, the bus driver transported the stamps for us, and my father would collect payment the next time his travel route took him to that particular store. I've tried to add up all the nights he spent away from home, but it's too many, especially when I include the war.

If he could do all that, certainly I can do this year in Vietnam.

Sunday, May 28, 1972
DAY 19:

While Sundays feel different here in Vietnam than they do back home, there is a familiar slowing of the weekly rhythm on the day of rest. More members of the unit tend to find their way to the beach. Meetings typically don't get scheduled. Not having a Mohawk mission today allowed me the opportunity to stay up most of the night trying to get through on the MARS line. It can sometimes take between one and three hours to get a MARS call connected through all the civilian radio operators. Last night it took me four and a half. It was about one in the morning before I finally connected to my parents in Charleston, which meant it was one in the afternoon there. I asked them to get the message to Martha Anne to send civilian clothes. I didn't think I would need them over here, but just about everyone wears them when they are not on duty. The PX here on Marble Mountain is terrible, and the CO doesn't really want us going to the one in Da Nang. He's concerned there are numerous Viet Cong mixed into the flood of refugees in the vicinity of the city.

I'm really looking forward to my mission tomorrow. It's finally my turn. Each of the pilots gets to fly to our secondary base in Ubon, Thailand on an orientation flight, typically in their first month in the unit. Because it is our auxiliary base, it's available to land if ever we are running low on fuel returning from a mission and the Marble Mountain airfield is socked in with bad weather or otherwise unavailable. The orientation mission to Thailand is really a glorified shopping and dining excursion. We don't even fly with an observer in the cockpit, but instead two pilots go over together. I might be able to pick up some good civilian clothes while I'm there.

I'm only telling Martha Anne right now that I've come to an important decision. I just can't see myself being away from her like this for another year. When I get back to the States, I'm going to ask for a drop from active duty maybe into the reserves or something.

Monday, May 29, 1972
DAY 20:

Dear Martha Anne,

Today was really a day. I went to Ubon, Thailand for a D-model check-out. It was unbelievable. I really regret that I'm not in the Air Force. They certainly know how to live. I had dinner in the officer's club which was really nice and then I went shopping. I spent nearly $200. I bought two suits (one dress & one double knit sport suit), two pairs of knit slacks, two sport shirts and a Spud party suit. The Spud suit is a 131st unit party suit made like a one-piece flight suit and made of a black material. I also bought a gold puzzle ring for me, a ring for you and a bracelet, and a pair of earrings for my mother.

Thailand was really different. You go to a place to buy clothes and it is a fabric shop with a tailor. You pick out the style from a magazine and then they measure you. You go to a shoe store and they draw your feet on a piece of paper and tape measure it from your toes all the way up to your ankle in sections. This way you get a shoe tailored to your foot.

You should see the temples in Thailand; they are really beautiful. I only regretted that I did not have a camera. Even some of their trucks were so decorated with chrome until they looked like something from the movies. My 10 hours there went by so quickly and we were back at Da Nang and in the war again. Oh, yes, I had a terrific steak supper in Thailand for $2.50.

My steak was very tender, tasty, cooked perfectly and about 2 lbs. I could not believe it. It would cost you at least $10 in the states. I'll soon be mailing the jewelry to you. Send a checkbook as soon as you can. Allow me $150 per month in checks. I'll let you know if I spend more or less. I really got about $250 worth of jewelry for $40.

I love you very much and I wish you could share some of my good times over here with me but I don't want you to even know of some of the days. I love you with all my heart.

Love always,
Joe

Tuesday, May 30, 1972
DAY 21:

Just days into the motor officer job and I am sick of it already. The collection of misfit soldiers that they have sent to work in this motor pool is depressing. But I'm dedicated to attacking the challenge. Patton was forced to sit as a decoy on the coast of England surrounded by a shadow Army while the D-Day invasion was planned and executed without him. However inglorious it is, this is my war and my mission, so I am determined to attack it with everything I've got.

Reinforcements arrived today in the form of Staff Sergeant Larry Dubose. He has run a motor pool operation before, and he has ideas about how we can quickly get vehicle maintenance to be a higher priority in the unit. For an officer in command of anything in the Army, from a detachment to a division, the relationship with your top noncommissioned officer can make or break you.

Dubose came to the 131st by way of a transfer from another unit located nearby. Like me, he has been a member of an MP unit in the past, so we found some common ground today when we met.

Like many of the sergeants, he has a mustache, and his salt and pepper hair has just enough gray to convince me that his eleven years in the Army have not been that easy. Even though he grew up in rural Texas, his accent isn't that strong. I know a little bit about Texas from my days stationed at Fort Wolters. He is just five-foot-seven, but he has a presence about him that I think will quickly command the respect of our mechanics. He's actually a little older than I imagined he would be—probably in his early thirties. I actually think that is a plus, too.

Wednesday, May 31, 1972
DAY 22:

In short order, Sergeant Dubose has schooled me on the intricacies of a functional motor pool. His experience is invaluable, and I am thankful to have his expertise. He told me about the critical importance of weekly preventive maintenance checks and services, which he calls *motor stables*. We devised a plan together, and I'm taking on the unpopular task of implementing it. We spent the entire morning in the motor pool trying to get our new motor stables organized.

This afternoon, one of my men got an Article 15 punishment. He was assigned to our motor pool two weeks ago and has been AWOL ever since. I think I only laid eyes on him once prior to this afternoon, and my conversation with him did little good. His name is Private Reynolds, and he is a young Black kid with track marks on both arms. He doesn't have any more rank to take away, so they docked his pay and put him on extra duty. It'll probably take more effort to track him down for extra duty than we'll ever actually get work out of him.

I already had my mission briefing this afternoon, and shortly after dark, I must fly a SLAR mission over North Vietnam. There'll be no rest when I get back, since I've been assigned duty officer responsibilities tonight. At least I can use the opportunity on duty at the orderly room overnight to try and call Martha Anne.

Thursday, June 1, 1972
DAY 23:

Last night while I was the on-duty officer, I tried twice to get connected on the MARS line to Martha Anne. Both calls eventually failed to get through, so once again I'm missing out on hearing her voice. After a really long day yesterday, it didn't get much better today. I finally put my head down on the pillow in my hooch at eight this morning. Then at half past noon, my platoon leader woke me up and told me I had to take an annual aviator written exam at one fifteen. I barely had time to grab a bite at the mess hall before reporting to the test room. We were provided a four-hour block to take it, but I finished the exam in three and a quarter. Thankfully, I passed.

With no night mission scheduled, I took the opportunity to watch the movie at the officer's club. It was *Kotch,* starring Walter Matthau. Very enjoyable. The storyline made me wish Martha Anne and I already had a baby or at least one on the way. We've got plenty of time to work on that when I get back from Vietnam.

It's really hard to not hear Martha Anne's voice on a regular basis. When she was still at Shorter College in Rome, we spent some serious time on the telephone. One month while stationed at Fort Hollabird near Baltimore, I amassed a $238 phone bill making calls to her in Georgia. I would have preferred her at my side. But once early on in our courtship, I stood in her parents' living room in North Charleston waiting to take Martha Anne on a date. Her mother pointed a finger at my chest. "She will not marry you until she is finished with her degree." So we waited.

If I could just get a couple minutes of clear connection on the phone, hearing her voice would put my mind at ease. In her last letter to me she said she was going to send me a cassette tape with a recording of her talking to me. I cannot wait.

Friday, June 2, 1972
DAY 24:

Each Friday, the 131st convenes an officer's call—a weekly meeting of every available officer in the unit. The room gets crowded because we have many more officers than a normal company due to all the pilots. At my first one, I was just a spectator sponging up information. Today, however, I was the newly christened motor officer, so I actually had a speaking part. To start, either the CO or the executive officer (XO) leads with some general comments. Then, the batting order commences with the operations officer first, followed by the imagery interpretation chief, then the aircraft maintenance officer, the supply officer and, lastly, the motor maintenance officer briefing. The tail-end placement is indicative of my esteemed position in the unit.

I'm determined to change the unit's maintenance culture, but today I was outranked by everyone in the room except for a couple of warrant officers and three other lieutenants who had actually been in the unit longer than me but had less time in rank.

When it came my turn, I rose and used the most confident voice I could muster. First, I announced that the nineteen vehicles on the deadline report a week ago when I took over had been reduced to sixteen. With the arrival of some repair parts, that number could be as low as fourteen before the next officer's call. Then I pulled out my prepared bullet points and laid down the new motor pool ground rules.

"One, motor stables are required weekly at zero eight hundred every Saturday morning, and anyone not conducting the preventative maintenance on their assigned vehicle on Saturday will be denied use of the vehicle for the next week."

"Two, the motor pool will remain locked, and no vehicles will leave that enclosure without the signature of me or my motor sergeant, Staff Sergeant Dubose."

"Three, there will be a guard at the motor pool twenty-four seven with orders to shoot anyone trying to remove a vehicle without written permission."

"Four, no pleasure trips with unit vehicles will be allowed to any non-mission-essential destinations."

"Five, all vehicles must be returned to the protection of the revetment area when the mission is completed. Any vehicle damaged or destroyed because it was left outside the revetment will result in the driver and the officer in charge of that vehicle being placed on charges for loss of government property."

"Staff Sergeant Dubose and I were both in the Military Police—myself with the 198th at Fort Stewart, where I conducted line-of-duty investigations. Dubose performed similar inquiries while stationed in Texas. I really have no problem initiating investigations."

It was over in less than five minutes, and I sat down in the incredibly silent room. I am not sure what I expected, but my ground rules seemed to have sucked the air out of the room. Major Smith added nothing to my comments and did not stop me once I got rolling. These ground rules were exactly what Dubose told me was necessary to stop the abuse of our vehicles and get them repaired. I'll just have to take the heat if need be.

The meeting concluded not long after I spoke, and the backlash came quickly as Captain Chapman, my platoon leader, cornered me. Apparently, he was the one who left the three-quarter-ton truck outside the revetment, which led to its destruction by mortar fire. I didn't know this until he approached me after the meeting. Chapman went on and on, detailing my ignorance about how things were done at Marble Mountain long before I got here. He told me I needed to be careful who I threatened. He finished his spirited talk with a warning: "I'm going to get you."

Saturday, June 3, 1972
DAY 25:

Today, Dubose suggested we grill on weekends down at the motor pool to build some *esprit de corps* among the men. They have been working hard on these deadline vehicles and deserve some recognition. Being the savvy sergeant that he is, Dubose was able to get some chicken leg quarters from the cooks in the mess hall, so we shut down work early this afternoon. A previous unit, probably the Marines, built a grilling pit at the motor pool area out of large stones and concrete. There were even built-in steel rods for a metal grill rack to sit on and a compartment hollowed out for charcoal. I sent a couple guys out to get some. When they came back with the charcoal, I helped Dubose cook the meat over the coals. The men had a cooler full of beer, and even the cooks made it down after they served dinner in the mess hall, bringing with them containers of coleslaw and mashed potatoes.

Later, after everyone had a good start on their second piece of chicken and probably their third or fourth beer, I overheard two of our men bragging about taking two bags of charcoal from the side of the road. I ordered them to immediately get into a three-quarter-ton truck. They gave me looks conveying both surprise and annoyance. It couldn't have been much more than a mile from the base before we arrived at the place where they stole the charcoal.

On the way, I lectured my guys: "First, charcoal doesn't cost that much. Second, it's hard to win the hearts and minds of the Vietnamese when we run around stealing stuff from them. Just because we carry guns and have a lot of powerful vehicles doesn't give us the right to take things. That makes us no better than the Viet Cong we are fighting." My men sat silently on the ride out of the base, and I could tell that they were not enthusiastic about this trip.

We approached the Vietnamese family who had the roadside charcoal stand, and they spoke very little English. We had no translator with us, so we did the best we could to communicate what we were doing. We paid them for two bags in South Vietnamese piasters and they tried to hand us two bags. We kept declining, and I kept explaining. This greatly confused them. In the end, I'm not sure they had any idea why we paid them and took nothing in return. The whole trip took less than fifteen minutes before we were right back at the motor pool. But I hope that the men got the message that we can celebrate our hard work each weekend without stealing from the locals.

Sunday, June 4, 1972
DAY 26:

Today I had a conversation with our supply officer Captain *Slim* Bumgardner, who is actively trying to starve himself out of the Army. He's certain that he'll be discharged if he can just get his weight below 130 lbs. At over six feet, he is already rail thin, and he is having trouble dropping those last few to get under his goal weight. His long sideburns highlight his large protruding ears, and the thick mustache that grows over the corners of his mouth is certainly out of regulation. Like many of the troops at this point in the war, I don't think Slim is too concerned about hair regulations. He is one of the 131st officers who never flies combat missions, and through an elaborate system of official hand receipts, he has signed for millions of dollars of equipment, including the planes. So for this reason, Slim purportedly convinced the commander that he is too valuable to fly missions. Slim isn't the only one crafty enough to avoid flying the dangerous Mohawk missions. Many of the seasoned officers in the 131st have carved out staff positions and make similar claims.

Monday, June 5, 1972
DAY 27:

When I woke up this morning, I went right to work on my new garden spot. I used an entrenching tool to carve out small holes into which I dropped the seeds. The row of revetments behind my hooch has a double row of fifty-five-gallon drums on the bottom with a single row of drums balanced in the middle, forming a higher wall of protection. This staggered alignment leaves open areas of sandy, exposed soil where I built my little bean and okra hills. I planted in eight of the drums, and even though they don't get direct sunlight all day, my main concern is that most of the soil is actually just sand. I could have really used some cow manure to enhance it because I'm not sure how well these seeds are going to take. I did fill a pitcher of water and soaked the sandy seed mounds. We are getting plenty of heat now, so I expect the sprouts will pop up soon. We'll see what happens.

I guess I owe just about everyone back home an apology. I wrote them and complained about them not writing me this morning, and then wouldn't you know it: I got a letter from Roy, one from Lindler, one from Mama, and three from Martha Anne this afternoon. Some of the letters were over ten days old, so I guess the mail system carries most of the blame. I don't have time to write everyone back before I head out on my mission this afternoon.

Tuesday, June 6, 1972
DAY 28:

Yesterday afternoon I was flying north at least four miles off the coast and above 10,000 feet when, over my left shoulder, I spotted an area in the ocean near the shore that looked like an island thick with trees and vegetation. I have twenty-twelve vision in my left eye and twenty-ten in my right. Even from that distance I could make out a number of small flat-bottomed sampan boats partially concealed under netting and could plainly see the outline of the body of a ship in shadow on the ocean floor. I immediately placed a call to the air boss, gave him the coordinates, and requested fire. I had mission points further north, so I continued on with my route, but on the way back down I made a point to fly a closer path to it. Sure enough, I was able to confirm my original suspicions, but it would have been impossible for me to identify it as a large freighter ship without seeing the outlined shadow on the sea floor. The surface camouflage was just too good.

Today is the anniversary of D-Day. This afternoon I thought a lot about my father. He was involved that day in one of his toughest days. He's always been quiet about it. But not long before my departure for Vietnam, I did get him to talk a bit. He told me he manned a dual 20-millimeter anti-aircraft gun on a landing craft vessel that shuttled medical supplies into the beaches and shuttled wounded Americans back out to the hospital ships waiting offshore. His craft made six trips back and forth to the beach. When I asked him which beach, he said they went to all of them, but he did say that on some of the beaches you could walk from the vessel to the beach on the backs of dead American bodies floating in the water. His boat only picked up the wounded and stacked the stretchers on the floor while my father provided cover. After each trip back to the hospital ship, they used a shovel to remove the empty brass casings from below his gun and throw them into the ocean before bringing on more ammunition and more medical supplies. The only injuries he suffered that day were some minor burns on his legs from all the hot brass falling from his gun. After six round trips, they removed my father to get something to eat, since he had been at it all day, and he was the only one not to be wounded yet on his vessel. On the seventh trip to the beach, the vessel never returned to the hospital ship. A German artillery shell directly hit it while it was in the surf. My father is the seventh son of an Irishman, and he has always counted himself lucky—and none more so than that day.

McGovern Wins in Four States

By Mike Feinsilber (UPI)—Like a prairie wind, George S. McGovern swept primaries in California, New Mexico, New Jersey, and his home state of South Dakota Tuesday and predicted "the same fresh spirit" would lift him into the presidency. Less conspicuously, President Nixon also triumphed. His one-sided victory over Rep. John M. Ashbrook, R-Ohio, a conservative critic of Nixon's disarmament, defense, welfare and China policies, assured the President of enough GOP delegates to win renomination.

U.S. Planes Attack Hanoi Power Plant

SAIGON (UPI)—The U.S. command today reported American warplanes bombed a rail yard and smashed a highway bridge with electronically-guided bombs in the closest raids to the Chinese border ever ordered by President Nixon. The strikes were part of 270 raids inside North Vietnam on Tuesday and the heaviest attacks north of the Demilitarized Zone (DMZ) since May 28 . . . In the Central Highlands, American B52s carried out 15 raids Tuesday night and today against Communist troops pulling back from Kontum. Allied forces had fought the North Vietnamese for 12 days before forcing them out of Kontum, located 260 miles north of Saigon.

U.S. Rejects Demand to Return to Talks

PARIS (AP)—The United States and South Vietnam today rejected a demand from North Vietnam and the Viet Cong to resume the Vietnam peace talks Thursday. The allies said Communists had given no indication that they were ready to negotiate seriously, and they still sought a military solution to the war. The allies suspended the conference indefinitely on May 4.

Wednesday, June 7, 1972
DAY 29:

Dear Martha Anne,

I received no mail today but considering all I have received in the last three days it is all right. I read your letters over and over. The envelopes get all worn and torn. Hey, how about a little perfume once and a while.

I'm sending an article out of the Stars & Stripes. The Navy gets all the credit in this case but it was LT Tallon who told the Navy exactly where the ship was hiding. It had slipped in during a thunderstorm at night when we couldn't fly and the Navy's radar doesn't work too well. I gave them six-digit coordinates of the ship's location. It was hiding behind some hills on a small island in a cove. They couldn't pick it up on radar but old eagle-eye Tallon saw him from 10,000 feet in the air. You can tell my father about it and show him the article. I thought about him yesterday on D-Day. It is discouraging not to get any credit but they don't want to tell them how we found the ship. I also had it on my sensor so that was forwarded to Saigon. I guess the mines & the blockade won't stop every ship. Some are very determined to unload their cargoes.

Much love from your lover and husband,

Joe

The original *Stars & Stripes* newspaper clipping.

(Transcription on next page)

STARS & STRIPES

Mystery Ship Spotted

SAIGON (UPI)—The cruiser Newport News spotted a merchant ship lying off the southern coast of North Vietnam, apparently unloading cargo on a beach. A UPI photographer reported from the Newport News that US Navy ships watched the cargo boat for several hours last Friday but took no action against it. The photographer said officers aboard the cruiser would not tell him what type of ship the merchantman was, or if it was actually unloading cargo. Military spokesmen were not available for comment. President Nixon ordered the seven biggest harbors of North Vietnam mined May 9 to prevent the use of dock facilities in delivering war material to the Communist nation. Military sources have indicated foreign ships within North Vietnamese territorial waters would be halted or fired on. Some sources have speculated that Soviet, Chinese, and other Communist and neutral nations would order their ships to unload at coastal beaches in order to beat the minefields. The US Navy has maintained officially that its only job in connection with the "blockade" is to warn away ships from the blockade. A news release issued Saturday said that a Soviet trawler was warned not to sail into Vinh harbor and thanked the US ship that issued the warning. Spokesmen had not reported the sighting of the merchant ship on the beach north of Dong Hoi, about 50 miles north of the demilitarized zone. The UPI photographer was told that the Newport News "got word that a merchant ship was unloading on the beach into junks," and the cruiser and her destroyer escort of about half a dozen ships sailed to the area.

Thursday, June 8, 1972
DAY 30:

Dear Martha Anne,

I never have told you this but I prayed my heart out almost for a full year before I met you and started dating you. My prayer was for God to give me someone who could love me as much as I could love them and he answered that prayer. I know our love was conceived in Heaven and that we will be together again. I know you have worries and are nervous over my being in danger. Just remember that I never fly alone. I always have God as a copilot and you in my heart. With a crew like that I could start the best airline in the world.

Seriously, dear, I love you and miss you terribly. I would be with you right now if wishing could make it so.

We had a farewell party for Major Davis today. Major Smith is my new CO. It was my first time to eat lobster. I like crab a lot better. Lobster is tougher than crab and not nearly as sweet.

I'm so glad we are married. I only wish we were married two years ago. You could have gone all the way through flight school with me. I love you desperately and pray for our reunion to be speedy. I love you.

> Much love from your lover and husband,
> Joe

AP photo by Nick Ut used with permission from the Associated Press

B52s Hit Enemy Depots

SAIGON (AP)—Waves of U.S. B52 heavy bombers swept over North Vietnam in a second day of heavy attacks against enemy supply depots Friday. Others struck near Saigon against elements of an enemy regiment menacing the capital's western flanks . . . Close to Saigon, a South Vietnamese bomber trying to flush out the enemy at the district town of Trang Bang accidentally dropped napalm on young children, villagers and government soldiers, killing or wounding about 20 persons.

Friday, June 9, 1972
DAY 31:

I spent the entire day at the motor pool pushing the men on these deadline vehicles. Major Smith seems to be very supportive, and Dubose and I have scheduled our first weekly motor stables for tomorrow. We will be inspecting each of the operational vehicles, documenting the faults, and taking corrective actions. Getting everyone in the unit who uses a vehicle to participate should help my job considerably.

I received my first cassette recording in the mail this afternoon from Martha Anne. It's wonderful to hear her voice, especially since we have had such trouble connecting on the MARS line. I just listened to her again.

"I wish I could think of something to say—some way to tell you how much I miss you. All I can say is that I'm really planning for New Year's to celebrate our anniversary. I have the room at the Holiday Inn reserved for us. Since we won't be together on our actual anniversary, we'll celebrate that day. I've been thinking about things we can do while you're home, like go look for seashells that we can add to the collection. I've got a starfish, you know. And I've got several new conch shells and some pretty complete, whole sand dollars. I want some unusual ones though.

We can maybe go to Charles Towne Landing if it's not too cold. I don't want to sit inside the whole time you're home. Of course we'll see your parents, and we'll have dinner at mother's house at least once. You better get your request in because she'll make whatever you want. I just want to say how much I love you and that I miss you more each day. You're my complete life and the only one I care about. Without you, I just exist until I hear from you or I know you'll be back with me. I love you more than you'll ever know. I love you more than I've ever let you know. But when you come home it will be different. I'll let you know."

Martha Anne

[End of audio]

I fear I'm going to wear it out, but I keep rewinding the cassette to listen to the last couple minutes over and over. I'm going to prepare a recording tomorrow to send back to her. I'm too tired tonight to do a good job of it.

Vann: A Soldier's Soldier

By Peter Arnett and Horst Faas, Associated Press Writers, SAIGON (AP)—No man served America in Vietnam longer than John Paul Vann. He was firmly convinced of the ultimate rightness of America's mission, saw Vietnam's problems with brutal clarity, and had the courage to act and speak up about them when things went wrong. Vann was a leader of men not by virtue of his rank or position, but by his drive and fearless personal example. That was why he was on a helicopter flying to the beleaguered highlands city of Kontum Friday night. Once more he wanted to back up the will to fight of the Vietnamese troops defending the city . . . He did not reach Kontum. The helicopter went down in flames, and Vann, 47, paid the final price like 55,967 other Americans in Vietnam.

Saturday, June 10, 1972
DAY 32:

This morning we held our first Saturday motor stables. We had some turnout, but unfortunately, none of the platoon leaders showed up. The commander didn't even show up. I think he got caught up in Saigon and didn't get back to the unit in time. We did the best we could with the folks who did show up. I didn't stay at the motor pool myself very long this morning, as I had an early afternoon mission. I flew with Specialist Yarborough as my observer, and everything was going well until we arrived at our last mission point. As we were turning around, Ho Chi Minh's revenge claimed me as a victim. I couldn't hold it any longer. There is literally nowhere to go *number two* in the cockpit. It's not the first time I've had the diarrhea since I've been in country, but this is by far the worst, since it struck in the air. On the flight back to Marble Mountain, I just had to marinate in my soiled flight suit. Yarborough, ever straight-faced and stoic, asked, "Are you going to make it?"

I meekly responded, "I'm thinking about ejecting and letting you fly back on autopilot." But I wasn't serious. The fever and cramps have wiped me out. By the time I got back to the flight line, I struggled to get back to my hooch. I immediately took off my flight gear and went to the showers to wash everything out. The head of aircraft maintenance, Captain Godwin, sent a runner over to my hooch to tell me to come back and clean out the aircraft. I referred to Godwin as *Chicken Bone Six* since he recently announced at the officer call briefing his anger at pilots leaving their chicken bones in the Mohawks. I told the soldier to relay to Captain Godwin that he could burn the aircraft for all I cared. I couldn't move away from the latrine for any reason. I didn't even get out of bed to eat dinner at the mess hall. By late evening, I felt so bad that I went to the clinic. They gave me some pills that have some amount of morphine in them to control the cramps, and with that they've grounded me from flying for two days.

Kim Phuc Recuperates in Hospital

EDITOR'S NOTE: An Associated Press photograph of an unidentified little girl running naked down a road after being hit in an accidental napalm strike was featured in American newspapers. AP correspondent Carl D. Robinson traced the girl to a Saigon hospital.

By Carl D. Robinson, Associated Press Writer, **SAIGON (AP)**—Nine-year-old Phan Thi Kim-Phuc is recuperating in a Saigon children's hospital but the memory of being caught and burned in napalm strike at Trang Bang two days ago lingers in her memory. Her mother and father are nearby, comforting her with

(cont.)

love, food and medicine. Their eyes are red from tears over the death of their 2-year-old son who died later the same day from severe burns . . . The children went off to play near the pagoda, leaving the parents at home . . . The South Vietnamese bombers came in for a run, and it was so close the children scrambled into a trench outside the pagoda. Soldiers warned the children they had better leave and together the group started running down the road. Another South Vietnamese bomber flew over and its canisters of napalm splattered sticky balls of fire across the road. The napalm set Kim-Phuc's clothes afire. She and her friends kept running, screaming at the flaming horror and searing pain of her back. They reached nearby government positions where soldiers poured water over her burns. Later, her mother came down the road, carrying her seriously burned brother. A soldier stopped the mother and draped his rosary around the boy's neck. The child died a few hours later.

U.S. to Shift Vietnam Units

WASHINGTON (AP)—To cut U.S. troop strength in Vietnam to the 49,000-man level ordered by President Nixon for July 1, several Air Force and Marine fighter units will be shifted to Thailand, Pentagon sources said Saturday. Although this will have the effect of removing several thousand airmen and support personnel from Vietnam, they still will be able to carry round-the-clock air strikes from their new bases. American troop withdrawals have continued despite the two-month-old North Vietnamese offensive but the pace has slowed somewhat. As of last week about 60,000 GIs remained, leaving nearly 11,000 more to come out in the next

(cont.)

three weeks . . . U.S. forces in Thailand, now numbering nearly 40,000, and the 42,000 navy men offshore aboard 7th Fleet ships, are not included in the Vietnam troop total. The Pentagon sources said the four Air Force and three Marine F4 Phantom fighter bomber squadrons remaining at the big American base in Da Nang will move to Thailand in the next few weeks.

Churches' Board to Question U.S. Role in War

NEW YORK (AP)—The policy-making board of the National Council of Churches—already on record as opposed to the war in Vietnam—Saturday adopted a resolution to question the legality of the U.S. role in the conflict. The action was taken on the concluding day of a two-day meeting of the 250-member general board, which represents 33 Protestant and Orthodox denominations totaling about 42 million members.

Sunday, June 11, 1972
DAY 33:

Our bunker is no more than 150 feet from my hooch. It's amazing how fast I can cover that distance when properly motivated. Like most of our serious mortar attacks, last night it started well after midnight. I was in a deep sleep, and I have no idea how many mortars had landed when the sound finally woke me up. I threw on my boots but didn't bother to fully lace them up. I grabbed my steel pot helmet, my frag vest, and pants, hitting a dead sprint to the bunker. None of us have weapons, as the unit doesn't trust us to keep them on our persons. The weapons are all stored in the unit arms room. I didn't even have my .38

pistol, which I sometimes sleep with after night missions. Our bunker was well-dug years before by the Marines and is lit by a single electric bulb. With a row of bench seats on either side, we can squeeze at least eight men in there shoulder to shoulder. Last night we had four, all of us pilots. There are no apertures to look outside or return fire. So we all just sat around listening to the thud of mortars outside. About fifteen minutes after the incoming stopped, we took that as an all-clear sign and returned to our hooches to try to salvage some sleep.

We were hit by medium-sized 81-millimeter mortars. Seven aircraft were hit and three destroyed—all from my platoon. These planes cost about $4.5 million each. Two people were wounded but not seriously. Fortunately, no one was killed. Given the extensive damage to our aircraft, it's highly likely that someone inside the compound helped them mark the aircraft locations.

This morning, I went over to check on the condition of the Mohawks—both the ones that were hit by mortars and the one that I bombed during my diarrhea-enhanced mission yesterday. Now that I can walk a distance from the latrines, I wanted to see if I could help clean the cockpit seat. Captain Godwin informed me that the plane was already cleaned by two of his aircraft maintenance soldiers. I asked what I could do for them, and he suggested beer. So, I immediately purchased two cases of beer and brought them back to say thank you. I have a feeling I'm going to hear about this incident again.

Dear Martha Anne,

This is my second letter to you today. I'm trying to make up for yesterday. I really feel a lot better today, even though I'm still weak. I tore the return address off of your letters and burned them today. I am keeping the letters but I don't want you to get some harassing mail if one of the letters got misplaced. I may package them up in a couple of months and mail them home. I want to keep them all so if I ever think of leaving you again, I can reread these letters and remember this year.

I love you so very much. I am so excited to have received my first tape. I want to hear your voice so much more. I may try to call you tonight. It sure is a fast three minutes on the phone when I call you. When it is night here it is morning of the same day over there. I go through a day first and then you get your turn at it. I can hardly wait until Christmas. I love you; I need you; I want you; right now! Keep the faith baby, 'cause I'm coming home.

Much, much love,
Joe

Monday, June 12, 1972
DAY 34:

This morning, my hoochmaid stopped by to clean up, as she typically does. I had my soiled flight suit hanging outside. I tried to rinse it out on Saturday, but in my condition, I did a really poor job. Extreme heat and the residue of Ho Chi Minh's revenge were a potent combination. My hoochmaid speaks no English, but she held up the flight suit and exclaimed, "Number ten! Number ten!" The number one meant good, so this garment was the opposite of good. She took it away to clean it. They have a well-established system here. The hoochmaids are not supposed to handle any money, and they get searched coming and going on the base. So I typically pay the unit clerk directly the equivalent of eight dollars in piasters each week for services like laundry, shoeshining, room cleaning, and bed making.

This afternoon, I worked in the motor pool with the men helping to turn wrenches while Dubose was in my office trying to sort out our mess of maintenance paperwork. This has been our normal pattern over the past couple of weeks since Dubose has some experience with paperwork, and I have no desire to learn it. A commotion in the tool trailer interrupted our afternoon rhythm. I ran over with a couple of men and discovered the two soldiers I assigned to the trailer in an all-out fistfight.

Specialist Sutton, a young athletic Black man, was grappling with Private First Class Clark, a skinny white guy with a moustache.

I managed to quickly get into the back of the trailer, grab their shirts, and crack their heads together like coconuts. It didn't knock them out, but it stunned them long enough for us to get in between them. They were both working inside a silver-sided forty-foot trailer filled with both our tool sets and our repair parts. All of these items are quite valuable on the black market, so I learned quickly to both restrict its access and keep it safely locked. That immediately cut down on a lot of our theft problems. To solve the potential for future disputes in the trailer, I ordered a barricade to be built in the center of the tool trailer—a Berlin Wall constructed hastily out of wooden pallets and plywood sheeting. Going forward, Sutton will be in charge of tools and enter through the double doors in the rear of the trailer. Clark will be in charge of the repair parts and enter through the single side door up front near the trailer coupling.

When I got back to the office with Dubose, we shared some stories working with MPs in the states. I told him about a time back on Fort Stewart in 1970 when we were called to a fight at the enlisted club on post. Fortunately, I was accompanied by two big burly MPs. Sergeants Hester and Waters were each in the six-five to six-six range and each a solid 300 pounds. The Green Bay Packers would have been happy to have either one of them. As soon as we entered the club, a soldier approached Sergeant Hester and told him that he wasn't supposed to be there since it was a club only for enlisted. Hester grabbed the soldier with both hands around the collars of his shirt, lifted him off the ground, and threw him, all in one motion. The soldier flew in the air at least fifteen feet across the top of the bar and hit the wall behind with such force that he left a dent. It wasn't a perfect chalk outline, but there were clear indentations in the sheetrock where his head, chest and some of his limbs made contact. He crumpled into a quiet heap on the floor. That took the starch out of the room. After that, dispersing the rest of the soldiers and shutting down the enlisted club for the night was not a problem. "Sir," Sergeant Hester said, "if you get the ringleader first, the others will usually fall in line."

I didn't expect to still be breaking up soldier fights here in Vietnam, but I'm learning that there are a lot of things I didn't expect to be doing here.

Dear Martha Anne,

I have been having good and bad days at the motor pool but the situation has improved 100% in the last 10 days. I just got two new mechanics this week. We now have enough people to keep up with the work, and I can quit pulling wrenches. My mother would never let me work on our cars, so I have learned a lot in the past month.

I love you with all of my heart. I hope I get a drop and can come home to you early, but I just wouldn't plan on it yet. It all depends on what the president is going to do before the election and how many troops get left here. We are supposed to be down to 49,000 by 1 July. Our neighbor units are being consolidated and two units are going home. I wish we would go too but so far it looks like Mohawks have an important role to play here. I love you very much. When you go to bed at night hold my pillow and say a few kind words to me and pretend you are holding me. It helps me a lot.

Much, much, much love,
Joe

Newest City Is Chartered; Council Meets Thursday

By Jack Leland, Evening Post Staff Writer, CHARLESTON—North Charleston received its charter Monday and Thursday night will hold its first council meeting as the state's newest city. Mayor John E. Bourne Jr. received the charter from Secretary of State O. Frank Thornton in Columbia. He and his six councilmen were

(cont.)

sworn into office by Gov. West. The new mayor said plans already are being formulated for merging the remainder of the county's North Area into the new municipality. That would mean a population of about 95,000 and make it the state's second largest city.

Reds Fire On Refugees

SAIGON (UPI)—Communist troops opened fire today on a ragged column of 1,000 refugees fleeing the provincial capital of An Loc and killed 12 civilians and wounded 30, field reports said. Newsmen who reached the scene shortly after the attack said the Communists fired a barrage of mortars onto Highway 13 while the refugees were trying to flee from An Loc, 60 miles north of Saigon . . . The reports said the refugees—mainly old men, women and children—ran down the highway as the mortars screamed into them and the chunks of shrapnel flew through the air. One old woman, shrapnel cuts across her body, died in the arms of her young granddaughter, the reports said. They said a young boy, hit by shrapnel in his head, was cradled in the arms of his parents while a South Vietnamese medic tried to stop the bleeding.

Tuesday, June 13, 1972
DAY 35:

This afternoon many of us gathered on the roof of our hooches to watch something I've never seen before. A Sikorsky CH-54 heavy-lift helicopter landed at our airfield to pick up the severely damaged

Mohawks from the mortar attack. My hooch-mate Pat and I sat on lawn chairs to watch the whole operation. They attached cables to sling-load one of the wounded Mohawks, and as the CH-54 lifted off, the cables tightened. At about 100 feet off the ground, the plane started to spin underneath the belly of the helicopter. The chopper continued to rise and the Mohawk continued to spin. We weren't sure if this was normal or not, but it didn't look right. All of a sudden, the helicopter pilot cut loose the sling load, and the Mohawk crashed down on the airfield. Pat and I groaned in unison while he joked, "That's gonna leave a mark." We've had five Mohawks destroyed by mortar fire since I've been here, which includes the three hit on Saturday night. We are starting to run short of aircraft. With so many more pilots than Mohawks, I'm not sure how much flight time I'll be getting in the next few weeks.

I also spent time this afternoon carrying pitchers of water out to my okra and bean plants. They've broken through the ground and sprouted little shoots. I've got to try and keep the water on them in this heat.

Wednesday, June 14, 1972
DAY 36:

Major Smith is not happy about the damage from the mortar attacks. From this point forward, he has ordered us to fly an extra mission leg off the airfield if we come in after dark. This only takes about an extra five or ten minutes to execute. We are always flying back in from the north, usually coming in off the coast. Now, if it's dark, we will fly a right angle inland on a SLAR mission. All the other missions we fly are for the greater Army good—higher commands and units we never see or interact with. This mission will be personal and for our own protection. Because the Viet Cong are expected to be setting their mortars up just before midnight, we hope that our incoming Mohawks will pick up their movements.

Dear Martha Anne,

    I have duty officer tonight. I didn't know about
it until about 7 pm. I'm taking the place of the guy
who got hit in our last mortar attack. He is better
but still not fit for duty. I hope to get a few hours

sleep this time. One of my men was attacked and cut by a soldier tonight. He had caught the soldier in his room going through his locker. I had to go to Camp Horn on the other side of Da Nang. It was quite an experience. It was the first time I have been through Da Nang after dark. It was about 10 p.m., and I kept expecting to get shot at but we passed without incident. I was thankful.

I love you so very much, and I do enjoy your letters too. You have often sold yourself short. I think many of your letters are great. I also love you for what you are and who you are. You don't need to apologize or make excuses. I love you freely. My only hope or desire is to gain your love in return. I'm so glad you are giving it all back to me. You have made my life full and rich. These past 11 months with you have been the best of my life. I love you and need you so very much.

Much love always,
Joe

Thursday, June 15, 1972
DAY 37:

I'm finding myself spending more and more time in the motor pool. Even long into the evening after the repair work has slowed, I've stayed in the office down there for extended hours, at least when I don't have a night mission. My office has air conditioning and is the only cool spot anywhere around the maintenance bays. Tonight, we cleared off my desk and played four-handed pinochle, which is a game my family likes to play. Dubose and I were partners and on the other team were Specialists Mop and Elkins. We weren't playing for money—nothing more than pride, I guess—but the others agreed to play anyway. There is a group of captains in the unit that plays poker for pretty high stakes. They seem to be out for blood in their games. I don't much like trying to take money off the enlisted men at all, so we play for fun or really low stakes down in the motor pool. Dubose told me tonight that he is working on getting a chess set in our office too.

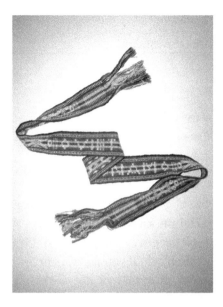

The men gave a headband to Dubose and me today. It's stitched with the words *VIET* and *NAM* in white block lettering over the top of stripes of red, yellow, blue, and black that unravel into loose threads at the ends. All of the men in our motor pool—our *misfits*—now have them. They've just recently taken to wearing them around the maintenance bays while working on vehicles. All four of us had them tied around our foreheads while playing pinochle, like a bunch of hippies.

I just received my second cassette tape from Martha Anne today, and this time she placed the recorder on the table at a family dinner. My sister Lindler was there, and my brother Roy, my mama, my daddy, and Lindler's husband Freddie. When we were playing cards in the motor pool office today, I thought about those times after dinner when we'd get out the pinochle deck. The new recording made me miss them even more.

Lindler:	What time you miss Joe, Martha?
Martha Anne:	All the time.
Lindler:	I guess you do. You had him around the house all the time the last month, didn't you? He didn't have time to come in and take off his work clothes. I don't miss Freddie when he goes out of town all the time. He'd be at work anyway. I miss him sometimes at night, but if he goes on a weekend, then I'm just in misery the whole weekend.

Roy:	You got nobody to nag at.
Mama:	Martha starts work on Monday.
Freddie:	Where?
Mama:	Belk's
Roy:	I'll have to go buy my clothes there now that Martha's there. Have to put me a sales price tag on them or something.
Mama:	Ha, she can't change the price. But she'll have to let you know when they've got a good bargain.
Roy:	Yes, why don't you let me know when they got some pants that look decent except just plain old Puritan white and black. If you do work in the men's department, please let me know when they've got some pants in my size. Size Puritan white and size Puritan black is all they ever have when I go over there. All the other sizes, they've got every color in the book: plaid, checks, everything. My size they got plain old drab color.
Lindler:	Martha Anne, now don't you go and play this tape for your momma and daddy and let them laugh at us.
Daddy:	That's what she wants it for.
Martha Anne:	No, I'm not going by there.
Daddy:	That's why she's not going to talk on it.
Mama:	We doing all the talking. She needs to do a little of it. I forgot to tell Joe in the letter I wrote him that Gaynell and those kids are coming back to Charleston.
Martha Anne:	I told him.
Mama:	You did?
Lindler:	Me too.
Martha Anne:	I figured he'd already heard.

Mama:	I couldn't think of any news when I was writing.
Roy:	If he don't start getting mail soon . . .
Martha Anne:	He did. Well the letters that I read today said he finally did get some mail.
Daddy:	Did he say he got the batteries?
Martha Anne:	I asked him on the phone the other morning and he said no.
Roy:	Well, we're going to have to get some carrier pigeons.
Lindler:	They'd have to be awful strong. They'd get plenty tired.
Daddy:	They might make it. They'd do just like Paul Revere did. He rode through the town hollering, "Here come the Yanks!"
Freddie:	No that was the Brits.
Mama:	I think you better not repeat your history. You're not up on it.
Daddy:	I thought they rode down Broad Street yelling, "Here come the Yanks! Here come the Yanks!"
Lindler:	No, they might've said that during the Civil War or the War of Northern Aggression.
Mama:	Joe will laugh at all this history when we don't know nothing about it. He's an expert on it.
Daddy:	He thinks he knows a lot more than he knows.
Mama:	He's pretty smart when it comes to history.

[End of audio]

◀×

Dear Martha Anne,

You're right about God being the only other one to know how much we love each other. Sometimes I feel I love you so much that even I don't know. I said I would leave the Army before I would leave you again, and I still mean it. I don't ever intend to put you through this again or for me to endure the heartache of being away from you. I had to do it when you were in college because I promised I would let you finish school with your class. I don't have to put up with this separation being repeated.

I have all I want from the Army. I have my flight experience and have seen enough of this world to last me for a long time. I do think this separation will strengthen our love and bring us closer together. I think we now realize how much we mean to each other.

Martha Anne

I look at your pictures and I remember you at the time each one was taken. The one when you were just 19 and not sure of me or yourself. The one of you for your senior album you were proud and poised. The one made at Ft. Rucker when you were applying for teaching jobs.

I loved you in all three times but I love you more as I see the picture of you in my mind. I see a beautiful young bride waiting at the airport for her man. Then I see you as I walk down the steps. You can no longer wait but run to meet me and I throw my arms around you and sweep you off of your feet and hold you and kiss you so much. That is the picture in my mind right now and it keeps me going forward.

Every day is a milestone. It is one less day for us to be apart. I can hardly wait until we're together again and I don't have to say goodbye. I never was good at saying goodbye even when I was small. I used to cry when we left Uncle John Wyatt's after Thanksgiving because I loved to be with them. I now cry inside at the thought of being away and apart from you. We are going to make it somehow. I look at my calendar and realize that it has almost been six weeks since we parted. I hope the next six months go as quickly.

Much love as I can send,
Joe

Friday, June 16, 1972
DAY 38:

No matter how hard we work in our unit motor pool, there are some repairs that are simply beyond our capabilities. For these more difficult jobs, we utilize a general support shop run by South Korean civilian contractors that most of us refer to as *Philco Ford*. This morning I met Mr. Moon, the Korean in charge, and it didn't take long to figure out how to grease his wheels. Wearing a bright floral print Hawaiian shirt and chain-smoking cigarettes, Mr. Moon was my first point of contact when I arrived at the shop. He is short and stocky with salt and pepper hair and is very clean-shaven. His shop office is small but centrally located in a giant garage, so it affords him a 360-degree view of all the repair bays. When he opened his office door, the familiar smell and haze of a thousand past smokes hit me in the face. His cigarettes smelled particularly awful, so I asked him, "What brand do you smoke?"

"It's some Malaysian brand that tastes like shit," he replied.

He told me American brands are available on the black market, but they are too expensive at $25 a carton. I thought immediately about the two carton per week cigarette ration that I never use. I could buy cartons through the military for just $2.

I cut the small talk short and made an excuse to get out of his office and back to Marble Mountain. Once back, I went straight over to our little PX and purchased two cartons of cigarettes. I hate cigarette smoke. Once when I was fourteen years old, my father tried to send me to the store to buy him cigarettes. I told him I wasn't going to go buy him coffin nails, and he was so angry at my insubordinate response, he was about to beat me. My mother intervened and wouldn't let him because she couldn't stand the fact that he was smoking either. He quit as many as thirty to forty times in a twenty-five-year period. He finally quit smoking for good when I was a sophomore in college because he had throat surgery, which he thought was cancer. It actually was abscessed tonsils, but nonetheless, he made a deal with God that if he survived that surgery, he would quit smoking. And he did. But he switched to chewing tobacco.

This afternoon we had a formation and inspection by Major Smith that even included the officers. Not many of the other officers are enthusiastic that we have to show up to the Friday formations like everyone else. I think it will improve the discipline in our unit, which is sorely lacking. The CO says he is going to put the same kind of command influence on participation in our Saturday morning motor stables.

U.S. Jets Fly 340 Strikes Over North

SAIGON (UPI)—American warplanes flew more than 340 strikes over North Vietnam, blowing up three MIG fighter bases among other targets, but stayed beyond 50 miles of Hanoi where Soviet President Nikolai V. Podgorny is visiting, the U.S. command said Friday . . . In South Vietnam, the U.S. command announced it was pulling out one of the two remaining American ground combat brigades from the war zone leaving the job of guarding the big Da Nang air base to a South Vietnamese division that had been routed during the battle for Quang Tri.

Saturday, June 17, 1972
DAY 39:

It was very hot and humid today. My men have been working hard on getting many of the deadline vehicles operational, so between that progress and the stifling heat, we decided to close the motor pool early. For a third Saturday in a row, we fired up the grills and threw some hamburgers on before the majority of the thirteen men—this did not include me—piled into a deuce-and-a-half to head to Da Nang. They wanted to do some shopping at the large military exchange on the Da Nang Air Base. They might have even stopped by the Sergeant Major's brothel on the way.

I spent the evening hours relaxing at the officer's club, which is one of the few places that has excellent air conditioning. I was watching a showing of *The Sting* when Dubose tracked me down. "Sir, we've gotta go to Twenty-fourth Corps Headquarters. Our men are locked up."

"What happened?" I asked.

"They've run over a gook on the I Corps bridge."

"I'll go get my gear and see you at the arms room," I said, as I was wondering to myself why our higher headquarters would be holding all of them when only one would have been driving.

Back at my hooch, I quickly gathered my flak vest and helmet while I changed into jungle fatigues. It was a short jog to the arms room, and I covered the ground quickly in long strides that reminded me of my glory days on the high school track team. Dubose was waiting for me when I arrived, so I skipped the small talk with the armorer and grabbed as much firepower as possible. I certainly was not going to get caught in a firefight and be outgunned, so I strapped two canvas bandoleers, each filled with ten magazines consisting of twenty-rounds across my chest.

Our arms room has quite a few of what we call *bastard weapons*. These are odd pieces that have been passed around by units that have come and gone during the course of the war and aren't registered on our property book. Dubose cradled one of these bastards—a pump action 12-gauge shotgun. Not to be outdone, I picked up a Thompson submachine gun with four extra fifty-round drums of ammunition. I glanced at my pistol holster just to make sure I still had my .38 pistol on my hip, and we moved our personal arsenal out to the Jeep. The armorer was the only one in the unit who knew we were leaving base at that time and where we were going.

Dubose gunned the Jeep toward the main gate. I looked up at the Marble Mountains looming in the late dusk when Dubose made the sharp turn to clear the end of the runway. The sudden motion dislodged the passenger seat and sent me flying. I managed to grab the bar on the dashboard as I was falling out but still banged against the road surface, tearing a gaping hole in my fatigue trousers and a half dollar-sized hole in my right knee. I totally scraped up a good pair of boots, too.

It probably only took Dubose a couple seconds to stop, but it felt like an eternity.

"Damn, Lieutenant. Do you want me to take you to the dispensary?"

"No, let's get our people first."

"They were working on this Jeep today. I assumed they'd already pinned this seat back in. Sorry about that," Dubose said.

"Don't worry about it. It's not the first time I've been run over by a vehicle."

The closer it got to midnight, the more active the enemy likely would be, and I did not want to be out riding the roads all night trying to resolve the situation. We left the main gate of our base and headed north up the main supply route. As we drove, I thought about the first two times I was run over. As a five-year-old living on Bull Street in Charleston, I eagerly awaited my father's return home from work. He sold yeast and coffee for Standard Brands in those days in a step-van delivery truck with dual rear tires that we called *The Yeast Truck*. Our driveway wound around the property in the shape of the letter C. With only one seat in the cab for the driver, I liked to jump into the open passenger side and ride around the driveway. We always did a long lap around, which was a treat for me and returned to park in the same rough-hewn area of packed dirt and coal cinders.

One time, as my father slowed down at our normal parking spot, I decided it was time to jump out. I fell under the edge of the truck, and the dual rear tires ran over my legs between my knee and ankle. Not realizing I had been run over, my father came around the truck to discover me crying and rolling in the Saint Augustine grass. He picked me up in his arms and carried me inside.

I convalesced on a surplus World War II Army cot downstairs near the kitchen. Back then, you didn't go to the hospital unless you were severely injured. Since Dr. John Shugrue's office was just around the corner, it was not a big deal for him to make a house call that same afternoon. Though no x-rays were taken, Dr. Shugrue determined that my legs were not fractured. All I wanted to do was play outside that summer, but instead, I was laid up on the cot. The bruising lingered for weeks and even six months later, it was so painful that I'd have my older sister Lindler sit on my legs to try and ease the pain.

By the time I was in second grade, we had moved to Woodlawn Avenue in North Charleston where I often walked to the neighborhood school down the street. On Pearl Harbor Day 1954, it was already very cold for an early December day in Charleston with ice in the mud holes along the edge of the pavement. I was bundled up in a thick coat with a hat that came down over both my ears and fastened underneath my chin. Even at that age I had feet big enough to fit a pair of hand-me-down World War II paratrooper boots. With those thick soles and heels, I stomped and shattered the ice. I thought I was really tough.

That morning I walked across the street to get my friend, Ronald Parnell. When we came out of his house, my father rode up and drove us to the busy intersection of Woodlawn and Dorchester Road, where we got out. He quickly drove away and off to work.

Ronald shouted, "The last one to cross the street is a rotten egg!"

I wasn't going to let him beat me across the street, so I took off running. Before I got to the other side, a lady in a Studebaker flew around the corner, did not stop for the crosswalk, and ran flat over me. I put my hands out in front of me to try to break the blow against the fender. When I did that, I fell over backwards, and my legs went under the wheels of the car as she came to a stop on top of me. Those were the same legs that had been run over years before by The Yeast Truck, and now I had a Studebaker parked on top of me. The lady got out and looked down at me exclaiming, "Oh, I'm on top of you!" She got back in the Studebaker, cranked it, and reversed back off my leg.

A schoolteacher stopped and put her heavy winter coat over me. Soon an ambulance arrived to take me to the hospital. In the 1950s, the ambulance service was run by the same people who worked for the funeral home. People were leery of riding in those ambulances that could get you coming and going, in life and in death. Ambulance service was all pay as you go, and there were transport charges. On the way, they stopped by my house to pick up my mother to make sure they got paid.

I had a knot on my head from hitting the pavement and a bruise on my chest where the fender of the car hit me. Fortunately for me, the thick soles of my paratrooper boots prevented my ankle and foot from being crushed. Once again, I had no broken bones from being run over. About the third day after it happened, the hospital doctors put a cast on my leg from my toes to my mid-thigh to stabilize my twisted ankle and knee.

Back then, the old Roper Hospital in downtown Charleston was constructed of wood and it had broad porches with banisters. The nurses rolled me outside on the sunny days so I could see people and be in the fresh air. They nearly froze me to death out there. Every morning at six o'clock sharp, the Coast Guard station across from the hospital played reveille. It was my first glimpse of the military lifestyle—waking up to the sound of reveille breaking the morning stillness. I got sent home the week before Christmas.

Miss Beautyhorn, my second-grade teacher, brought the entire class to my house to sing Christmas carols. My classmates and Miss Beautyhorn were very kind to me, and they seemed truly relieved that I survived. We didn't have a porch, just a little stoop, so I went outside and sat on the stoop in the freezing cold and listened to them sing carols to me. Besides the music, they brought two other gifts to me— pneumonia and the measles. So shortly after their visit, the pneumonia brought hacking and coughing up phlegm and the measles felt like a million little ants gnawing on my skin. Out of necessity, I taught myself how to use a coat hanger and a yardstick to run down inside my cast to scratch areas that I could not reach. It absolutely drove me nuts, and I turned eight in that cast. When it finally came off, I had to learn to walk again. For the second time in my young life, I had paid a visit to the undercarriage of a moving vehicle and lived to tell about it.

When we arrived at the XXIV Corps Military Police station, I left the Thompson submachine gun in the back of the Jeep. I wanted to come in showing strength, but I did not want to appear ridiculous. After all, I still had the bandoleers of ammunition strapped across my chest, and I had my M-16 rifle in hand and my .38 on my hip. My pistol holster, which did have beautiful Western-style, tooled black leather, was now scraped with deep grooves and scratches from our

Jeep mishap. I had to check my .38 and M-16 with the desk sergeant before I could proceed back to the lockup cells to see my men. I wanted to hear from them first exactly what happened.

I was happy to find out that one of my best and most trusted men in the motor pool was driving the truck—Specialist 4th Class Seabolt. We call him *Mop* because of the long floppy hairdo he wears that exceeds any regulatory definition of a military haircut, but by this point in Vietnam, haircut regulations are a low priority. I can easily look past the hair because Mop's work ethic is top-notch. We use him much like a sergeant to manage the other mechanics in our motor pool.

Mop explained to me that there had been a disabled vehicle on the bridge, and a Vietnamese man on a moped swerved into Mop's lane to get around the disabled vehicle. The moped had actually hit our truck, and the man had been conscious and able to walk away from the scene. Mop said he was driving between twenty and thirty miles an hour at the time of the accident. This report was much less serious than what I was initially led to believe when Dubose pulled me away from the officer's club.

By that point in the evening, it was after nine and a good three hours since the incident occurred. As each moment passed by, I was concerned about getting back to the safety of our base before the Viet Cong got active. I returned to see the MP desk sergeant out front where Dubose was waiting. Like Dubose, this man was a staff sergeant, and I was hopeful that Dubose—a former MP himself— was able to grease the skids for a quick release by having a congenial sergeant-to-sergeant conversation.

I approached his desk and asked, "I've come to get my people. What do you need me to do?"

"I'm sorry L-T, but I need your commander before I can release these men," he replied.

"I am their commander. They're members of my motor pool section."

"These men were speeding and almost killed a civilian. They were doing sixty miles an hour on the I Corps bridge."

"How did you clock their speed?" I asked.

"The MP unit that brought 'em in said they had to do sixty just to catch up to them."

"Well, how far did it take your MPs to run them down?"

"They caught up to them just after the end of the bridge and pulled them over."

"I've done some traffic work for the MPs myself back at Fort Stewart, and you know as well as I do that pursuit is much faster than the vehicle you're chasing. If my truck was really driving sixty and your guys were pursuing at sixty, they would still be out there chasing them now. They got them right off the end of the bridge. Come on, Sergeant," I said.

"They are also charged with leaving the scene of an accident."

"Was the guy killed?"

"No."

"Was the guy conscious?"

"Yes."

"I gave them a direct order not to stop for any reason between Da Nang and our airfield because our vehicles are being stripped of parts. They were following my orders."

"The rule is simple. Their commanding officer has to authorize their release back to the unit," the desk sergeant said with some finality.

"You might as well call your commander down here. You're jeopardizing our mission right now. These men are a critical part of our mission at Marble Mountain. We fly most of our Mohawk missions at night and you know it."

For the first time, he looked at the dried blood on my forearm as well as the bloody ripped hole in the knee of my trousers. I think he realized that I was serious and did not plan to leave without my men. He picked up the phone and made a call to someone who sounded like his supervisor, and after a minute, he released the men to my custody. Before we left, we gave Mop the Thompson submachine gun for their truck, and our two vehicles convoyed back to base without incident.

5 Held In Plot To Bug Democrats' Office Here

By Alfred E. Lewis, Washington Post Staff Writer,
WASHINGTON—Five men, one of whom said he is a former employee of the Central Intelligence Agency, were arrested at 2:30 a.m. yesterday in what authorities described as an elaborate plot to bug the offices of the Democratic National Committee here. There was no immediate explanation as to why the five suspects would want to bug the Democratic National Committee offices or whether or not they were working for any other individuals or organizations.

Sunday, June 18, 1972
DAY 40:

Given my minor injuries the night before, the medics wrote me up to not fly for at least forty-eight hours. So instead, I found myself today once again focused on the motor pool. After the morning formation with the commander, I visited Mr. Moon once again during a parts run to the general support area. This time, I gave him a brown paper bag with a carton of Winstons and a carton of Salems. "Try those and see how you like them," I said. He glanced quickly left and right through the glass windows of his office, as if checking to see if anyone witnessed this transaction and then slid the cartons into his desk drawer. He thanked me, but nothing else was said about the cigarettes nor was any agreement formally made.

Dear Martha Anne,

You remember Camp Christian, don't you? Remember you came up for the weekend. You know, I think that weekend was the point in my life that I looked at you differently than ever before. I suddenly became attracted to you like a moth to a flame. It was on that bus ride home that you went to sleep in my arms. That said to me that you trusted me and it meant a great deal to me at that time. My father picked us up from the church and about one minute after we left, that car driven by a drunk raced through the churchyard and went between two iron posts on the walkway between our church and the educational building. It was right where we had been sitting on our suitcases. I don't know if I ever mentioned this to you but I felt that our lives were spared for some reason that day. I never dreamed at that time we would be so happy together. It was about two months later when I asked you to marry me.

I guess I had better cut out this memory lane stuff before I relive our entire lives together. I just enjoy looking back on some of the days we have shared. I love you so very much my dear wife. I can't really understand how I managed to win your heart.

I wish I could send myself in this letter,

All my love,

Joe

Monday, June 19, 1972
DAY 41:

We haven't heard anything from Major Smith or the MP unit, and it seems like we probably won't. My sore knee is a steady reminder of Saturday night. Before I went to the motor pool today, I spent some time watering my okra and butter beans. They aren't looking good in this heat. We've also found a way to get some additional repair parts. By some quirk of the property book long before I arrived, we own a very large, rough-terrain forklift in our motor pool. This thing is so big that the tires on it are over six feet tall, and when we add steel pipes on the ends of the tines, we can even lift small buildings with it. We recently got a couple requests from other units on Marble Mountain to move things with our forklift. Today, I sent Specialist Asbell over to the heavy lift helicopter unit on the other side of the airfield. They fly Chinooks, which are affectionately referred to as *Shithooks* by the soldiers. Asbell took a shopping list of parts to acquire before agreeing to move anything with the forklift. Sure enough, he came back with a slew of additional parts for our wheeled vehicles.

Dear Martha Anne,

I had a busy day today. I am still not flying. My knee is improving but it sure drains a lot. I get a lot of yellow fluid out of it. I have already soaked through two bandages today.

I really enjoyed your letters, one of them was especially great. I didn't know I would miss you so much either. That is why I am thinking about leaving the Army. It is not because the Army has not been good to me; it is because I just don't want to leave you again. I think of you every day. I only want you and no other woman will do. I don't want any of these girls over here. They are real cheap, and I think all of them are prostitutes. I guess I'm old-fashioned, but I married you and not anyone or everyone else. You have been, you are, and you will continue to be the only woman in my life.

I miss you. I need you. I think of you. I dream of you. I want you. I lust for you. I had better stop before I commit sex through the mail.

I do love you with all of my heart,
Joe

Hurricane Agnes Hurls Tornadoes Into Florida: 13 Dead, 20 More Missing

PANAMA CITY, Fla. (UPI)—Hurricane Agnes hurled deadly tornadoes into inland Florida and raked the Gulf Coast with high tides and howling winds before plunging inland Monday 50 miles east of this resort city. The season's first hurricane killed seven persons in Cuba and at least six in Florida, four from tornadoes, and perhaps as many as 20 more persons were missing . . . Much of the Deep South was placed under tornado and flash flood warnings as a result of the dying storm, which was downgraded at dusk to a tropical storm.

Tuesday, June 20, 1972
DAY 42:

I'm no longer grounded for medical reasons, but nonetheless, my name didn't come up on the mission board today. I spent the whole day in the motor pool with Dubose. As the afternoon work slowed down, Dubose pulled out his chess board. As we got a game under way, I told him about my attempt at a garden plot outside my hooch. He talked about a garden patch his family kept in Texas and asked me to bring him some okra, but I had to admit I am still a long way from a harvest. I told him about how I first got started with gardening. It was back on Bull Street in Charleston when I was just five years old. Our landlord owned a landscaping business with a hothouse on the property. He called me his *yard angel* and taught me how to graft and grow camellias and how to tend to roses.

Dear Martha Anne,

Do you remember that weekend we went to Chattanooga? We saw the wax museum of the presidents, the inclined railway, Lookout Mountain, the battlefields, and that little restaurant near Rock City. I watched you eat your sandwich and I kept wishing we were married and on our honeymoon. I always spent a lot of time watching you. I wanted to see every movement you made. I wanted to see the twinkle in your eyes. Remember the picture I took of you on Lookout Mountain. I carried that picture until I nearly wore it out. I used to carry it dove shooting with me. I would put it on a fence post or a corn stalk near where I was standing so I could look at you. I even put it up in the library at the Baptist College when I was working at the desk. I know a lot of people thought I was crazy but it was just love. I love you even more now.

Until now you have never said you wanted to have my baby. Maybe it is pride or something but a man wants a son to carry his name. We have not seriously talked about children yet. I think we should wait a few months after I get home so we can play around and go places before you get pregnant. I think everyone knows by now that you weren't pregnant when we got married. I had a few people make such remarks when we planned our wedding right after your graduation. I guess it is just human nature to say such things. I think we should have our children while I'm still in the Army, but we can wait. I don't want any children until we are both completely ready for them. It is a lot of responsibility, and I'm ready. I think this time alone will mature both of us a great deal. We may have some children by accident but I would prefer planning them. I think it will be a lot of fun and a lot of trouble. I

know I will be a nervous wreck by the time you deliver
our first child. I can see me now. I'll probably wreck
the car or something. I think the main thing you have
to realize is that before you have a baby you will be the
center of attention. You will get about anything you
want until the baby comes, and then the baby becomes
the center of attention. I just want you to know that
I will still love you just as much, if not more, but it
will appear just the opposite to you. The first two or
three months after the first baby I'm sure you will
think I have cast you aside like a worn-out shoe. I'm
going to try to do my best to love both you and the baby.
I just hope you will forgive my shortcomings.

Much love always,
Joe

Wednesday, June 21, 1972
DAY 43:

I thought I finally was going to get back into a Mohawk tonight for an
evening mission, but it turned out to be a damaged aircraft waiting for
me. It's well known in the unit that the worst of the mechanics are sent
down to my motor pool to pull vehicle maintenance, but I'm starting
to grow concerned about the aircraft maintenance section, too.

Today's setback reminded me of the officer's call we had at
the end of last week. Captain Godwin, who is in charge of aircraft
maintenance, briefed the reason for the lack of compressed air in the
Mohawks. Each Mohawk is equipped with oxygen bottles that we use
for high-altitude flying. Ours are all empty. By Army regulation, we
are supposed to use the oxygen supply any time we fly higher than
10,000 feet in altitude. I know for a fact that I've flown up to 15,000
feet trying to avoid ground fire and have done so without oxygen.
Flying missions lower means a greater risk of getting shot down.

When Captain Godwin addressed the air problem, he told us
a story of taking the dysfunctional compressor pump to Da Nang
Air Base for repairs. He loaded the compressor in the back of a

three-quarter-ton truck along with a couple of his men. On the way and apparently unbeknownst to him, one of the men picked up the adapter pipe for the air compressor and fired it like a javelin into a raft of ducks floating in a rice paddy along the side of the supply route. After spending some time at Da Nang and getting the compressor repaired, they drove back to Marble Mountain and saw a dead duck floating upside down in the paddy where the pipe was thrown. Some of the pilots in the briefing room laughed out loud at this detail. So, now we have a functional compressor, but without the adapter pipe, which turned into a javelin, it is not possible to fill the oxygen bottles in the aircraft. I didn't find any of this briefing particularly amusing, and I don't like flying Mohawks that aren't fully prepared.

Dear Martha Anne,

I was supposed to fly today but my aircraft was grounded. I found some battle damage on the landing gear and they would not authorize me to fly it in that condition. It was really strange because that aircraft has been flown several times since our last mortar attack. It appears that the pilots in this unit are not pulling proper preflight inspections.

I am having a real problem at the motor pool. I have enough people now to get the job done, but I have not gotten any parts in 10 days. Philco Ford is our support, and they are changing their system, and they have stopped supplying us for the time being. When a truck breaks down it just sits there waiting for parts. It makes me feel so helpless. I cannot do anything about it except beg, borrow, or steal new parts.

With all the units leaving around us we don't have many people to ask for help. I'm afraid the 131st will be here when everyone else is gone. I would love to get a drop, but they are not sending any more Mohawk pilots over here. Things will really get hectic in October when about half of the pilots leave this unit. Maybe they will send the rest of us home, too. I really don't know what they are planning. I feel that everything depends largely on what the president decides in his next statement on the troop strength in Vietnam. I would like to see it cut to zero but I'm afraid that is too optimistic. I feel that a reduction below 30,000 men is almost impossible. It is getting so now that they don't have enough people to sort the mail.

How about Hurricane Agnes? Did she hit Charleston? I'm awaiting news from you every day on her. I hope to call you soon if I can get a connection with the states. So far this week they have not been making connection until after 9 p.m. here.

Much, much love,
Your husband Joe

Thursday, June 22, 1972
DAY 44:

Our company executive officer, Captain Fordiani, sent a driver down this morning to get the CO's vehicle. Major Smith had just returned from a flight mission, and Fordiani wanted to have him picked up on the flight line to avoid a half mile walk back in the sweltering heat. I refused to release the vehicle to the driver, since the weekly maintenance had not been completed. An angry call from Captain Fordiani immediately followed, demanding that I release the CO's Jeep. I refused again. Later in the afternoon, Fordiani and the CO's driver were personally in our motor pool completing the weekly preventative maintenance checks. I'm sure Major Smith ripped into them and sent them down to the motor pool. It was a great feeling to know that the CO was indeed supporting our efforts to improve vehicle maintenance. It did, however, make me realize that my isolation from the other officers in the unit is growing. Other than my roommates, I hardly spend any time with the other officers in the company. I spend an increasing amount of time with my men in the motor pool when I'm not preparing for or flying a mission.

Friday, June 23, 1972
DAY 45:

When I returned today with Specialist Mop to the general support area run by Mr. Moon, an amazing thing happened. We checked our unit parts bin, and it was full of new repair parts. I didn't see Mr. Moon in his bright floral shirt anywhere, so I went to his office in the center of the bays. No sign of him there either, so I slid another two cartons of fresh cigarettes into his desk drawer as a thank you.

When we got back to the gate at Marble Mountain, the guard began reprimanding Specialist Mop for being out of uniform. He was wearing the hippie headband with VIETNAM stitched in white block letters that all our men have been wearing with regularity around the motor pool area. We threw ours on early today as we rode back to base. The gate guard came around to the passenger side of the vehicle. I could see him hesitate, taking in the headband on my head and the lieutenant bars on my shoulders. He apologized, saluted, and waved us right through.

Today was an especially hot scorcher, and the men really suffer while working on the vehicles in this kind of heat. I'm thinking about changing to a day-night shift in the motor pool to give them some relief. The only thing that made it partially tolerable today was a slight breeze blowing in off the South China Sea. My knee is feeling better, but I still haven't flown a mission in a few days.

Saturday, June 24, 1972
DAY 46:

It's not until I report to the airstrip to conduct preflight inspections that I learn who my assigned observer will be for my mission. This afternoon, I flew once again with Specialist Yarborough. It's starting to become a pattern that we fly together, and I don't mind it at all. He's only about five foot seven or eight and maybe 160 pounds dripping wet. He's got sandy blond hair, a fair complexion, wears eyeglasses, and like so many of our soldiers, wears a mustache. It's mainly silent in the cockpit with him. Yarborough just does his job with no unnecessary chatter. He gives regular updates on what he sees, and he calls hot reports (hotreps) back to the air boss when we see a target that needs immediate attention. The imagery he collects flows back to the base in real-time if there is an airborne radio-relay plane. I never have to remind him to do a required task. Yarborough brings a competent self-discipline to his work that is refreshing. We're improving, but I certainly don't experience that attitude with many of the misfits in my motor pool who have been relegated to me.

Dear Martha Anne,

Today was a very busy day for me. We had an inspection at 7:30 this morning and motor stables at 7:45. I had a tree-lowering device class at 10:00, and a flight at 2:00 p.m. After my flight, I went back to the motor pool and my motor sergeant was having problems with one of the men—Private Reynolds. No punishment seems to work on this guy. He's still AWOL all the time. I think that I will have to get rid of this man or my motor sergeant will go nuts.

It has been two days since I have received any mail so I'm looking for a letter tomorrow. Please excuse this terrible writing because my hand is a little sore. In the tree-lowering class you hang in a parachute harness in the airplane hangar and you have to release your hooks and lower yourself to the ground with the device. It is practicing for the possibility of being caught in the top of a tree after you have bailed out of your airplane. I think it was a priceless class but I strained muscles I didn't even know about. You have to pull yourself up with one hand and release the catch on your right side and then do the same thing on your left side. The pack that we wear has 250 ft. of nylon rope in it so you can lower yourself at least 250 ft. Of course we only practice from about 10 or 12 ft. in the air but it takes a lot of straining to get out of that parachute harness.

I love you and miss you very much. I think of you constantly. My hope now is to return to you as soon as I can. I hope the president makes some earthshaking decision like the RVN's can fight this war okay without the Army personnel over here. I'm afraid that the Mohawks will be one of the last units to leave. I need you right now. I just can't be happy at all without you.

I love you just like you are,
Joe

Sunday, June 25, 1972
DAY 47:

It was supposed to be a quiet Sunday, so I spent three hours of my precious free time this morning wrestling with the MARS lines trying to get connected to Martha Anne. These connections are awful, but just hearing her voice would help me. It's been three days since I got a letter, and I worry so much about her. I'm pretty certain Hurricane Agnes passed through South Carolina, but I'm just not sure how bad they got hit and she's having to work that new job at Belk's. I gave up the effort just after the noon hour and grabbed some lunch before heading back to my hooch, where I promptly gave up watering my okra and beans this afternoon. I think it was the excessive heat, but it could have also been the soil was too sandy. Either way, I've declared total crop failure. It looks like I'm not going to grow those fresh vegetables I've been craving.

I tried the MARS line again tonight for another couple hours, but no luck connecting with Martha Anne. It feels lonely here, like we are all transients. I don't even like going to the parties with the other pilots. Everyone seems to have an idea of when the drawdown will affect us, but nobody talks about the war in terms of winning or losing. I laugh when I think of some of the things I said on my way over here just last month. It's all just talk, talk, talk about when we will be gone.

Monday, June 26, 1972
DAY 48:

Mop and I made another trip today to Mr. Moon's general support shop, where we parked our three-quarter-ton truck in a shaded corner to avoid the blazing sun. When I was walking toward Mr. Moon's office for my weekly meeting, I saw a Korean wrecker reversing in the direction of my truck. I ran toward it, waving my arms and yelling for him to stop. I was too late. The driver crashed into my front bumper, and by the time I got to his truck, he was desperately trying to explain something in Korean while bowing repeatedly. I couldn't understand a word he was saying. Almost immediately, Mr. Moon joined us, and since he was the only Korean there who spoke English, I turned to him and said, "I can't believe he didn't see my truck."

"He probably couldn't see you in his mirrors; he's not used to driving this wrecker," Moon responded. The Korean wrecker driver stood there shaking and spouting Korean phrases in clusters with an intensely anguished look on his face. Moon put up his hand, barked out a Korean command, and pointed to the maintenance bays.

"Why was he saying so much?" I asked.

"He was very sorry. He probably thought you were going to shoot him."

"Really. Why?"

"That's exactly what a Korean officer would've done. You've lost face 'cause he's damaged your vehicle. He expected to get shot," Moon said as he lit a cigarette.

I did have my pistol holster on my hip. Shooting him had not crossed my mind. By the time we walked to Mr. Moon's air-conditioned shop office, Korean mechanics were scurrying around the front of my truck like ants. In my meetings with Mr. Moon, I tolerated the overpowering smell of cigarette smoke in his office for two reasons. One, it is air conditioned, but two, it is also necessary to build a rapport with a man who clearly knows how to get things done when it comes to repairs. Unfortunately on this trip, he didn't have any new repair parts for me. He told me how most of the repair parts and newer vehicles were being sent to the Vietnamese units as soon as they came in. He had my parts requisitions, so he told me he would set aside any of those parts if they came in. When we emerged from his office in less than an hour, my front fender looked better than the undamaged rear one. The Koreans had even taken out a stencil and repainted the bumper numbers.

Dear Martha Anne,

I'm flying again now and it really helps. I think if I could not fly, I would go completely crazy over here. I just plain hate to go to that motor pool. I wish every night that the V.C. would mortar the motor pool instead of the aircraft. I think I would even pay them for the help. The supply system has gone to pot over here. I cannot get any parts to fix my broken trucks. I think I'll turn in most of them for salvage. The Vietnamese get all new trucks and we get the old, worn out ones. I don't like this system at all. I hope we go to Thailand and leave all of these trucks here. I would be the happiest officer in our company.

I flew up north with my roommate, Pat, today. We got some very good imagery. It was a SLAR mission. He carried his camera and we have some pictures of North Vietnam and some of us by our aircraft after the mission. If they turn out okay, I'll send you some.

It is really hot here. I think July will be even hotter. If I do not live through this war at least you will know I'm in heaven because I've already served my time in hell. If you die over here and go to hell you would have to wear a coat when you got there. We are about a half mile from the ocean and when the wind doesn't blow it is very hot and humid. I really feel sorry for my mechanics. I have had three of them suffer heat exhaustion. I have to watch them like children. Most of them are 20 or younger and they seem to have very little common sense. One man is a Black militant, one a Jesus freak, one a drunk, one a marijuana smoker, and they all conflict with each other. They are constantly bickering with each other. My poor motor sergeant is about to go crazy. He told me yesterday he wants a unit transfer. If he leaves, I think I will too. I would rather fly helicopters 120 hours a month than run that motor pool.

I enjoy your letters so much. They are always the high point of my day. I would like to know about Hurricane Agnes a little more if possible. I worry about you being alone in a storm without lights or anything and maybe without a phone. I would love to call you but I have been unsuccessful all last week. I'll try again Wednesday night when I have duty officer. I just love to hear your voice. Do you remember some of those record calls I used to make to you? Some of them were for over two hours and cost over $30. I guess it's a good thing they limit calls from here to 3 minutes. They have a regular type phone to the states at the USO that you don't have to say over and all of that stuff. I hope to use it next Sunday on our anniversary. I love you more than the day I married you and more than the day I last saw you. It seems impossible for our love to increase, but it does. I love you more, and I don't know exactly what else I can say about it, except that it is a miracle blessed by God.

All my love always,
Joe

Tuesday, June 27, 1972
DAY 49:

When I returned to Marble Mountain tonight after flying a night mission, my post-mission routine was interrupted by an amazing sight. I actually heard it coming before I saw it. The engine props on the AC-130 were quite loud and distinctive, and as it passed by the end of our airfield, the Gatlin guns on the aircraft opened up on an island in the river past our base. Some call this gunship *Puff the Magic Dragon*, but we shorten it to simply *Puff*. As its guns opened up, it looked like a giant red firehose disgorging from the side of the plane—so many bullet rounds coming out at once. It did not sound like a gun at all, more like a revving engine. Multiple secondary explosions went off on the island as the hose of fire streamed down. We just stood in awe on the airfield and watched Puff work its magic.

Wednesday, June 28, 1972
DAY 50:

Dear Martha Anne,

You would not believe the day that I have had. First, I overslept and missed the company formation at 7:30. Pat's clock didn't go off. I got the clock from you this afternoon. Second, I had to explain to Major Smith why I missed the formation. Third, my motor sergeant is sick. Fourth, I had two missions this afternoon and flew almost to North Vietnam when my system failed. I had to return to base and get another aircraft and continue the mission. However, I exceeded the time block on the first mission, so I had to pick up the following missions. Due to aircraft shortage, I flew four missions instead of two. Fifth, I am company duty officer tonight and my motor sergeant is CQ. He needs to rest, so I will stay up all night. Sixth, I got back too late for supper, and the club's kitchen was closed.

Well it looks like I may be one of the last of the Mohicans. We are getting rid of nearly all American units over here. It looks to me like we are not going to move to Da Nang. Maybe we will get orders to go to Thailand. You can hear almost any rumor you want if you listen.

I love you so very much. I feel like a complete fool for leaving you. There must have been some way for me to have avoided this separation. Maybe we will all come home soon. I hope so. I just want to be with you

and not let you go. I think of you so much. Last night
I dreamed I was holding you and I woke up and found
my arms around my pillow. I need you so much it hurts.

Much love as I can send,
Joe

Nixon Slows Vietnam Pullout Rate

WASHINGTON (AP)—President Nixon slowed the Vietnam withdrawal rate Wednesday—to 10,000 troops over two months—but said draftees no longer will be sent to the war zone unless they volunteer. Nixon's action will cut U.S. force levels in South Vietnam to 39,000 by Sept. 1. This compares with a peak ceiling of 549,500 when he took office. The 39,000 figure does not take into account about 86,000 participating in the war from Thailand and the 7th Fleet off Vietnam. In May and June, troops were pulled out at the rate of 110,000 a month, but with the remaining force getting ever smaller and Hanoi's army continuing its Southern offensive, Nixon opted for a go-slower approach at this time.

Weyand Made Commander of U.S. Forces

WASHINGTON (AP)—President Nixon elevated Gen. Frederick C. Weyand to commander of U.S. forces in Vietnam Wednesday and announced a consolidation of Army and Air Force commands in the war zone . . . Weyand, a four-star general, will, as predicted widely, succeed Gen. Creighton Abrams as commander of the Military Assistance Command in Vietnam and as commander of the U.S. Army in Vietnam.

Thursday, June 29, 1972
DAY 51:

I flew a mission up the coast into North Vietnam today. It wasn't a much different route than many of my recent missions in that direction. I flew past the same stretch of coastline where I spotted the camouflaged freighter unloading cargo. Before I spotted that freighter, our pilots weren't taking enemy fire on that stretch of the coastline very often at all. Afterward, it was a different story.

Today's daylight mission was a late-June scorcher when it was more than 100 degrees in the shade. As is typical, I carried a hand towel to wipe sweat and wore thick gloves just to touch the blazing skin of the Mohawk as I climbed in. It was a routine SLAR mission plan where I worked my way up the coast, staying eight to ten miles at sea and above 10,000 feet. Once again, Specialist Yarbrough was my observer.

The coastline there is not smooth but contains outcroppings of land that sometimes placed my Mohawk within five miles. I was close to where I had spotted the Chinese freighter when the small screen on the left side of my dash alerted me that I was being tracked. The warning system was connected to a radar jammer hanging on my left wing. With its own diminutive propeller, the radar jammer generated its own power independent of the rest of the aircraft.

The dash display showed my plane in the center of a circle, and whenever the enemy anti-aircraft battery locked onto me, the display circle lit up the quadrant to give me an idea of its general direction. The front left quadrant was illuminated, which didn't tell me much since I knew that no enemy was going to be firing on me from the open sea to the front, right, and rear of me. This tracking notification had happened to me many times before. It was not uncommon for enemy batteries along the coast in North Vietnam to lock onto us as we fly our missions, but since we were unarmed and predominantly off at sea, they didn't fire on us often. This mission was different.

For the first time, I heard the unmistakable buzzing on my headset which notified me of a missile launch. The dash screen display changed instantly from a highlighted tracking quadrant to the bright-orange word *launch* flashing in all caps. The launch alert sounded like a rattlesnake, and it became a butt-puckering moment in the cockpit as Yarborough and I surveyed the coastline for any sign of a missile.

We were at least two miles in altitude and three to four miles off the coast, so I figured we had some time to react. I was the first to spot the missile because of its white tail exhaust. It was only a mile away from us and closing fast. At that moment, I tried a maneuver I'd never done before. The Split S was something that other pilots had talked to me about. Trading altitude for speed, I flipped my left wing over to invert the plane while at the same time starting a dive down toward the surface of the sea. I knew that the surface-to-air missiles could make no better than a three-and-a-half G turn, and I was starting to pull serious Gs as my speed increased from a cruising rate of 220 knots to at least 480 knots when I last glanced at my instruments. I felt the extreme pressure bearing down on my body, and even my toes started to tingle as if they were going numb. In the midst of this dive, I looked up through my canopy to see two amazing things. One was a Navy A-6 Intruder plane flying a sharply vertical trajectory headed quickly for higher altitude. I had no idea he was in the vicinity. The other was the actual missile that cruised between our two planes and looked like a small telephone pole with fins on the sides and its ass end on fire.

I exceeded the envelope of the aircraft during my turn and dive, so I started to pull the nose up between 2,000 and what too quickly became 1,000 feet above the sea. The aircraft did not behave normally at such a high rate of speed, and the surface of the sea approached incredibly fast. Yarborough calmly reported the altitude to me—900, 700, 500. I no longer wanted to trade altitude for speed. In fact, I'd trade anything at that point for more altitude, but I certainly didn't want to trade our lives. We dropped altitude so fast that for the first time in Vietnam, I found myself contemplating pulling the ejection handle, but we were way out in the water, so that thought evaporated quickly.

We finally leveled out at fifteen feet above the surface, as reported by Yarborough, who was watching the altimeter closely, but I did not yet have full control. The plane experienced a terrifying porpoise effect, and it tried to dive toward the water surface even as I fought it and pulled up on the controls. Our forward momentum from the dive was so great that the plane was behaving in ways I couldn't predict. Just as I thought we were gaining a few precious feet of altitude, the nose dove back down toward the water. Finally, after coming within a few feet of the water several times, the plane slowed and I regained more control of the Mohawk. I began a steady climb in altitude. At this point, we were headed in the exact opposite direction of when we started the Split S.

Yarborough, deadpan as usual, said, "Shit sir, that was close."

I wasn't sure whether he was talking about the missile or the water. We were less than a half hour from our intended turnaround point.

"This is our new turnaround point," I said. "We're taking our asses back to Marble Mountain."

I flew low on the surface of the water hoping to avoid further radar detection. At no time during the incident did I ever actually reach for the ejection handle. We were at least 100 miles into North Vietnam and, based on what I had heard about captured pilots and sharks in those waters, I knew ejecting in North Vietnamese territory was not good for one's health.

For some reason, as I flew low over the open sea back to base today, I couldn't help but think of my branch manager Major Canfield and a conversation we had almost two years ago. I can remember it vividly. He was the first person who convinced me to join the military intelligence branch to get the opportunity to fly the speedy Mohawks. Coming out of my basic officer's course, I tried to go directly to flight school, but he couldn't get me a slot. So instead, I ended up working as an MP on Fort Stewart. I felt like I totally missed my opportunity to fly when they asked me to give a safety briefing to what I was told was the last incoming class of fixed wing trainees. I was so upset that I immediately got on the phone with Major Canfield.

"I signed on to your branch to fly, not to issue damn traffic tickets!" I shouted into the phone. Canfield muttered something about the Army closing its fixed wing school at Fort Stewart because of the excess of trained helicopter pilots that the Army could simply transition to fixed wing. This was the very same man who told me that the Mohawk was the fastest plane in the Army and promised I would fly it if I joined his branch.

"I had my pick of branches but went with military intelligence because you made a promise!" I slammed down the phone. I didn't care if I got hauled up for insubordination.

A few hours later, I was summoned back to the phone in my MP office. It was Canfield. I braced myself.

"Lieutenant," he said. "I've got good news. I can get you in the next primary helicopter training course in Texas."

"What the hell am I going to fly helicopters for?" I barked. "What about the Mohawk?"

"You don't understand, Lieutenant. After you complete helicopter training, I can send you to the Q Course back there at Stewart."

"What's the Q Course?"

"Fixed wing transition. Complete helicopter first and you'll be slotted into the Q Course to convert over to fixed wings. They're shutting down the other fixed wing courses, but the transition course will continue. Report to Fort Wolters, Texas on Sunday evening by five. That's two days from now. How ready are you, Lieutenant?"

"I was born ready, sir! I was born ready and had a relapse!"

★ ★ ★

After such a stressful mission today, it was really exciting this evening to receive a cassette tape in the mail from Martha Anne. I wasted very little time eating at the dining facility before getting back to my hooch for a listen. I laid back on the bed and hit play:

═══════════ 🔊 ═══════════

Dear Joe,

It's now Monday night, and I just got home from work. I worked twelve to nine on Monday. The weather's terrible. The lights are out and I have a candle. It's about nine thirty and I have two candles, but I only have one that is burning. I'm not really sure when the lights went out, but the whole area out here is dark. It's been raining real hard. I think it's because of the hurricane that came in over Florida. It was supposed to hit somewhere around Panama City. So far, I haven't heard any reports. I was going to listen to the late weather and see how much damage it has done.

I got paid tonight for one week's work. I worked thirty-six hours, and I made fifty-five dollars. I really made sixty-six dollars and fifteen cents, but they took eleven dollars out for taxes. I'm not sure how much I'm making an hour. I'm going to check with them tomorrow. I guess I could divide it out and figure it. She never did tell me. They're paying me with a check this time. They usually just pay me cash. Tomorrow I don't go in until twelve. Usually, I'm off on Tuesday, but I switched with this lady, so I've got to work twelve to seven tomorrow night.

I got your letters from the twelfth and thirteenth today. I'm glad you're finally getting all your mail and have gotten all the back mail. It made me feel kind of bad that you'd think I hadn't written. Even when I was in Washington, I wrote every night. I'm glad your motor pool job is doing better. I know you have to spend so much time at it, that it's bad if it's a job you can't stand. I do have a phone in the bedroom now and still have a phone in the living room. But I use this one in the bedroom mostly. It's a lot better. When you called the last time, all I had to do was reach over and answer it.

I didn't understand what you wanted to know about the picture-taking with Senator Kennedy. I think I told you we were waiting outside the Hollings office for him to come out and take his picture. Lindler took it because I knew I would be too nervous to take it. Except she had trouble with the camera, and I thought we'd never get it taken. But it came out real well. All my pictures from Washington came out except the ones I took at night.

I hope you enjoy the newspaper clippings I send. I think you ought to keep up with what's going on. I try to send a variety of clippings and try to get some short ones and not ones that will make such a bulky letter. Really ones that you are interested in. The campaign news has kind of died down lately. I know it will be more interesting when the conventions begin. I'll send you news about that.

You were talking about in your long P.S. when's the best time to call. You can call anytime. I don't mind you waking me up in the morning just so you catch me. It doesn't bother me to wake me up at six or six-thirty or even five-thirty because I can go back to sleep and then get up. I think it's about twelve hours difference. That's the way I figure it. I figure when you call me at six-thirty in the morning then it's six-thirty that afternoon there. Or is it six-thirty the next day? I guess it's that afternoon. We had a big discussion about that at Granny's trying to figure out whether it's a whole day ahead or just twelve hours ahead. I never could get it straight in my mind.

When you call, it seems like we don't get too much said before you're saying goodbye. He obviously notifies you that the three minutes are about up cause I never know until you let me know. It seems like we just start talking when it's time to stop. We went to see The Godfather *the other night. It was pretty good except it was violent and gory. I just closed my eyes. I didn't watch all the shootings cause they did have quite a few shootings. The way they put it was they'd offer these deals. They offered an agreement that could not be resisted or something. We're going to offer you this deal you can't resist. The fellow would say that no he didn't want to sell out his company or no, he didn't want to do this, that, or the other. Once they finished with him, then he'd want to do it.*

I guess this tape's about over. I'll send you a better one on my other one. I was just trying to fill up the rest of this tape. I love you so much and miss you. It doesn't seem to get better. I thought I'd get used to being without you, but I don't think I ever will. I need you all the time. It's been so dreary today. I can't get too cheerful on this tape. It's rained all day, and I had to straighten the apartment. I love you.

Martha Anne

[End of audio]

=========== 🔇 ===========

Friday, June 30, 1972
DAY 52:

Today, we had our weekly officer call. Major Smith was happier than usual, and we soon knew why. He had the official report from the Puff gunship earlier in the week. When the ground unit inspected the island, they discovered twenty-three killed and seven wounded. In addition, nineteen secondary explosions were reported during the course of the air assault. We certainly had some quiet nights this week with no incoming mortars. Sometimes war just seems to be that simple—us or them. Fortunately, this time it was them.

Dear Martha Anne,

I got my pay voucher today. I'll give you the breakdown by the numbers.

[1] Amount brought forward from the last check.
[2] Basic pay

[3] Housing allowance

[4] Food

[5] Hostile fire pay from last month

[6] Family separation pay from last month

[7] Flight pay

[8] Hostile fire pay for this month

[9] Family separation pay for this month

This is about $100 more than I expected this month. The reason was because of $65 hostile fire pay from last month and $25 family separation allowance. This is good money but I would rather have you. I can't hold, kiss, or love money or have it love me back. You are all that counts. I wish I could be there eating anniversary cake with you. I think I'll put some of the icing from our cake on you and lick it off. Oh! I could just bite a big chunk out of you right now. I want you so very much.

I send all my love and kisses to you my darling,

Joe

U.S. Planes Soften Up Red Defense

By Arthur Higbee, SAIGON (UPI)—American warplanes softened up Communist defenses in Quang Tri Province today and two battalions of South Vietnamese paratroopers followed up with an airborne raid to the outskirts of the Communist-held provincial capital . . . The paratroopers are part of a 20,000-man force of South Vietnamese troops trying to recapture Quang Tri Province, taken by the Communists May 1 . . . The U.S. command, meanwhile, reported five American reconnaissance planes crashed or were shot down in the war during the week with two crewmen reported missing.

Saturday, July 1, 1972
DAY 53:

Last night around dusk, I walked over to the latrine on a mission and not the typical mission associated with latrines. The building is about 100 yards from my hooch and has a cement floor with cinderblock walls. The corrugated tin roof is pockmarked with shrapnel holes ripped in it from past attacks so you can actually see stars at night when sitting on the can. We have porcelain toilets and urinals, a rarity on bases in Vietnam. Most units have to burn their toilet waste in barrels using diesel fuel. We even have a 131st unit songbook with an ode to the commode called "Sam, Sam, the Lavatory Man:"

> *Sam, Sam, The Lavatory Man*
> *The Number One Proprietor of the Public Can*
> *He brings in the papers*
> *He brings in the towels*
> *And he listens to the rumble of the people's bowels*
> *Down, Down, Down in the Ground*
> *Hear those turds just a-rumblin' down*
> *Flip Flop Hear them Plop*
> *Sam's Got the Shithouse Blues*
> *Sam's Got the Shithouse Blues*

I carried with me a can of Raid from my hooch. As I entered the latrine, I flipped on the light. Hundreds of roaches scattered to find dark holes and cracks. I zapped the cracks with Raid. Out they came again. I went for the biggest and snatched it up with my bare hands. I plunked the roach into a glass juice jar and screwed the lid on tight to hold him until Saturday's main event.

When I awoke this morning, my roach was still kicking in the jar. The centerpiece of our unit organizational day was the roach race. I dutifully signed up my entry at the roach registration point. Each roach had to have an assigned number, so I chose seven in honor of my call sign—Spud Zero-Seven. I used a BIC Wite-Out brush and painted the number seven on its back wings. In the process of painting and measuring him, I managed to break off two of his legs. This seemed like a big disadvantage, but with the race about to start,

I didn't have time to locate a replacement.

A white rope defined the edge of the thirty-foot circle. In the center was a large can with the bottom cut out. The idea was for all the competitors to drop their roaches in the can. The winner would be the one whose roach crossed the outer ring of the perimeter rope. Once it crossed the line, the roach's coach was supposed to stomp it dead. The can was lifted and the roaches scuttled across the dusty ground. It didn't take long for all hell to break loose. There was a lot of premature stomping of roaches before they made it to the edge of the circle. Dust billowed all around as soldiers feverishly stomped on one another's roaches. Spud Zero-Seven, powered by two fewer legs than the others, not only didn't win, but he didn't even survive to see the rope.

Dear Martha Anne,

Today was the 7th anniversary of the 131st MI company. Tomorrow is our first anniversary. All afternoon the entire company has been partying and celebrating. There were volleyball tournaments, basketball shooting competitions, tug-of-wars, horseshoe contests, and a cockroach race. That was really something. I had the second biggest roach, but I broke two of his legs trying to hold him down to measure him. Needless to say, that certainly slowed him down. I didn't win the race but I stomped my competition into the ground. I had to fly at 5:30 this afternoon, so I missed the band and one of the two strippers. The enlisted men threw all the officers in a trailer of water. The trailer had ice and beer in it but all the beer was gone and the ice had melted. It was a cold bath. With all this celebrating, I keep wishing I were home with you for our anniversary. I would like for us to have a piece of cake after a dinner at the Trawler or someplace and then have a piece of each other at the Holiday Inn in room 808!

I love you very much and wish you a happy anniversary. I'm going to try and call you tomorrow if I can. I want to go to the USO at Da Nang and call you on a regular phone. It will cost more, but I don't care. I just want to talk without saying over. With my entire heart, mind, and body, I love you, you are my wife and the darling of my life.

I love you completely,
Joe

Sunday, July 2, 1972
DAY 54:

July seems to have brought with it a whole new level of heat. When I complete a flight mission, I quickly shed my stifling Nomex fire-retardant flight suit. The Air Force and Marines have one-piece flight suits, but the Army has two-piece suits, for some unknown reason. I assume an Army general at the Pentagon or somewhere in the chain of command decided the flight suit needed to be split in two in order to more closely replicate the Army's jungle fatigues. With an opening, one might assume that the ventilation would keep us cooler, but it still heats up like an oven. I try to spend most of my daytime hours wearing my lighter weight jungle fatigues or a pair of coveralls. These July days are so hot that if we kneel on the skin of the airplanes, we get burned. While flying my mission tonight, I sweated the entire time in my Nomex suit, and even though it was primarily dark and raining, the high humidity offered no relief. I kept a small towel draped over my shoulder in the cockpit just for sweat. After my daytime missions, I can literally pour the sweaty liquid sludge out of my boots.

Dear Martha Anne,

I just returned from North Vietnam. I was well into the North at 8:00 p.m. and I said to my observer, "One year ago at this hour I was married." That is really some way to spend your first anniversary. I have tried all day to call you, but so far, I have not been successful. I will try again tomorrow.

I love you with all my heart. I love you even more than the night I watched you walk down that aisle in your wedding gown. Maybe we can say our R&R in Hawaii is our honeymoon. I still don't feel like we have had a real honeymoon. I guess you could call some of our trips a honeymoon. The Grand Canyon was kind of like a honeymoon. The trip to Panama City was too.

Where do you want to live when I get back to the states? I have to know within the next four weeks. I was thinking of Ft. Bragg, N.C.; Ft. Lee, VA.; Ft. Lewis, Washington (state); Henderson Field, Hawaii. If I go to a post on the East Coast, I will get about 10 days travel time. I'll tell them I'm driving by car so I'll get the maximum time to travel.

Right now it looks like we won't be moving to Da Nang for a while. I hope we don't move at all. I am the motor officer and the movement control officer. I would be in charge of getting 211 people and all their belongings there and moving all our equipment. With the trucks I have it would take a miracle.

It has really been raining a lot here lately. I flew last night and tonight in the rain. I'm really glad I had all that instrument flying at Fort Rucker now. I would like to fly every day, but so far I'm only flying about four days per week.

I'm sending your letters back for safekeeping. I have to burn the envelopes because if they get in the trash you may start getting some mail from the VC over here. They are very tricky. If you are contacted in any way notify the air police at the airbase or the FBI. Do not try to lead them astray or play any games with them. The military has special teams to

track them down if you notify them of any contacts.
In the event that I'm captured, you will be notified
by an officer of the Army in uniform. You will not be
notified by mail or telephone.

I have to be getting ready for bed. I'm tired from a
busy day. I had a systems fail today so I had to return
for maintenance and then relaunch for another mission.

I love you so very much. I want and need you every
day. You are very special to me and have been for a
long time.

I love you with all I have,
Joe

Monday, July 3, 1972
DAY 55:

Exchanging cigarettes for repair parts from Mr. Moon has become a
weekly ritual. Mop was again my driver to Philco Ford. After the parts
run, we stopped by the USO office on base to use their telephone to
call Martha Anne, with no luck. I was so glad we connected on the
MARS line early this morning, since it was still our anniversary date in
Charleston's time zone, but we only got a couple minutes to speak. On
our way back, Mop and I stopped at a great little Chinese restaurant
located between the Han River and the heart of Da Nang. It's popular
with the Viet Cong, too, so we tried to get there after the lunch crowd.

The building does not look like a typical restaurant. The outside
walls and roof are covered by corrugated tin sheeting that resembles
crinkle cut French fries, looking more like an old tool shed than
a restaurant. Inside, the hot air barely gets moved around by four
decrepit ceiling fans that sway and click, an incessant rhythm loud
enough to be distracting. On the exposed studs hang a motley
assortment of framed landscapes. The dim lighting is made more
so by pointy shades that resemble rice farmers' hats. The floors are
bare and the hodgepodge of tables and chairs look like they were
salvaged from a dump. But I don't go there for the ambience. I go
there for the shrimp.

When we walked in this afternoon, the restaurant was packed with American soldiers in uniform as well as some civilian contractors. This was no surprise, as word spreads quickly when there's good chow to be had. We sat close to the front door, and as expected, we received our food incredibly fast from the kitchen.

Less than a minute later, we heard a deafening *whoomp*. A mortar hit just outside the back wall of the restaurant. Reflexively, Mop and I, as well as everyone in the restaurant, dove to the floor. Most of the corrugated tin sheeting on the back wall was now bent into the restaurant or completely blown off the wall studs. "You hit?" I heard people ask. "Damn, that was close."

My bowl of rice noodles was upturned on the floor in a puddle of brown sauce, a delicious shrimp roll nearby. I picked up the roll, plucked it into my mouth, and ran with Mop outside. That was the third time that restaurant had been hit by indirect fire since I've been stationed here, but that was the first time I was in it when it happened. We did not pause to pay our bill but hightailed it back to the base.

I've thought about it, and I've decided I'm not going to tell Martha Anne what happened at the restaurant today. I'll talk about the shrimp in my letter. We always liked to eat shrimp at Obie's Oyster Bar near Rome, Georgia, which was close to her college campus, or the Sandbar Restaurant at Folly Beach, just south of Charleston. I'm just not going to tell her what happened and stress her.

Dear Martha Anne,

I enjoyed talking to you so much this morning on the MARS line that I left here and went to Da Nang and tried to call you on the regular phone. They have closed the USO at Da Nang, so I could not use their telephone. I wanted so much to call you without having to say over.

I was going to eat at a Chinese restaurant yesterday, but I had to fly, so I ended up going today. I had egg rolls stuffed with shrimp and dipped in sweet and sour sauce. They were really good. It was the restaurant at Da Nang that was destroyed two weeks ago by a rocket. It is already repaired and in business again. A mortar puts a hole in a building, but a rocket puts the building into a hole. I did not realize how powerful they were until I saw some of the buildings they hit.

It is one day and one year since we have been married. I do not regret one minute of our time together. I only regret the time we are apart. I wish we could have married a year earlier. I love you so much. I need you every day. I get excited reading your letters and realizing how much you want me home. I want to be there even more than you want me there. I'll have to be careful not to squeeze you to death when I love you again. I just want to hold you so close until our bodies grow together. I don't want to leave you anymore. I didn't want to this time. I wish I were with you right now. I don't think I will spend much time sleeping the first couple of days. I'll be too busy loving you and making love with you.

I send you all my love,

Joe

Tuesday, July 4, 1972
DAY 56:

It's Independence Day, but it doesn't feel much like a holiday here at Marble Mountain. Often on the Fourth, we gather as a family at Folly Beach to have a cookout and spend time in the surf. I wonder if they are going to be at Folly again this year. When I got back to my hooch, I pulled out the cassette recording Martha Anne sent me from the fish supper in early June to listen again:

━━━━━━━━ 🔊 ━━━━━━━━

Roy: What kind of fish was it?

Freddie: Spadefish.

Roy:	There wasn't but two of y'all boats out there today, Freddie?
Freddie:	There was ten out there.
Daddy:	Tell Roy how close we were fishing out there together ten miles out in the ocean.
Freddie:	The boats was bumping together out there.
Mama:	Way out there where you can't even see land and you've got to bump together?
Freddie:	Well just two boats were mighty close to us. I guess there was about ten of us out there altogether.
Daddy:	We was just good buddies.
Roy:	I don't think I'd be that good. Only person I know that let you fish that close to him is old Joe. We fished off his head that time.
Lindler:	It doesn't matter. They still gonna bite his hook.
Daddy:	That's the Fulton in him.
Mama:	Well, I don't believe Joe ever caught any spadefish. But they sure are pretty fish.
Lindler:	Well Joe's never been out in the ocean like that, has he?
Roy:	Not that far.
Lindler:	He didn't want to go out in Freddie's boat. He's scared.
Daddy:	Freddie might drown him.
Freddie:	We got out there and back today no trouble.
Roy:	Just how wet were you when you got back?
Freddie:	Oh well, we were a little damp.
Daddy:	Oh yeah, oh yeah, tell Roy how come the thirty-gallon fiberglass gas tank wouldn't give us no gas today.
Freddie:	Full of water. I got a gallon of water out of it.
Roy:	How'd you know it was full of water?
Freddie:	I pumped it out. And I guarantee you it's running like a garden hose now.

Daddy:	We didn't use but twenty-two gallons, Roy.
Freddie:	Eighteen. Eighteen's all we used.
Lindler:	Thirty-five miles, eighteen gallons.
Mama:	Your car does better than that, doesn't it Roy?
Roy:	Yup, just a little bit.
Daddy:	We rode by them big yachts though, didn't we?
Freddie:	One of them boats had the same sized boat as mine for a lifeboat.
Lindler:	Freddie, you know not!
Daddy:	Sure did.
Lindler:	That musta been a sea-going yacht.
Roy:	If you out there, you better be sea-something. You're not gonna get me out there. If I get a spare minute, the closest I'm gonna get is about a hundred yards off the beach where the waves is breaking—me and Little Red Hen.
Lindler:	What's the Little Red Hen?
Mama:	His surfboard.
Lindler:	That's her name now?
Roy:	I can't hardly believe that you left them biting, and the time between when you got there and the anchor got down you done caught five.
Daddy:	Well if you got two foot off the spot, you done messed up.
Lindler:	They were fishing in the bed just like a bream bed Roy.
Daddy:	Then the sharks come in, you see.
Roy:	Sharks?
Mama:	And they could see the fish 'cause the water was so clear. Why they just didn't look for them and sit right on top of them?

Freddie:	No you can't see the bottom, but you could see way down in it.
Roy:	Y'all seen some sharks?
Freddie:	One of 'em took Pa's fish! He was bringing a spadefish in and the shark got it.
Roy:	What did you do then, Daddy?
Lindler:	He hollered.
Daddy:	Yeah, I said, "The shark's got my fish! Freddie, great day!"
Roy:	Well, you couldn't hook the shark?
Daddy:	The shark caught the fish. He didn't catch the hook!
Roy:	Well, it looks like he'd've swallowed the fish and then you'd have the shark.
Daddy:	Oh no, he bit him off.
Mama:	And that was the biggest one, evidently.
Roy:	The biggest one always does get away.
Freddie:	Na, the biggest one I had on.
Roy:	Now how did you have the biggest one on that got away?
Freddie:	I had two big ones on that got away. They would have gone about five pounds apiece, I reckon.
Roy:	Well that's all you catch out there, spade and black bass?
Freddie:	That's all that was biting today.
Roy:	So you didn't catch no cane-cracking, line-singing fish like Joe catches?
Freddie:	Nope.

[End of audio]

With all that talk about fishing by my family members, it really has me itching to go fishing over here. Dubose is looking into renting us a boat for the motor pool men to go out in.

Dear Martha Anne,

Happy 4th of July. I guess you had today off. I had to work just like any other day. I hope I get to come home for Christmas. I certainly would hate to spend my holiday season over here. You cannot tell a holiday from any other day. We did have a fireworks display tonight. They fired a lot of flares. I guess the VC could throw in a few mortars for good measure.

I'm getting your letters pretty regularly now. I'm so glad my mail is straightened out. You cannot imagine how demoralizing it is to not get any mail. Your letters keep me going. They are always the special time of my day. I can hardly wait until mail call. I read them over and over. I'm returning your letters so you can save them for me. I don't have any place to store them over here. I haven't put the cards on the banner yet because I thought we were going to move to Da Nang. It now looks like we will be staying here. I'm certainly glad about that. I don't like the idea of being hit by the larger 122 mm rockets. So many units have left Vietnam until it is getting to the point where there are very few Americans left. If the president keeps this up, I will be the only American left in Vietnam. I guess that is the way everyone over here feels. I certainly hope that we are all home soon. I feel that now it is a game of numbers. The American troops no longer fight over here. We only try to protect our own bases.

Much love always. Your passionate husband,
Joe

Wednesday, July 5, 1972
DAY 57:

Dubose learned from another local unit just how easy it is to rent a fishing boat. We agreed that he'd take a number of the motor pool men with him today and then I'd take another group on Friday. I've caught literally thousands of fish in my life, but it's hard to believe I could be catching fish in the South China Sea this week. The first time I remember going was when I was five and we were living on Bull Street in Charleston.

Bull Street wasn't south of Broad Street, where the cream of Charleston society resided. It was where working-class families lived, like our neighbors—the LaCroix family. Mr. and Mrs. LaCroix had no children of their own to help with chores, so in the winter, they paid me five cents per bucket to move coal—three to bring the coal in and two to take the cinders out. Besides the pay, Mr. LaCroix thanked me for my work by taking me fishing. I always thought he liked talking about fishing more than actually going, but on those occasions when he decided to go, I was excited to walk the three blocks down Rutledge Avenue to the edge of Colonial Lake, located right in the middle of the city. Though it looks more like a pond than a lake, its waters are salty and fed by the nearby Ashley River on the west side of the peninsula.

Typically, there were never more than a half dozen others fishing there, and reflecting back on it, I guess I know why. We never really caught anything besides eels—long, smooth, silvery eels that fluttered back and forth on the hook like an overeager dog's tail. First time I caught an eel I thought it was a snake, and I was shocked when Mr. LaCroix put it in his bucket to take home. Once back at home, I watched him skin and debone the meat. Mr. LaCroix then cooked some of the leftover bait shrimp in a pot over the open fire while Mrs. LaCroix fried the eel in the house. I had just one or two small bites of that fried eel because, as I have said ever since, "a little bit of eel goes a long way."

Dear Martha Anne,

I just returned from a mission. It is 9 p.m. and I'm tired. I wanted to write several people tonight but it looks like I will only write you. I'm eating some corn chips you sent me and drinking a 7Up. I didn't get any supper tonight. It is the only thing I don't like about these late afternoon and early night missions. I have lost 10 pounds since I have been in Vietnam and at this rate, I'll lose 10 more soon. In cases like this, your food is a real lifesaver. They keep the hunger away until the mess hall opens again.

We had a good day at the motor pool today. My motor sergeant went fishing all day and I only had four men, but we got 4 trucks and a tug back up off of deadline. That is to say we fixed them and I do mean we. I got pretty dirty myself. I have been going to Philco Ford to get parts the last few days and I get results. I guess I need to do a little back-patting because I deserve it. I think we are the only unit in I Corps with some of the parts I got today. Everyone has been out of them and we could not get any no matter how hard we tried. I went to the manager of Philco Ford yesterday and told him I had to have the parts and today I got them.

I'm planning a fishing trip Friday. I don't care about catching fish as much as I want the day off. I guess I should have joined the Navy or Coast Guard. I like small boats a lot. I really enjoy the water.

I remember some good times with you at the beach. I guess water makes a man hungry for a woman. Maybe it is the salt air or just the fact that they have on less clothes than usual. I hunger for you, my love. I need you near me all of the time. I guess I'm being selfish, but that is the way I feel. I want to watch your movements, the way you walk, talk, breathe, eat, and everything. I just love all of you.

All my love always,
Joe

Thursday, July 6, 1972
DAY 58:

I received a letter today from Uncle John Wyatt and Aunt Myrtle, which was a pleasant surprise. Sounds like the weather's hot there in Bishopville, too. It was this time of year when I used to head up to their place to spend a few weeks every summer. When I was five, he bought me my first Daisy Red Ryder BB gun. He taught me how to shoot it, practicing on homemade targets behind his house. His son was a little jealous and didn't think kindly of the fact that his father had purchased a five-dollar BB gun for me, but I loved him for it. Making the distinctive ping noise of a BB going through a metal pie plate target always brought a smile to my face. In his letter, he asked me if I'd fired my rifle at the enemy yet. Around Marble Mountain, we hardly ever draw our weapons from the arms room, much less return fire on the VC.

One fall when I was still in college, Uncle John Wyatt invited Roy and me to an opening day dove shoot behind his place. To get ready for the dove season, Roy and I shot skeet near our home in Charleston. When we arrived just in time for Aunt Myrtle's lunch at his house, we reported our diligent preparation at the skeet range. I asked him if he had done anything to prepare for the start of the season. He drawled, "Boys, I don't need to get ready. I was born ready and had a relapse."

I don't think I was ready for the heat today, since I still have a pounding headache late at night. Felt like it was over 120 degrees this afternoon in the motor pool. Even my flight mission got cancelled out at the last moment. I can't wait to get out on the water tomorrow with the guys for a little fishing.

Friday, July 7, 1972
DAY 59:

The fish weren't biting much, but I finally caught a ten-inch fish, which turned out to be the biggest of the day. While on the water, we took the boat out to a small one-acre island not more than a mile off China Beach. Before getting out, we conducted a recon by fire which means we basically shot up the island vegetation, and when no one returned fire, we assumed that it would be fine to hit the beach. We also devised a shooting game using sand crabs as targets. The object was to flip the live crab as many times as possible without killing it. If you didn't aim just below it in the sand, then you ran the risk of annihilating the crab. Taught by my sharpshooting uncles like John Wyatt and Willard, I've always taken great pride in my marksmanship, and I was able to win the contest by flipping a crab seventeen different times before destroying it. I wish I could have taken the entire day off, but I have to report to the airfield for a night mission tonight. I'm looking forward to writing Martha Anne later.

Dear Martha Anne,

What a day today was! We went fishing this morning. That is, I went with seven enlisted men from the SLAR section of the 131st. We had a great time, but we only caught four fish. We went swimming for 2 hrs and cooked steaks on a grill and heated c rations and drank cokes & beer. We didn't really care about the fish as much as we wanted to have a good time away from here. We came back a little early and took a steam bath and had a massage. That was really good. The steam bath & shower got all the salt water & sweat off, and the massage took the soreness out of our muscles.

I also had to fly tonight. That is a different story. I'm just a little sunburned and tired, so I didn't feel much like a night mission. I got a good bit of weather/ instrument time. The thing that ruined my flight was my GCA here at Da Nang. They vectored me through 3 thunderstorms. One of the storms bounced the aircraft around like a toy and flashed lightning in my eyes, so I could hardly see. I was sure glad to get my wheels on the ground tonight. I have never flown in such rough weather before. I have flown in some bad weather at Ft. Rucker, but today was the worst so far. Well, I'm safe at Marble & mighty thankful. I'll say an extra prayer tonight for this one. I have been praying for this war to end every night since I've been here, and I also thank God for another day of life. You really never savor the taste of life until you have come face to face with death. It gives you a zest for living that sheltered people will never know.

I love you constantly. I can't help but talk about you. I know people get tired of my constant praise for you & your love. I can't help myself. I love you completely and forever.

Much love from your husband,
Joe

Two US F4 Phantom Jets Downed Near Chinese Border

SAIGON (UPI)—Two US F4 Phantom jets were shot down by Soviet-built MIGs between Hanoi and the Chinese border, the US command announced today . . . All four crewmembers are missing, the command said. A total of 62 US aircraft have been downed by MIGs in the Vietnam war, while American planes have shot 150 MIGs out of the sky. Since the air war began eight years ago, 994 American aircraft have been downed over North Vietnam by MIGs and antiaircraft fire, 58 of them since the start of the current offensive March 30. Since March 30, a total of 67 American fliers have been reported missing in North Vietnam. The Command also announced that 12 122mm rockets hit the US air base at Da Nang today, killing one American and causing "light materiel damage."

Sunday, July 9, 1972
DAY 61:

I can't believe that Martha Anne's anniversary package made it here so quickly. I've got another brand-new cassette tape to listen to. It's perfect that it arrived today because I have more time to listen. I close my eyes when I listen and pretend that she's sitting next to me talking.

"Joe, it's Sunday night, July second and I've just gotten back from the beach. It's our first anniversary. I wanted to send you a tape and tell you what I've been doing and tell you how my day went. I'm sure it was a lot better than yours. Yesterday I was supposed to work from nine thirty to six, but I decided before I went to lunch that I didn't feel particularly like working. So at lunch time, I just decided that when I went to lunch, I wouldn't come back. I waited until two o'clock to go to lunch so I could at least get a few hours in. And then I left. I had to go to the commissary anyway because I wanted to make some blondies to take to the beach today, and I needed to get a couple of things. There wasn't any way I could go to the commissary and get back to work anyway, so I just went on. When I got home, I called the store and told them that I couldn't make it back to work. I was sorry that something came up at home. So I stayed home yesterday afternoon and sewed. I made myself a new Bermuda outfit that's real cute that I wore to the beach today.

I was sewing yesterday afternoon when mother called. She wanted to know if I wanted to go out to eat, so she and daddy took me out last night to the Sandbar for shrimp for our anniversary. It was real good. I think they're getting better. They have added a whole new floor upstairs, so we sat upstairs to eat. We found out today that your mother and father would have gone if they had known. I thought they were going to the beach this morning, but they went on Saturday morning instead. I didn't realize that they were even over there yet, but it was real late when we went out to eat.

I stayed up late last night fixing the blondies to take to the beach. When I went to bed, it was after twelve o'clock, so I opened the card from you that you said not to open until July second. I've been dying to open it ever since I got it on Friday. So, I opened it, and I went to bed and figured you would call this morning. I think I kind of dreamed about you calling because I just knew you would. Obviously, you couldn't get a line through because you didn't call. Anyway, I hope you call tomorrow morning because I want to talk to you. I know you've been trying to get a call through. I really am eager to talk to you, not that we get to say that much, but I'd just like to talk to you.

Guess what? When I got to the beach and we got in good, I discovered a dozen roses—six reds and six whites—in a blue vase with a pretty red bow. There was this pretty card on it, and it said, "Come rain or shine, I'm glad you're mine. Happy Anniversary to the one I love, love, love." Then it was signed, "With All My Love on Our First Anniversary, Love Joe." And that was in your handwriting, and it had been cut out of a letter obviously and taped onto this other card. So it was a personal signature from you. It was a real cute card, so I'll put it on my door and save it for you to see. I'm going to keep this card, and I'm keeping the one you gave me and taping them up on the door. Plus, I'm keeping the cute little Charlie Brown card you sent to me the other day saying that I was the best form of entertainment. And that's pretty good if I even beat Airport *because that's a pretty exciting movie.*

The thing about work is, I didn't mean to walk out on people, but I was so tired of working. I don't particularly like working in the men's department. I knew I had a lot of other things yesterday I'd rather do than stand there. I don't really have to work, and I know it. So I just decided I wouldn't come back after lunch and be tortured for three more hours. I really appreciated the break. I think I'm going to work until August 1st and then concentrate on studying some.

Oh, another thing. Your daddy wanted to know if you called from your airplane. So I promised that I'd ask you whether you called from your airplane when they get a phone call. I don't think you can do that, but he somehow had it in his mind it is possible to call from your airplane over the radio somehow over here. So let me know about that.

There's really not much more to say except that I love you. I want you to know that I'm thinking about you constantly and I'm here waiting for you. I want you to know that I love you and that my whole life is centered around you. This past year has been the happiest year of my life. Our year together was really together because we saw each other a whole lot. I feel like I've learned a lot about you in this year, and I hope you've learned a lot about me. I love you and I love you some more. I'd give anything to have you back here lying next to me. I'd love to have the warmth and security that you offer."

Martha Anne

[End of audio]

═══════════ 🔇 ═══════════

I'm so glad that she liked the roses for our anniversary. I had to enlist my parent's help to make that delivery happen.

Dear Martha Anne,

I tried to call you tonight but I got no answer. It was about 7:30 a.m. in Charleston, so I figured you were at the beach with my parents. I hope that was the case and you are all right. I just wanted to say hello and hear your voice again. I missed you so much this weekend. I didn't fly yesterday or today, and time has really gone by slowly. I feel like my watch is running in slow motion.

I love you and miss you so very much. I find it difficult to imagine that we have to wait 5 ½ more months before we see each other again. I know why my father wanted out of the Navy so much now. He spent 36 months away from my mother. He also went 9 months without any mail. I guess I don't have too much to complain about. I can call you and write you at will. I get your letters within 10 days and packages too. The last package took 6 days. I think that is a record. I need you very much. Keep writing and sending me packages & tapes. I love you very much. I love you, I love you, I love you, I love you!

Much love always your husband,
Joe

Monday, July 10, 1972
DAY 62:

When Dubose returned from a visit with the first sergeant today, he had written orders for the two of us to become leaders of the new mobile reaction force. My roommate Pat McGarvey will share the extra duty with me. With the last full combat brigade leaving Vietnam in June, individual units can no longer rely upon an increasingly rare infantry detachment to secure our base perimeter. It's now an organic function.

There are other lieutenants in the unit with fewer extra duties who can be assigned this task, but instead it has come to me. We are asking for volunteers to serve on this force, even though I doubt we'll have any takers. Most are just counting the days until the war ends or their tour is over so they can ship home.

Since I wasn't scheduled for a mission tonight, I took a trip over to the arms room this afternoon to check on my assigned weapon. Working for Captain Slim's supply office is a Cajun sergeant from the Louisiana bayou named Boisclair, but we just call him *Frenchie*. He has a heavy Creole accent and French-styled moustache to go with it. He is the gatekeeper to the unit's weapons.

Today I noticed that he has about twenty-five Ho Chi Minh sandals mounted to the walls of his office. Most of the sandal soles are constructed of tire treads and vines or old cord strings as the straps. I questioned him about them and asked him if he was making them or collecting them.

"I picked dey up off dead gooks," he replied. "Two, three nights a week I go on night patrols wid da recon from dey First Cav."

Even though I didn't say anything, he could tell I didn't approve.

"It's not like I'm taking dey ears," he said.

This is not Frenchie's first tour in Vietnam. He strikes me as very strange. Most guys in the unit are trying to get on that silver bird back home and are doing as little as possible to get themselves killed. Frenchie seems to be waging his own personal war against the Vietnamese.

None of us carry weapons as we walk around the base at Marble Mountain Airfield. Due to the high number of fratricide incidents and accidental discharges, the higher command thinks it is safer to keep the weapons locked in an arms room unless we are under a significant attack. Because of this policy, the supply personnel have never assigned weapons to individuals in the unit. Until getting assigned as the leader of the reaction force, I had no reason to care about this policy. But I certainly care now. We will *have* to get weapons assigned for the men who volunteer for our force.

Dear Martha Anne,

I went to the movie tonight but left after the first reel. It was not a very good movie. I felt my time would be better spent writing the one I love. I'm afraid I'm having emotional problems. I don't enjoy being with my fellow officers. I feel almost hostile toward them. All I want to do is think about you or talk about you. I can talk about you for hours on end but other conversations bore me. I guess you occupy most of my thoughts all day long. The last week has really been slow for me. The days just seem to get longer and the nights shorter.

Love always,
Joe

Tuesday, July 11, 1972
DAY 63:

Today the first sergeant provided us with a list of volunteers, and we eliminated anyone who had not earned an *expert* on their rifle in marksmanship training. From his initial list of thirty-five, we paired it down to twenty-five. Out of the thirteen soldiers we had working for us in the motor pool, all but one volunteered to serve on our reaction force.

Dubose and I sat down at the chess board this evening after a particularly hot and humid day. On these July nights, the air conditioner in the motor pool office is a special blessing. I am not on the schedule to fly a Mohawk mission tonight, which is a relief given how many hours I spent in coveralls today. Our chess board is neatly arranged on top of an old wooden Army field desk in the center of the office. Two or three evenings a week, we square off. We take turns playing the role of the Russian Boris Spassky or the American Bobby Fischer, and we even take turns winning since neither one of us is good enough to shut the other one out. The chess board is worn from use, and a few of the white pawns were lost long ago. So, we cut the tips off used spark plugs to replace them.

Dubose broached the topic first. He thought it strange that an OIC [officer in charge] and an NCOIC [noncommissioned officer in charge] were both assigned to the reaction force from the same section.

"I bet Captain Fordiani is still ticked off about that incident with the CO's Jeep," I said.

"Not just that, you really lit a fire last month when you laid down the law in that officer meeting. All of those captains are probably out to get you."

"I know Chapman is. He told me he was," I said. "We're probably the least popular guys in the unit right now."

"I don't really care, anyway. We've gotten most of the vehicles off the deadline report, and the first sergeant seems to be pretty happy with the motor pool." Dubose seemed genuinely satisfied.

While I still see the other lieutenants who are my roommates almost daily, I spend most of my free time and working daylight hours with the soldiers in the motor pool. Other pilots have even questioned me as to why I spend so much time with the enlisted men. Since I started off as a private when I entered the Army in 1969, I guess I just feel more comfortable with them. Plus, these are the men who work every day to get our vehicles repaired and help me be a successful motor officer. They may be the misfits of our unit, but they are working hard for me.

Despite the fact that the mobile reaction force is a potentially dangerous job, we feel like there is a lot we can control. Dubose's prior experience with the military police will be helpful, and I can use some of my basic infantry training experiences to prepare our security force.

Dear Martha Anne,

The motor pool is looking better. We are making progress. We are getting trucks running every day. I'm going to turn in some old clunkers this week. They always break down and we don't need them. I can get rid of 9 trucks all together. That will reduce our workload and the number of parts we need. It will help us a great deal. I have been waiting until after we moved to Da Nang, but I don't think we are going.

I have not been scheduled to fly for four days now. We are really short of aircraft. I don't see why we stay here. I hope we get stand down orders before Christmas. I would give up my R&R for a 4 month drop. I don't care where they station me after here as long as we are together. I need you all the time. I sure do miss you.

I pray for peace every night. I want to come home to you soon. I wished to be there for our anniversary but that wish didn't come true. Maybe I'll be home to stay by Christmas. I'm seriously thinking about voting for McGovern just to get out of this place. Maybe Nixon will wind this up if the election looks close. I don't know if you told our Senators I was here but I wish you had. You could have told them to end this mess now. This is our country's longest war and we don't see an end over here. I only hope the Americans will discontinue their policy of troops everywhere that calls for them. The only thing I dread now is if I have less than 6 months here when we leave. I will probably get sent to South Korea. I would prefer the 225th Mohawk unit in Hawaii. Could you imagine two years in Hawaii? You could learn to hula while I learned to surf. Well, all this is dreaming and not reality yet but it sure is great to dream. I love you so very much I cannot explain it.

Much love always, your husband,
Joe

Title Match Adjourned With Fischer In Trouble

REYKJAVIK, Iceland (AP)—Bobby Fischer made his opening assault on the Soviet Chess fortress Tuesday night, but world champion Boris Spassky repelled it and left the American with a tough fight for a draw when their first game was adjourned. The first game of history's richest world chess title match was called after 40 moves and 3 hours and 34 minutes of play . . . Fischer has played Spassky five times in the past. The three times he played the black pieces he lost. Playing white he was able to salvage two draws, but he has never triumphed over the Soviet.

Wednesday, July 12, 1972
DAY 64:

To prepare our new reaction force, the next logical step in the process is to assign, clean, and fire the weapons. In the humid tropical environment, one of the serious challenges is rust. It is just a matter of time before everything next to the ocean rusts. Even the magazines must be taken apart and cleaned. A rusted magazine spring can cause an improper feed, jamming an M-16 after firing just one round, instantly converting a slick semi-automatic modern weapon into a single shot, bolt-action relic.

Once we cleaned our assigned weapons today, we took our team down to the rifle range at the end of the base. Past the end of the runway, a large dirt berm piled by Marine Corps bulldozers provides a backdrop for the targets. The men had to zero their assigned weapons, which meant adjusting the sights to how they personally fired. The two M-60 machine gun crews had never fired one, so we provided some weapons familiarization and instruction as well. There is no shortage of ammunition available at the end of this war, so we were able to get in as much range practice as we could in a very limited time. I don't think many of these men on the volunteer list have fired a weapon since being in country.

Dear Martha Anne,

I am sitting at my desk watching the date in the corner of this letter. I keep wishing it was 12 December. I want you so much I can hardly stand it. I miss you, your body, your boobs, your bottom, all of you. I can't imagine how I left you for this place.

The motor pool is looking better. Things are improving all the time. I'm starting to get some parts now. We have only 6 vehicles to work on. The rest are running. That is a record. I hope to get down to zero by next week, if possible.

Tonight was boss night at the NCO club. My motor sgt. carried me over there and tried to get me drunk. He didn't succeed, but he almost did. I usually don't drink any alcoholic beverages at the Officer's Club, but he was buying and I kept drinking. Needless to say, I'm feeling no pain. They had a good band called the Horoscopes. They also had some topless dancers. One had boobs almost as big as yours. They sure made me homesick. I sure do miss your boobs. I love your boobs. I can hardly wait until we are together again.

I put a water pump on a ¾ ton truck today by myself. I really feel proud. It did not leak a drop. I will be able to do some of the repairs on our car when I get home from over here. Being the motor officer does have certain advantages.

I received a letter from you and a card today. They were dated 6 July. It only took 6 days to reach me. It is an improvement over past mail service.

I was scheduled to fly tonight but my mission was cancelled. We have a new mission that takes us further up north. It should start to get exciting in the future up there. I hope the new Paris peace talks result in something concrete. So far, they have established absolutely nothing.

I love you with all of my heart. I am faithful to you always. I love no other woman. I only want you and your body. I want you to turn it all loose on me. I can barely wait until we are together. I love you, 1 love you, I love you, I love you.

Much love always,
Joe

Thursday, July 13, 1972
DAY 65:

On the main road north today, I rode again with Mop to the turn-in point. As an officer, I never drive on these errands, so I'm able to take in the scene. There appears to be more and more displaced refugees along the roadsides this month. Pockets of Vietnamese walked on the shoulders of the road, and at times, traffic slowed us to ten miles per hour or less. We were driving along at a snail's pace, when from out of nowhere a young Vietnamese cowboy jumped onto the running board of our three-quarter-ton truck and snatched the sunglasses right off my face. His fingernails scratched my cheeks and the bridge of my nose. My anger erupted as quickly as the blood pooled out from under my skin. I cursed the boy, but he was long gone and there was nothing I could do. We couldn't stop. You just don't leave your vehicles in that part of the road unless it's an absolute necessity. Damn cowboys! I have been warned about this, but I was a little naïve about their level of audacity until this afternoon. I don't think Mop has seen me this mad since we started working together. When we got back to the motor pool, I set aside a ball-peen hammer to carry with me in the cab of the truck on future missions outside the wire. If anyone tries to reach into our truck again, he will eat a face full of that hammer.

Dear Martha Anne,

Today was quite a day. I spent most of the day turning in an old three-quarter-ton truck. You have to go through the third degree to get rid of a truck. The Vietnamese & Koreans are running the turn-in point and I have never been unnecessarily delayed so many times in one day except the night we got married. I had reached the point that night where I was almost on the verge of fighting. I just wanted to get away with you and show you how much I loved you. It seemed like there were a thousand delays, but we did make it.

I went to the movie tonight. I haven't been going for a while because they were rather bad movies. Tonight we had George C. Scott in *Hospital*. I don't think I ever want to go to a hospital again. I think I will deliver our children. It was really tragic. This one lunatic thought he was the avenging angel for a man who died next to him. He just kept arranging deaths that looked like hospital mix-ups. It was really weird.

I am thinking of you nearly all of the time now. I long for the time when once more you will be in my arms. I just want to hold you so close so you will know how I feel for you. I love you with all my heart.

> I love you, Past, Present, & Future.
> Much love always,
> Joe

Woman is Selected Democratic Chairman

MIAMI BEACH, Fla. (UPI)—George McGovern accepted the Democratic presidential nomination early today with a pledge to beat President Nixon on Nov. 7 and to halt the Vietnam bombing on Jan. 20, the day of his inauguration . . . "I have no secret plan for peace," McGovern said in a reference to Nixon's 1968 promise to end the Vietnam War. "I have a public plan. As one whose heart has ached for 10 years over the agony of Vietnam, I will halt the senseless bombing of Indochina on inauguration day. There will be no more Asian children running ablaze from bombed-out schools. There will be no more talk of bombing the dikes or the cities of the North. Within 90 days of my inauguration every American soldier and every American prisoner will be out of the jungle and out of their cells and back home in America where they belong."

Actress Denounces Bombing of Dikes

TOKYO (AP)—Actress Jane Fonda has gone on Radio Hanoi and denounced the US bombing of dikes in North Vietnam, the Vietnam News Agency reported today. The agency said the broadcast was directed to "all the US servicemen involved" in raids against North Vietnam. Earlier, the agency reported that Miss Fonda had visited an area east of Hanoi where dikes had been damaged by US planes.

Friday, July 14, 1972
DAY 66:

Dubose and I had to report today to a meeting of the entire joint security team. A major has been placed in charge, but he was just echoing commands from a full colonel back at the 11th Combat Aviation Group's headquarters. One command that shocked me was the directive that our men are supposed to shout *dung lai* three times before firing on anyone in the wire. This word means "halt" in Vietnamese, even though I suspect the order is an attempt to limit the number of friendly fire casualties. We have American soldiers who sneak out to the edge of the minefield at night to exchange money for drugs by throwing satchels over the wire to local drug dealers. I told Dubose that if anyone yelled *halt* or *dung lai* before firing a full magazine at a target in the wire that I would shoot him myself. As a supplementary reaction force, we will only be called to man fighting positions along a section of perimeter where an attack is already in progress, and I'm not going to lose a man because he compromises his position screaming *halt* repeatedly.

Dear Martha Anne,

    I flew today for the first time in a week. I have had one mission cancelled after another. It is really weird. I have used the time to put the motor pool in order. We now have less than 5 trucks on deadline. I can hardly believe it. I feel certain that better days are coming for that job. I can get almost any part now. Things are looking a lot brighter. I now have to turn my efforts toward getting this entire company registered to vote. I also am the assistant reactionary force commander. That means when Pat McGarvey is flying, I am responsible for the 25-man force that will challenge any aggressor forces we receive here. Since I have been here, we have not received any ground attacks, so that should not present a problem.

I am finally getting rid of trucks. I am so glad to see them go. They are real junkers that need repairing constantly. I want to get down to 24 reliable vehicles. I feel that this is a sufficient number to sustain our operation here.

I have also won some money playing poker. I never play for much, but that seems to be the only card game anyone over here is interested in. We usually play for nickels, dimes & quarters. That usually means if you lose, you only lose about 5 to 10 dollars. I have been winning 15 to 20 dollars nearly every time I play. I don't really understand how I end up winning. I guess I'm just lucky. I'm getting to the point now where I'm afraid they will think I'm cheating. Actually poker is just another card game to me and I play to win. I have always played any game that I played to win.

I'm writing this letter in bed. I keep wishing you were here with me. I think I will vote for McGovern just to get out of here. If I'm not through with this tour by election time I will probably vote for the candidate that will bring me home. I want to be with you again. I'm so tired of sleeping alone again.

Much love always,
Joe

Saturday, July 15, 1972
DAY 67:

As the mobile reaction force, we can be called to fill a gap in the perimeter anywhere an enemy attack has penetrated the wire. The primary defensive perimeter is composed mainly of wooden towers containing machine gun emplacements with interlocking fields of fire. A series of cyclone fences with rolls of concertina razor wire span the distances between the towers, and land mines are placed there as well. One hundred to 200 meters behind all these defensive obstructions are the secondary fighting positions that we will be asked to man in the event of an attack. In the many months since the Marines turned this airfield over to the 131st, the secondary fighting positions have been untouched.

Dubose and I devised a plan to improve these secondary positions. In six- to eight-hour shifts, we plan to alternate who leaves the motor pool with a team of men from our reaction force to work on about forty to fifty positions. The front walls of the fighting positions are being reinforced to be three sandbag rows thick with a sheet of corrugated steel in between each of the rows. The back wall will be two bags thick with a single sheet of corrugated steel in between. The biggest improvement is the addition of reinforced overhead cover, which consists of cross-stacked sandbags on top. With this overhead cover, we are much less susceptible to injury from rocket and mortar attacks.

I took the first shift today and fortifying the old fighting positions was especially labor intensive in the mid-summer tropical heat. Filling sandbags is never easy work. Fortunately, we were able to acquire thousands already filled. A local Marine unit pulled out earlier in the year, leaving large piles of sandbags on our compound. We are very grateful to have them but moving the free sandbags has been an issue. By hand, we loaded and unloaded a dump truck load this afternoon. When the men started to complain about the work, I told them, "You can either sweat or bleed—take your choice. My goal is that you go home alive and not in a body bag."

Sunday, July 16, 1972
DAY 68:

After my last week on the ground, it looks like I'm starting to get more flight missions again. Mission notification in the 131st is a simple process. Conveniently, a daily posting is placed on the ready board in the mess hall. There are two places each pilot is guaranteed to visit at least once each day at Marble Mountain—the mess hall and the latrine—sometimes one right after the other. The powdered eggs and bland food with zero seasoning haven't gotten any better since I've been here.

Once my name and flight time appears on the ready board, I know to report to the briefing room ninety minutes prior to my mission.

There, the flight operations officer briefs me on my mission objectives and provides a map showing exactly where I'm supposed to go. Since I always head north to collect imagery of North Vietnamese objectives, the ops officer also warns me of potential areas of enemy anti-aircraft fire. Next, I receive a briefing from the imagery interpretation officer, who outlines the targets the imagery shop wants us to capture. At the end of these briefings, he hands me a sealed, black, soft-sided zipper pouch called the *mission packet*, classified *Secret*. Inside are all the coordinates of critical checkpoints. It is to be returned intact after the mission.

An hour prior to my mission this morning, I arrived at the airfield staging area to draw my aircraft. We call it *the pen* since it is bordered on three sides by portable concrete barriers. These barriers, known as *revetments*, are supposed to protect the planes from indirect fire, but without overhead cover, a well-placed mortar round can do significant damage. We don't fly the same Mohawk each mission, and our technical observers frequently change as well. So, it is incumbent upon me to get quickly acclimated to both.

At about four this morning, my assigned observer Specialist Yarborough was already waiting on me to do our preflight checks on the aircraft. Yarborough and I have flown missions together quite often, so we are comfortable working together. Our objective each mission is to get in, collect our imagery and get out, preferably without being seen. Checking fuel levels is critical. The Mohawk has a 300-gallon main fuel tank in the center of the plane with two 150-gallon wing tanks, but we can only fill them halfway. Anything more and we cannot get the lift needed to take off on the short runway at Marble Mountain.

Finally, after completing our preflight, we get into our ejection harnesses and survival vests before climbing on board. The parachute harnesses have rings for the legs and a vest with belt buckles to secure around the chest. I always have to let the straps on mine all the way out to fit me. Seems all of my gear is too short. After our harnesses are secure, we zip on the survival vest, sealing it with a Velcro binder running alongside the zipper. The black nylon survival vest has a series of small pockets from neck to waist with useful items including fishing line, nets, hooks, lures, shark repellent, crackers, flares, a radio with extra batteries, ammunition for our .38-caliber pistol, and a first aid kit with bandages. Also strapped to the vest is a pilot survival knife, much like a miniature Marine Ka-Bar, and a .38-caliber revolver pistol in a canvas holster. Inside my vest in my breast pocket, I carry the New Testament Bible my cousin gave me at the airport. And I always carry my checkbook in case we get diverted to Thailand, where I might actually do some shopping and eating. The cockpit has two gull-wing door hatches—one for each of us. Once inside, we leave both hatch doors open to provide some relief from the heat while we complete yet another engine start-up checklist. We have a routine, and we try to stick to it so we don't miss a step.

Focusing was tough after yesterday's work hauling sandbags. I was exhausted and my muscles were sore. Plus, we were sweating our asses off. But once we fired up those twin turboprop engines, it was easier to get focused.

When the chocks were pulled, I left the protective revetment area and taxied to the navigation point. The *nav point* is a known location that we use to program the coordinates for our mission. Typically, there are anywhere from eight to sixteen points we must hit during the mission. Today's mission required only ten, but the weather was going to be poor. Yarborough checked the SLAR equipment while I fired up the onboard computer to input the locations from the black mission packet satchel. I've been flying nothing but SLAR, as opposed to infrared missions, the entire time I've been here. Infrared requires the plane to fly directly over the mission points, so at least with SLAR we can take imagery from a greater—and hopefully safer—distance.

After this detailed preparation was complete, it was time to get the plane in the air. I backed my aircraft as far as I could. We have a 500-foot apron added on to the end of the main runway, which is comprised of a material we call *PSP*. Left by the Marines, this temporary metal grating is filled with circular holes to make it portable. But portable has become permanent, since the Mohawks require 2,300 feet to take off, but our airstrip is only 2,000 feet long.

Pitch black skies coupled with sticky, wet humidity, and ominous cloud cover rolled in as we sat poised at the back of the apron. I made my typical call to traffic control:

"Marble Mountain Tower, this is Spud Zero Seven on checkpoint requesting takeoff."

The tower instantly replied: "Roger, Spud Zero Seven, you are clear for takeoff."

Our runway is parallel to the South China Sea, with the imposing Monkey Mountain to the north and the pair of Marble Mountains directly to the south. Depending on the wind direction, we take off either north or south but always into the wind to get more lift. Last night we took off to the north. After I received clearance, I revved the engines to full military power before releasing the brake and making my run for takeoff. I felt Yarborough's silent presence in the seat next to me. He is an observer in the truest sense of the word during takeoffs and landings. With the two turboprop engines humming, I popped my foot off the brake and prayed that we would have the necessary lift by the end of the airstrip. The nose gear lifted off the ground and the air gripped the wings, snatching us up off the ground and into another mission.

Monday, July 17, 1972
DAY 69:

I didn't have to fly a mission tonight, and since I left the motor pool earlier than usual to perform my voting officer duties and help register soldiers to vote, I went back to my hooch to write and respond to some letters. It was another scorcher today. With the air conditioning on full blast, the hooch is one of the few places to get cool on Marble Mountain. Before I got into writing letters, I listened again to Martha Anne's cassette recordings from our anniversary:

"Got your phone call a little while ago. I was in between recording sides one and two of this cassette, and I had stopped to clip some newspaper clippings from the Sunday paper when the phone rang. I was in the living room sitting on the floor, so I ran back here into the bedroom to take the call. I was sure glad because the TV was on in the living room and the connection was so bad. I couldn't understand all that you were saying except I could understand when you said you loved me. And I believe you understood that I had received my roses. You kept saying something about January second. At first, I was worried because I thought you were trying to say that you wouldn't be

home for Christmas or something. Or maybe it would be after January until we could get together. Then I figured out after you hung up that maybe you were saying that on January second we could celebrate our anniversary because it would be a year and a half. So I'm just hoping that is what you were saying. If I were to find out now that you couldn't be home for Christmas, it would be terrible. I've gotten all worked up about Christmas. In fact, I think about it a whole lot. I think about ways I'd like to fix up or decorate the apartment and things I'd like to buy you for Christmas. Different things to make it a really happy Christmas. If you're not home, it will be nothing. I can't think of anything that would disappoint me more. If you have to check about leave or whatever you have to do, please do it.

I hate that we can't be together for our first anniversary. That's why I'm glad you called today. And I'm glad you remembered to give me roses. I was really surprised. I didn't know you had planned on that, and they're really beautiful. The red ones are gorgeous. I'm looking at them now. I've got them set up on the dresser. Flowers on one end and your picture on the other. I'm laying in bed looking at them. I miss you so much. I wish you were in bed here with me. I'd give anything to have you here with me. I keep this constant pain or emptiness in my chest when you're not here with me. It was a little bit worse today. I knew you couldn't be here for our anniversary, so I'd already determined to have a good day even though I knew you couldn't be here."

Martha Anne

[End of audio]

========== 🔇 ==========

Tuesday, July 18, 1972
DAY 70:

They called us together again this afternoon for a meeting of the reaction force leadership at a conference room in the officer's club. When I walked in, I couldn't believe my eyes. Standing there was a captain named Harvey Wilson. He is one of the reaction force sector commanders and was shooting the bull with some other officers. Back when I was in advanced rotary wing training at Fort Rucker, Harvey

Wilson was the designated student company commander. He was a captain back then too, and his sandy blond hair is still cut into an extreme high and tight, which accurately reflects his airborne-all-the-way mentality.

When I was a fellow trainee at Rucker, he tried to make me clean up the training classrooms by removing cigarette butts and empty drink cans. I told him that "I'm a commissioned officer, so I don't have to do it. And I'm not going to do it. I had to do that stuff when I was a private, but I don't have to do that stuff as an officer. I'll straighten up the chairs, but you can get the smokers back in here to clean up their own butts."

I was a new lieutenant, but his higher rank didn't matter to me. Back in basic training at Fort Leonard Wood, the drill instructors forced about 200 of us to line up shoulder to shoulder on the parade field and cut the blades of grass with our fingers. In the evenings after a long day of training, we had to go clean up office buildings by dumping ash trays and conducting police calls. I paid my dues. I wasn't paying them again.

But Harvey didn't share my mindset. After my refusal, he was out to get me. The tension between us continued for about two weeks, and I tried to avoid him. Then, one afternoon after flying, our entire training class was forced to stand in formation for a haircut inspection by a major. Harvey walked just two steps behind the major as he inspected the lines of the formation. When the major got to me, he started to talk about Colonel Bill Tallon. He went on and on about how great it was to work for Colonel Tallon, and he finally asked if he was my father. I just said "yup" and left it at that. The major moved on with his inspection, and Harvey Wilson whispered to me, "Your father signed my orders in Vietnam." After that, Wilson treated me with regard.

This afternoon, Harvey was talking to the other officers in the conference room about extending in Vietnam to get a command. He was willing to do an extra six months just to get a combat command on his resume. Just as soon as he finished saying it, a couple of members of his unit came to retrieve him. We learned a little later that his CO was killed and the XO severely injured on the same helicopter mission. Harvey Wilson was immediately named company commander of the helicopter unit. I guess he got his command wish.

Dear Martha Anne,

I think I will request Ft. Bragg when I leave here. It will give me a chance to work in area studies and maybe Latin America. I could use some of my experience in that area when working on my masters. I don't know if I will stay in the Army or not. If I do stay in that means two more years away from you at a minimum. I will have at least 3 short tours that are not accompanied by you. Right now I don't even like the thought of being away from you for a whole year. It has now been 2 months and 10 days since I left you and I don't think I will last until Christmas. I just want to be with you again. I want to hear you talk. I want to feel you near me. I have this hollow, hungry feeling inside that only you can satisfy.

Much, much love,
Joe

Wednesday, July 19, 1972
DAY 71:

King Korn

In addition to voting officer extra duties, I have also been assigned as the assistant yearbook officer. As we brainstormed funny phrases today to caption photos of the 131st, Mike labeled me *King Korn* under one of my pictures in the yearbook and, as an homage to Ho Chi Minh's revenge, he captioned *I've got toilet paper in here* under another photo of me standing beside a Mohawk holding my mission packet. I don't know whose idea it was to make a unit yearbook, but I am glad we found the unit's old spud description. No one is quite sure who the original author was, but it had to be a Mohawk pilot. Like the family Bible, it has been passed down over the years that the unit has been stationed in Vietnam and makes for a powerful opening to our current volume.

131st
Military
Intelligence
Company
Nighthawks
yearbook
cover

Excerpt
from book
below

DEFINITION OF A SPUD

A man of vision and ambition, an after-dinner speaker, a before-dinner speaker, before and after dinner guzzler, night owl, able to fly all day and fill out reports all night and still appear fresh the next day; is able to sleep on the floor and eat two meals a day to economize on expenses so he can entertain his friends at the Spud Club.

He is able to entertain wives, sweethearts, hoochmaids and Mothers without becoming too amorous in public, date "Doughnut Dollies" and at the same time keep out of trouble; drive through snow 10-feet deep at 10 below and work all summer filling sand bags without acquiring B.O.

He is a man's man, a model husband or bachelor, a fatherly father, a good provider, a plutocrat, a Democrat, Republican or "New Dealer" when it's necessary, an "Old Dealer" and a fast dealer, a technician, a politician, a mathematician, an expert OV-1D mechanic and engine fixer, and an authority on anything and everything. He is an accomplished stenographer and typist, able to rip out 150 words per minute and keep a cigar going. He attends all meetings, conventions, funerals, visits hospitals, jails and the drug rehabilitation center, contacting and soothing the feelings of wayward Spuds, and every commander in the Army, drives a government car, truck, tractor, trailer, sweeper, crane, palouste unit or oxygen cart, and is ready to compute mileage, drift, ground speed, JP-4 consumption per-block-per-minute, wear and tear on the tires and depreciation on the paint job.

He has unlimited endurance and frequently over-indulges in wine, women, song, and gab; he knows a wide range of telephone numbers almost as well as he knows his air machine; he knows the very latest jokes and stories; he owns the latest car, an attractive hooch with bar and air conditioning, sexy hoochmaid, an extensive wardrobe, and an Air Force oxygen mask. He belongs to all clubs, pays all expenses at home plus old age pensions, social security deductions, income tax, tobacco tax, luxury tax, and the heavy liquor tax.

He is able to stick his neck out by answering any questions with authority, and then pull it back before it is chopped off. He is an expert talker, dancer, liar, traveler, aviator, fornicator, prophet, poet, bridge player, and poker hound; an authority on palmistry, chemistry, physiology, psychology, aircraft accident prevention, cats, dogs, OV-1D's, and birth control, etc . . . He sees all, knows all, and is able to tell his boss "no" in such a way that takes 10 minutes and leaves the boss with the impression that he has done him a big favor; he is able to say all without telling anything or committing anybody.

He is Shit Hot!

Dear Martha Anne,

Today I started working at the motor pool then I went flying. Afterward, I worked on the company yearbook with Mike McClendon. He is in charge of the project. I just helped him write some captions for the pictures. It is not an easy job. I always thought that the yearbook at school was not much to it, but now I realize it takes a lot of work.

Would you like to have some silk to make an evening dress? If you do want some let me know how much and what color. I can get Chinese or Thai silk. They are both good quality. I also may buy some emeralds. They are good investments. A good $350 jewel over here is worth about $1400 in the states. I may need you to put some money in my checking account if I decide to make such a large purchase. I will call you if I do.

I love you so very much. I had a headache about 30 minutes ago but now it is gone. I always feel better when I write you. I feel like I'm talking to you almost. I try to picture you in my mind as I write. I have looked at those picture cubes over & over. They hold a million memories. Each picture is worth at least a thousand words. I have many memories of that hill by Cooper Hall. The one we slid down on the trays. The one I tried to get you to pose on for me. I did finally get a picture of you there. I remember those steps and that porch outside Cooper Hall where I used to wait on you. I also remember your father trying to move your things up those stairs. I thought he would have a heart attack. I also remember that you were living on the third floor of Cooper Hall when I first asked you to marry me and be the mother of my children. I don't think I will ever forget that night. It sure was cold. You were wearing my coat and I was in a vest and shirt sleeves. It was around midnight and we had been double dating with Sandra and Tom. We had gone to Martha Berry's house of dreams. You were my dreams then and you still are today. I loved you then but I love you even more now. You have made me very happy.

All my love always,
Joe

Actress Jane Fonda broadcasted an anti-war message via Hanoi Radio, one of a series. This message was directed to US pilots.

HANOI—"This is Jane Fonda. I have come to North Vietnam to bear witness to the damage being done to the Vietnamese land and to Vietnamese lives. Just like the Thieu regime in Saigon, which is sending its ARVN soldiers recklessly into dangerous positions for fear that it will be replaced by the US government if it fails to score some strategic military gains, so Nixon is continuing to risk your lives and the lives of the American prisoners of war under the bomb in a last desperate gamble to keep his office come November. How does it feel to be used as pawns? You may be shot down, you may perhaps even be killed, but for what, and for whom? Eighty percent of the American people, according to a recent poll, have stopped believing in the war and think we should get out, think we should bring all of you home. The people back home are crying for you. We are afraid of what must be happening to you as human beings. For it isn't possible to destroy, to receive salary for pushing buttons

(cont.)

and pulling levers that are dropping illegal bombs on innocent people, without having that damage your own souls. Tonight when you are alone, ask yourselves: What are you doing? Accept no ready answers fed to you by rote from basic training on up, but as men, as human beings, can you justify what you are doing? Do you know why you are flying these missions, collecting extra combat pay on Sunday?"

Thursday, July 20, 1972
DAY 72:

Dear Martha Anne,

Would you believe I fly almost every day now? It looks like I'm going to be flying this coming Sunday too. That I don't like. My one day in the whole week that I'm off and I have to fly. It looks like they could do all the fighting and flying in six days and give us Sunday off. Well, at least I'm getting flying time and experience. I hope to get 300–400 hours flight time if I stay here a complete year.

I will be filling in my preference statement soon. I will probably choose Ft. Bragg first and Hawaii or Ft. Lewis, Washington second. I can't make up my mind if I should stay in or get out. I'm afraid if I don't get out then I won't have a choice any longer. By the end of my next tour I would have 10 years in the Army and probably three or four kids.

I love you very much. They closed the PX at Marble Mountain yesterday and I'm getting low on stationary. I'll have to go to Da Nang Air Base and get some.

Much love,
Joe

Friday, July 21, 1972
DAY 73:

Mop and I drove north on the road to Da Nang this morning to turn in a vehicle at the port. Since I've been in Vietnam, getting soldiers to cut their hair short is just not something that we do in the 131st. It's one of those things for which we say there is *no percentage in pursuing it.* Men are draftees who don't want to be here, so insisting on things like tight military regulation haircuts can get an officer fragged. Just a few weeks ago, a first sergeant in one of the other units near us was cut in half at the waist by a booby trap. Someone rigged a claymore mine to the door of his hooch. Haircut standards aside, Mop remains one of the few self-starters that I have down in the motor pool. He's also a very reliable driver.

On the road north, Mop's hat blew off and was immediately sucked out of the open window to the side of the road. I was in the second truck riding shotgun in the turn-in vehicle, so I didn't see it happen. Since I adamantly refuse to allow stops on the road north and since we were destined for vehicle turn-in, Mop didn't miss a beat. Any stopping on that road risks Vietnamese civilians stripping away the pioneer gear or any other items not welded onto the vehicle. We couldn't afford to lose essential equipment that would jeopardize a smooth vehicle turn-in. Mop didn't stop, which was good.

On the way back, the hat was long gone, so I told Mop we could just go over to the PX at XXIV Corps to buy him a new green patrol cap. The PX is comprised of two prefab building units cobbled together. Inside, the shelving looked like Mother Hubbard's cupboard. There were a few bars of soap and some random toiletries, but the place was pretty well cleaned out. Our small PX back at Marble Mountain closed last week, and it was clear that this one at XXIV Corps was not receiving any resupply. The uniform clothing items were long gone too. I told Mop that we would get him a new hat made by one of the Vietnamese mama-sans back at our base. He left the building a minute before me as I continued to search in vain for stationery.

When I stepped outside, I saw that Mop had his heels locked as he was being chewed out by a full colonel. What apparently started when the colonel saw Mop without a hat outdoors spiraled quickly into a bigger issue. The colonel didn't like his shaggy long hair or the unauthorized gold chain hanging around his neck. To add to the grievance of the gold chain, the colonel pulled it from Mop's shirt only to discover an even more offensive peace symbol dangling from the lanyard. I strode quickly into the colonel's line of sight to deflect the attention from Mop only to be locked at attention once I claimed Spec-4 Seabolt as my own soldier. The colonel recapped for me all the ways that my Spec-4 was out of regulation. Then, looking at me, the colonel noticed I was wearing a non-standard black hat with my very standard looking olive drab green fatigues.

"Why are you wearing a black hat, lieutenant?"

I replied with what I considered an honest answer, "We Mohawk pilots wear black hats because we're badasses, sir!"

Well, that was not the answer he was looking for, and his ass-chewing vitriol reached a new volume. He demanded the name of my unit and commander, which for some reason I actually answered truthfully. When he finished, we wasted no time getting in the vehicle and heading back to Marble Mountain.

As soon as we pulled into the motor pool, Dubose ran out to our truck proclaiming, "The old man needs to see you and Mop right now, sir. What happened?"

I shared quickly with Dubose that we had just come from an angry full-bird colonel at XXIV Corps. I told Mop to stay at the motor pool. Major Smith had gotten a call from the colonel, but thankfully when I arrived, the CO told me to describe for him what happened from my point of view. I told the story in brief, and I made sure to emphasize that Mop was following a direct order from me not to stop the vehicle for any reason. I also summed it up with my personal assessment that they have too many colonels at XXIV Corps with nothing to do.

To my relief, Major Smith agreed that there were too many excess colonels running around. He also wasn't upset that I didn't end up bringing Mop with me to his office. He decided two things in response to what he had heard. One, the unit's pilots are no longer allowed to wear black hats off the base anymore. Two, we had to punish Mop for being out of uniform.

"What type of punishment do you recommend for Mop?" Smith asked.

"Sir, we should promote him to sergeant." Taken aback, the CO asked me to explain my rationale. I shared just how much of a self-starter Spec-4 Seabolt really is—how he organizes and takes charge of the work in the motor pool when Sergeant Dubose and I are not there.

"I use him as my driver for all of our vehicle turn-ins because he can be trusted to follow orders, not stop, and get the vehicles to the turn-in point on time and in proper condition. He's actually been filling the role of buck sergeant down in the motor pool for quite a while, and the results are outstanding with the improved vehicle maintenance."

Saturday, July 22, 1972
DAY 74:

Our simple mission today was to pick up parts at the Da Nang Air Base. Mop borrowed another soldier's hat this morning, and I made sure not to wear my black one. The July heat and humidity has not let up. None of our vehicles has air conditioning, and the air circulating in through the windows was so hot and sticky that it felt like we were driving into a blow dryer. Still, at least it was airflow. But making the parts-run to the airport across the river rather than the depot meant we had the opportunity to eat at our favorite shrimp restaurant. Of course, last time we were there it got blown up, but they were rumored to be back in business the next day.

As usual, we crossed the Han River via the I Corps bridge, and we wound our way through the streets of Da Nang. Nearing the portion of our route that intersects with the corner of Blood Square, we noticed numerous locals running toward it. Black smoke billowed up over the row of houses separating our three-quarter-ton truck from the main square. It was ten in the morning, the time of day when many women and children shopped in the downtown open-air markets. As we crept along the road leading through the square, we saw the burning hulk of a passenger bus still smoldering. People were crying and dazed—most of them women and children. Some partially burned civilians walked around aimlessly looking in all directions as if they had misplaced something. The smoke poured from the bus in a terrific black column.

The foggy haze in the air carried a noxious smell I recognized— charred rubber. But with it was another smell, fouler than anything I've ever experienced. It was the smell of burning flesh and human guts.

I felt queasy and, for a moment, I thought I might vomit. I tamped down hard on the sensation and harder on my instinct to command Mop to stop the truck so we could help. Mop looked at me, a wordless exchange that communicated volumes. The standing command, one I have repeated countless times, was never to stop and engage the local population for any reason. We watched the children cry and the locals call for help in Vietnamese. Mop and I navigated our vehicle through the humanity gathered at Blood Square and continued our parts run.

Dear Martha Anne,

I got a letter from you today telling me how much you missed me. It started on the first line of the first page so I know you have it bad. In about five months we will be together again. I hope we can last that long, but I don't know. I keep thinking I won't make it that long without you. You see, I need you too. I keep looking at those pictures you sent me and they certainly bring back a lot of memories.

I guess you will be retiring from Belk's next Saturday night. I have thought about your safety there quite often. Especially since you told me about those three drunks. I feel much better now that you are in the linen dept. again. I wanted you to keep busy this summer but I don't want you endangered. I love you and worry far more about you driving to and from work than I do about my flying in a combat zone. More Americans were killed on 4th of July weekend car wrecks than have been killed over here all year. That is tragic. I'm glad I got those new tires before I left. If you keep the correct pressure in them and keep them balanced, I don't think you will have any trouble. I wish I had shown you how to change the tires. If you have a flat in an out of the way place just keep driving slowly until you get to a service station. You can drive 10 miles without doing any major damage and I would rather

buy a new tire and wheel than look for another wife!
I guess I worry too much about things that probably
won't happen. I love you so much.

Much love always,
Joe

Sunday, July 23, 1972
DAY 75:

During my mission this morning, I just kept thinking about the
beach. I was trying not to think about the smells and the screams I
saw yesterday. I thought I might go to China Beach this afternoon,
but I have an upset stomach. It started yesterday and hasn't gotten
any better. I didn't eat breakfast or lunch. Part of me would like to
float out past the breakers on my back to the little island where we
shot crabs and pretend that Mop and I had a nice drive yesterday
and enjoyed a shrimp lunch.

My family rented a place earlier this month on Folly Beach. I
wish I were there. When I was a small kid, we went out to Folly on
day trips to visit my aunt and uncle at their cottage. It was a two-
bedroom place with a screened-in front porch just big enough for
two grown people to sit. Nobody had air conditioning, so that porch
was the best place to catch a breeze, if there was one.

One of my favorite things to do at Folly Beach was to catch blue
crabs. We tied raw chicken necks on strings with lead weights and
threw them into the rock groins in the surf. It was best on incoming
tide, but we learned how to catch them on the outgoing tide as well.
We had to watch our step so we didn't cut our feet on the barnacle-
encrusted rocks. When pulling the crabs in on the string, we had to
pull steady but not so fast that they released the chicken and swam
away. Once we filled a good portion of a five-gallon bucket, we'd head
back to the house to cook and clean them.

My uncle boiled those blue crabs until the instant they turned
bright pink and then dumped them on his picnic table in the back
yard. He dug a hole in the ground at the end of the table using his
posthole diggers and then showed us how to clean the crabs. Then
Mama, Daddy and I would clean and pick out the crab meat to take

home to make deviled crab and crab dips. We just slid the empty crab shells and claws off the table and into the hole. My uncle just sat back in his chair drinking beer and watching us work that pile of crabs.

The memories at his beach cottage aren't all fond ones. One afternoon our family was walking back from the beach with our beloved Chihuahua named Mitzy. She was dark tan, energetic, and knew the way back to the cottage. She trotted ahead of us, crossing the last street by herself. A woman in a black Studebaker ran right over Mitzy in front of the whole family. The old woman driver had silver hair and glasses and was smoking a cigarette. She offered to take Mitzy to the vet to see if anything could be done, but it was clear Mitzy was already dead when we picked her up. Mama, my sister Lindler, and I were crying, and I remember wishing that cigarette she was smoking would give her lung cancer and kill her. My dad took the posthole diggers and dug a small grave behind the cottage. We wrapped Mitzy in a beach towel and buried her there.

Dear Martha Anne,

Today is Sunday and I had my usual Sunday morning mission. I'm beginning to think it is my special mission. I was going to the beach this afternoon but I had an upset stomach. I had also planned to call you but I started playing basketball and by the time I got a shower it was too late. I'll try tomorrow night and that is a promise.

I don't know if I have told you or not but we are going to move to Da Nang. We don't know exactly when yet but it will be soon. It won't change my mailing address. I have really been busy these last two weeks. I find that the week is gone before I know it. I think it is because I'm doing 3 or 4 jobs now instead of one. I don't have much time to stop and think. I do think about you though. I was talking to Mike McClendon tonight. We were trying to decide if it was worth staying in the Army. He said leaving your wife was bad but leaving his little girl when she was just starting to do things

was worse. I don't like most of the Army brats that I
have run into, so I don't think I want our children
subjected to the kind of kids that live on most posts.
The more I think about it the better I like the idea of
teaching history or military science. I just want a job
that lets me be with you some every day of every year.
I need you, woman, I really do. What I'm saying is that
all of this that I have worked for these last few years
means nothing to me without you. I will probably never
do anything more personally satisfying than flying,
but you are more important than anything else in my
life. I'm not a rich man, so all I have to give you is my
love and someday soon, my time.

I need you and love you more each day I live,

Joe

Monday, July 24, 1972
DAY 76:

Today during our weekly officer's call we learned the details of the
Saturday morning attack in Da Nang. The Viet Cong exploded a
bomb underneath a civilian passenger bus, killing twenty-nine and
wounding at least eighty. The explosion happened just thirty minutes
before Mop and I passed through the square. Detonated at the height
of the morning shopping hour, the bomb was sent as a message by the
Viet Cong that their own government in the South cannot adequately
protect them. This was my first experience seeing firsthand why they
call that area of Da Nang *Blood Square*. As horrific as the sights and
sounds were that day, it's the smell of burning human flesh that I
hope never to experience again. I can't shake the thoughts of that
burning bus and all those screaming people. My stomach hasn't been
right for days now. I want so much to bury these thoughts. I just want
to hold Martha Anne and pretend none of this happened.

I sat in the operations area for two hours today trying to get a
call to go through to Martha Anne, but to no avail. I've applied for
Christmas leave, and I had a conversation with Major Smith about it

today. He said I'd get one or the other—Christmas or New Year's. He said that any day now we should expect to get orders to move the unit to Da Nang Air Base. That move will probably be temporary as they are supposed to move our whole unit to Thailand to run missions from there. It's all a guessing game and rumors are flying around daily. As the movement officer for the unit, I certainly prefer to get the move done before the wet rainy season begins a month from now.

Wednesday, July 26, 1972
DAY 78:

Dear Martha Anne,

I'm so tired I can't see straight. I was scheduled for one mission and I ended up with three tonight. I started my preflight at 6:15 p.m. I then got word not to take off until 9 p.m. I started my engines at 8:15 p.m. and started my run-up checks. I took off at 9 p.m. and landed at 11:45. It would have been later but I did a high speed dive to get back quicker. That is why it is tomorrow and I'm trying to write you a letter.

I love you very much but it's 1:30 a.m. and I'm beat. I worked all day in the motor pool. I got a letter from you today and it was great. I'll write you the night of the 27th if I get back from flying in time. I'm going on a mission with Mike McClendon. I love you very much.

Much love always,
Joe

It is always a relief at the end of our short runway to lift the nose gear off the ground and then feel the air grip the wings. As soon as possible, I turn toward the water and the relative safety of the open sea. Only large caliber anti-aircraft (AA) fire and surface-to-air-missiles (SAMs) can touch us out there. The US Navy controls the sea. At night, we see flares and illumination rounds going up around the perimeters of American bases as force protection security measures. Often, in the distance, we see the distinctive glow of the B-52 strikes. We call them *Arc Light strikes*, and since the B-52s fly in teams of three, parallel triple rows of bombs light up the horizon as they explode. During my mission tonight, I saw both the base illumination and distant B-52s. What was undoubtedly hell on the ground was beautifully serene from my distance. Seeing the illuminations of war in the night sky was a potent reminder for me to get on the radio with the air boss shortly after takeoff. The air boss controls the active air space in Vietnam and provides pilots with the latest positions of enemy activity to avoid.

With the side-looking airborne radar (SLAR) equipment, I'm able to fly a few miles off the coast at 10,000 feet in altitude and still collect viable imagery. However, it is critical at this distance to remain steady. I lock into autopilot mode when we approach the vicinity of target points since it is impossible to hold the plane steady enough with the manual hand controls. The darkness and overcast weather don't stop us from collecting SLAR imagery. Normally, my observer works the imagery controls while I hold the plane steady and on course. Tonight, I had my copilot and former training classmate Mike McClendon riding in the observer seat next to me. Conditions were challenging, so I resisted the urge to give him vertigo like Mike once did to me in training. I was totally reliant upon my instruments tonight, as thick clouds moved in this evening while I was waiting for takeoff. It felt like flying in a bottle of ink.

Thursday, July 27, 1972
DAY 79:

Dear Martha Anne,

I just returned from not flying a mission. Let me explain. I was supposed to fly at 5 p.m. today but I had a chip light on #2 engine and had to abort. I had that fixed and cranked again only to lose my altitude indicator. On my 3rd crank I had operations come out and cancel my take off because I was too late starting. Needless to say it was 2 ½ very frustrating hours on the ramp. I was going to try again but the guy that is flying now is picking up my missions. That is what I had to do last night.

I'm sorry I didn't get to talk to you. I have been trying now for two weeks and I either get no answer or they can't make the connection. You said you saw *Billy Jack*. Well, I saw it over here the 2nd week I was in country. I enjoyed it very much. It has a lot to say about how we treat people in our country today. I'm afraid the people that need it most will not see it.

I slept late this morning, and boy, did I need you. I woke up several times needing you by me. I would just like to wake up with you beside me in the mornings again. I sure do enjoy watching you sleep.

Much love always,
Joe

Friday, July 28, 1972
DAY 80:

The main supply route runs north up a strip of land bordered by China Beach on the east and the Han River to the west. I can see the river in spots along the road, but the vegetation is too thick to see the South China Sea. Even if we don't cross the I Corps bridge toward the city of Da Nang, the road leads to many destinations: the port to turn in a vehicle, the Philco Ford general support maintenance shop, or the PX, which may even be closed by now. Today we left to pick up parts at Mr. Moon's Philco Ford shop. As usual I rode shotgun, which gives me plenty of time to survey the area.

Refugee camps are overfilled with Vietnamese. A whole village gets burned down and the survivors pour in. Our forces provide temporary housing for them, more like tent shantytowns than homes. It isn't so much a steady stream as it is pockets of refugees moving around. At our officer briefings, we hear that the Vietnamese are just leaving their destroyed villages in the countryside and clustering around American bases seeking protection from the VC. It must be even worse down south around Saigon. Some refugees pull or push carts by hand. Others have water buffalos hitched to their rickety carts. They all move slowly. Mostly women, children, and old men. Fighting age Vietnamese men are not among the civilians. I keep the ball-peen hammer in the door of my truck, and I find myself scanning the landscape for potential dangers looming along the roadside, gripping the handle of the hammer as I do.

Along the sides of the road are small field tables stacked with clear bottles of gasoline for sale to the many buzzing moped drivers weaving through the traffic. I've also noticed the increased number of charcoal salesmen with the increase in refugees this month. Charcoal here isn't like the briquettes we are accustomed to, but it's burned wood about two fists big. Refugees use this to cook their food on open fires. On the left side of the road heading north is a hospital for injured South Vietnamese soldiers. Out front we often see amputees hobbling about or sitting in wheelchairs. One afternoon when my soldiers from the motor pool were on the road, one of these wheelchair men was pushed in front of their three-quarter-ton truck. They came to a stop and waited for the man in the chair to clear the road. Little did they know, Vietnamese were grabbing the pioneer tools and anything loose off the rear of the vehicle.

Last week, US engineers bulldozed one of the biggest shantytowns along the road to Da Nang—an effort to cut down on the number of people along the military route. What was a bustling makeshift city is now a field littered with the remnants of temporary buildings. A few days ago as we passed the area, my eyes locked on a vision that I just can't shake. Amidst the strewn sandbags and cinder blocks was a single copper pipe crooked at the top like a shepherd's staff. A meager stream of water spilled from the pipe. Under it stood an old Vietnamese man, naked, washing himself, his gray hair, moustache, and goatee thin and scraggly under the drizzle of water. He may have been a *dah wee*, that is a village leader or chief. But just then he looked meager and vulnerable. How had it come to this for this man? What was I doing here passing down that road through his country?

Saturday, July 29, 1972
DAY 81:

Dear Martha Anne,

It is 2:40 a.m. and I just returned from a very long mission. This letter will count as yesterday's letter. I'm having a slight problem answering letters this week because of my busy schedule. I hope you will explain it to our family that my letters may thin out for a while. This is the morning for your last day at Belk's but it is Friday afternoon in North Charleston. How is the new city doing? I can't believe John Bourne was named mayor. I always thought that your father was going to be the first mayor of North Charleston the way he knows everyone who comes in and out of that post office. No matter who sees him on the street, they love talking to him. How is your brother's Pizza Hut doing?

I love you with all my heart, mind, body, and spirit. I am counting the days till I get back to you.

Much love,
Joe

Sunday, July 30, 1972
DAY 82:

After a busy week, I finally got some rest time this afternoon. I took out my New Testament and read the entire book of Acts while lying on my cot. The last two days I have been so overloaded I can hardly believe I made it to Sunday. I've been working in the daytime at the motor pool and flying at night. The last three times I have flown something always happens to my aircraft. It has taken me four to five hours each night to get a plane ready to fly. I started at six o'clock yesterday evening and it wasn't until eleven thirty when I took off on the mission. I'm bone tired. Especially my behind. Those Mohawk seats are very hard and my rear is raw. I don't have to work today, so I slept until ten o'clock. I was sitting around thinking about my very first flight with the military, which happened before I even started basic training.

Naïvely, I thought that I would get to come home on weekend passes to Charleston while I was in basic training. Instead, the first thing they did when I arrived at Fort Jackson was take all my civilian clothes, box them up, and mail them to my parents. They were having trouble with new soldiers going AWOL during basic, so we were only allowed to wear Army-issue clothing.

The second big surprise came two days later when they told me I was being shipped to Fort Leonard Wood in Missouri for Basic and Advanced Individual Training (AIT). Much later I'd learn that the military slang name for Fort Leonard Wood is *Fort Lost in the Woods*, but looking back on it now, I get it. Between Columbia and St. Louis, the plane made six stops. In the St. Louis airport, I was transferred to a private air charter service for flight directly to Leonard Wood. It was only me and one other recruit—Dan Taylor—on a DC-3 twin propeller tail dragger. We called it that because the cockpit was so much higher than the tail on the runway.

The plane touched down on a dusty stretch of dirt runway carved into a vast pine forest of the Missouri Ozarks. Not another soul was in sight. We stepped out and watched the plane taxi back to the end of the runway, line its wheels into a dirt rut and take off. The heat was scorching, and I shielded my eyes as the dust from the DC-3 prop enveloped us. When the dust cleared, we saw no flight tower but only a limp windsock to indicate this was an airfield. Dan Taylor and I walked 300 yards to a single Quonset hut—the only manmade thing in sight—hoping to find some answers. The Quonset was empty except for a green Army field desk containing a black Bell telephone with a rotary dial. Behind the desk and phone was a painted wooden sign on the wall with numbered instructions. The first read:

1. *If you are on orders, call your command.*

My eyes drifted down to the second item on the list, since this did not pertain to us.

2. *If you are in basic training, call 5-3435 for transport.*

I stopped reading after the second paragraph and picked up the phone to call. It was there in that remote and strange place that the reality of my situation hit me—I was now in the US Army. That was a full three years ago in the late summer of '69.

Dear Martha Anne,

I love you more and more. I can hardly wait for our 5th anniversary to see if I love you 5 times more. Don't feel like you are the only reason for my wanting out of the Army. It is getting so that officers don't mean anything anymore. You don't have any authority over your troops. You can threaten action but they know it usually will be a verbal slap on the hand. We have to treat them like spoiled kids. I can only see increased trouble and problems for an Army run this way. It will mean defeat after defeat. The discipline is terrible in this company and it is a Mohawk unit. I felt when I got into a M.I. Company everything would be above normal. This company is so far below normal that you have to look up to see the bottom. The officers & senior NCOs have their little groups. There is one group of 4 captains that play cards together and they schedule us so their card game won't be interrupted. I always felt that M.I. was above the rest of the Army but I was wrong.

No matter what I do or where I go you are on my mind and in my heart. You are the flame for my torch. You are my S.T.P. You make my engine purrrr . . . I love you!

I give you my everything. Your husband forever,
Joe

Monday, July 31, 1972
DAY 83:

Dear Martha Anne,

I keep saying we are going to move but it keeps
being delayed. I don't want to move to Da Nang. I would
rather stay here or go to Thailand. I hope to turn in two
trucks tomorrow. That will mean we only have trucks
that run. It will make my job of moving us a lot easier.

Pat McGarvey is in Thailand so I now have his jobs
as well as mine. He doesn't do much so it won't be much
of an increase. He does fly a lot so I may get a few more
missions next week. I fly five different areas and soon
I will be flying six. It is better than the first two
months when I flew the same mission day after day.

The food over here is not very good. It makes losing
weight easy. I have been exercising some too, so when I
get home you will have Mr. America on top of you. I am
not really trying to become a Samson. I just would like
to tone up my stomach muscles. They are not as tight as
they were when I got out of O.C.S.

I look forward to every night when I write you
because it means another day is past. I'm wishing my
life away so we can be together again.

Much love always,
Joe

Tuesday, August 1, 1972
DAY 84:

We drove north on the road today to turn in a pair of vehicles. Two
men from my motor pool rode in the back of my three-quarter-ton
truck since we planned to visit the PX after turn-in. There was a cluster
of refugees on the road, which slowed us down, but we got the vehicles
turned in successfully. Then, at the Da Nang Air Base, I left the men

at the PX while I went to find Bill Latham, a family friend who was unfortunately gone on leave.

I'm not much of a socializer here, especially with the other officers. Everyone seems to drink too much. Sometimes I'll get a mixed drink, but usually I just drink a Coke. As many as I drink, I think I'll turn into a Coke can before I leave Vietnam. Over a game of pinochle cards tonight down in my motor pool office, Dubose and I talked about the stalled peace negotiations. I was upset that it seems they like to argue more about the size of the table or where people sit at the table than truly discussing the end of the war.

"What does that make us, the placemats on the table?" Dubose quipped.

"It probably means we are just the lukewarm leftovers," I said.

Bug Suspect Got Campaign Funds

By Carl Bernstein and Bob Woodward, WASHINGTON—A $25,000 cashier's check, apparently earmarked for President Nixon's re-election campaign, was deposited in April in a bank account of one of the five men arrested in the break-in at Democratic National Headquarters here June 17. The check was made out by a Florida bank to Kenneth H. Dahlberg, the President's campaign finance chairman for the Midwest.

Kissinger Holds Another Secret Meet

PARIS (AP)—Henry A. Kissinger, President Nixon's national security adviser, held his 15th secret meeting

(cont.)

on Tuesday with North Vietnamese negotiators in Paris. The secret meetings are believed to take place in a house provided by the French government in a Parisian suburb. The meeting was part of the parallel pattern of Vietnam talks: one secretly and irregularly, between Kissinger and the North Vietnamese, and the other semipublic every Thursday with four delegations representing the United States, South Vietnam, North Vietnam, and the Viet Cong.

Wednesday, August 2, 1972
DAY 85:

This morning a couple of our men in the motor pool tied up their dogs. I asked them exactly what they were doing since I've always seen these dogs get free range around our vehicles.

"Sir, the MPs are coming around shooting strays today," he said.

I had no idea they did this, but apparently to prevent the spread of disease, a security detail circulates through each compound once every ninety days or so and shoots any dog not claimed by an owner. I love dogs, so I definitely don't love this policy. Then again, there are a lot of things we are doing over here in Vietnam that I don't really understand.

Dear Martha Anne,

I just returned from talking to you and I certainly do feel better. I feel as happy as I have felt since I left you. I guess it is a combination of things. Today 13 months ago we were married. I love you at least 13 times as much as I did then. I now have nearly completed three months in Vietnam. Do you realize that at least ¼ of my tour is up? How about some good news? We are starting to get drops again. The officers in our company are getting around 30-day drops. I don't know what it will be like 6 or 7 months from now but I hope I get a drop.

I have a mission to fly tonight so I will be getting dressed to fly in a few minutes. I watched one reel of the movie and decided I had better write you because I may be too tired when I get down. It looks like another 18-hour day. The good thing about these busy times is it sure helps the time pass more quickly.

A happy 13ᵗʰ monthaversary.
Your lover and husband,
Joe

Thursday, August 3, 1972
DAY 86:

Dear Martha Anne,

I don't know if I ever explained it to you before, but you can't talk about certain things over the phone. Troop locations, movements, stand downs, transfers, etc. are included. I'm certain it is an oversight on my part. The latest word is that we won't be moving to Da Nang. I am constantly confused by these changes. I don't think anyone knows what is happening. I'm losing men rapidly and they are not being replaced. I'm reluctant to say anything anymore because everything is changing daily. The P.X. on Da Nang Air Base was rocketed today. Now we don't even have an Air Force P.X. to go to.

I certainly enjoyed talking to you yesterday. It gave my morale a big boost. It was so frustrating not being able to call you for so long. I remember some of my telephone bills before we were married. Do you know I spent $105.00 one month talking to you? I guess I'm crazy or something but money never mattered when you were concerned. I just wanted you so very much I could hardly endure to be away from you. When I would leave you at Rome I could hardly see to drive for the tears in my eyes. I would always drive a little faster when I got near Rome on the way to see you, too.

I have to fly in the morning, so I'm going to end this letter before I remember too much and go AWOL. I think of you often and I am amazed that we have made it through this time apart. I thought I would be out of my mind by now. I love you and feel more a part of you every day. I need your T.L.C. every day. Much, much, much, much, love, love, love, love, love!

Your husband,
Joe

Friday, August 4, 1972
DAY 87:

Today, our unit got command guidance from a higher headquarters to no longer carry loaded weapons with us when we are off base and driving the main supply route. Apparently, the collection of colonels making decisions in our area are concerned about civilian casualties with all the refugees moving along the roads. It seemed to Dubose and me like a futile and misguided piece of command guidance, but at this point in the summer, there has been plenty of that to go around. This guidance, combined with the fact that the Da Nang PX was just hit hard, means none of my men are going to want to head out with me to get parts or turn in vehicles.

I'm flying missions nearly every day now, but I still have nearly everything down at the motor pool like I want it. Maybe by the end of next week we'll be set. I now have a man trained up on repair parts storage and a reliable tool-room man. I also have a shop foreman that I'm trying to get promoted. If we can get this jeep turned in tomorrow afternoon, it will feel like a great week.

Saturday, August 5, 1972
DAY 88:

Today I received a letter from my cousin Sandra and her husband Bob Gardner. It is great to hear from them. Last time I saw them was Thanksgiving 1970 while I was stationed at Fort Wolters. They spent Thanksgiving weekend at the Gardner family ranch in Winters, Texas, just 150 miles west of Fort Wolters. They invited me to join them and let me know there were quail coveys all around the watering holes at the ranch, so I stopped by the Morale Welfare and Recreation office on post and checked out a 12-gauge Winchester pump-action shotgun. I would have preferred a Remington 1100 automatic, like my shotgun back home, but I had to go with what they had on hand. It just didn't feel right showing up on a Texas ranch without a gun.

I didn't get on the road until late Wednesday afternoon. From a distance I saw the oil well pumpjacks bobbing up and down like dinosaurs. Gas was only thirty cents a gallon, and with no speed limit, my MGB got me there in less than two hours. On a desolate stretch of highway approaching Abilene, the only disruption to my relaxing drive was the occasional dead skunk in the road.

It was only the second time I had ever seen Mr. and Mrs. Gardner—the first being their son's wedding. Bob Gardner married my cousin Sandra in North Charleston in the early 60s, and at the time, I told them I would try to make it out to their family's ranch if I was ever in Texas. Despite their new-found oil wealth, the Gardners remained hardworking people. Mrs. Gardner worked at a café in downtown Winters. Mr. Gardner was a tall, bald-headed man with tanned, leathery skin, who always wore a cowboy hat. His hands were so rough he once smashed a wasp nest on a fence post with his bare hands and did not flinch.

Quail hunting on the Gardner ranch was like no other quail hunt I'd ever been on before. We could see quail running on the open ground because the sheep had eaten the grass down. Normally when quail hunting, I had to traipse through briers and underbrush while trying to keep pace with the dogs. We didn't have any dogs on the ranch. Instead, Mr. Gardner followed us slowly in his pickup truck to watch us shoot. The birds ran and hid in the cactus clumps like they were part roadrunners, so we had to throw sticks and stones into the cactus clusters to get the birds to flush out and fly. Even with the borrowed shotgun, I was able to kill sixteen quail. Bob only got one.

During the entire holiday weekend I spent there, the Vietnam War was not mentioned a single time. At that point, it didn't seem like I would ever get to Vietnam. I had a lot of flight training remaining, and the war was potentially ending at any month. Now, after all the talk of it being over back in 1970, I might be spending Thanksgiving two years later in Da Nang.

Sunday, August 6, 1972
DAY 89:

Dear Martha Anne,

I was going to write you last night but we were attacked by mortars and they declared a red alert. I'm the reaction force commander so from 11 p.m. until 2:30 a.m. I was busy. We did not have to defend the perimeter but we were on alert just in case.

My roommate George Davis came in from Thailand to have his plane worked on last night just as the mortars started falling. He waited until it was over to land. He is going back today and I hope he will be able to get the silk for you and the watch I want. I dropped my watch two days ago and broke it.

I've been thinking about R&R a lot lately. I think it would be better to take it in the 1st week of November or the last week in October. I don't think at this time I will have a complete year over here. Right now tours for officers are from 10 ½ to 11 months. I expect this to go as low as 9 ½ months. I may be wrong but what could happen if we don't take any R&R before Christmas is that we miss our Hawaii trip.

How is Freddie's shrimping business doing? It sounds like he should invest in the pizza business to me. I guess Thomas and Linda are very pleased with their results at Pizza Hut even though your brother puts in a lot of hours. I have felt for a long time your father should be running an Italian restaurant. Maybe Thomas will encourage him to retire from the post office and go into the food business. No matter how hard you work for other people you will only make a salary, but working for yourself, you can reinvest and expand as much as you want to. Col. Sanders started 15 years ago with one chicken place and today he is a multimillionaire. Food preparation is big now because people have the money and don't want to go to the trouble of cooking at home. I can remember when we were growing up that we only ate in a restaurant once or twice a month and sometimes not that often. Now most families eat out at least twice a week.

I think of you all the time. This morning I woke up wanting you so much you could not believe it! I held my pillow in my arms and wished with all my might it would be you. I look forward to the time when we're together again. I want to hold you so close until you can't breathe. I want to do everything to drive you to the height of passion. I just want you!

Much, much love,
Joe

Monday, August 7, 1972
DAY 90:

Today was a really busy day for me even though I didn't fly. I spent the morning reorganizing my reaction force. We had to assign some more weapons and get people onto the range to zero and quality on their rifles. The other night when our reaction force was called on alert, only twelve of the twenty-four assigned people showed up. We couldn't locate the missing men. That's when I learned that my coleader of the reaction force—Pat McGarvey—had neglected to check his force for people that were getting early drops. Thankfully we weren't called out to defend the perimeter, so I was able to limit the embarrassment of my inadequate force to the confines of the arms room.

This afternoon, Mop and I went to the Philco Ford shop and turned in a five-ton truck that has been a maintenance problem. We picked up a repaired two-and-a-half-ton truck they'd been working on for a couple weeks. It is great to get rid of these old clunkers that keep dragging down our deadline report.

When we got back to the motor pool, Specialist Asbell reiterated his favorite line for me that "rocks don't live as long as you have left in Vietnam, sir." Specialist Asbell is *short,* which means he is down to his final thirty or so days in Vietnam. Most soldiers start talking about being short when they have two months left or less. Asbell won't volunteer for the reaction force or any extra duty that is requested of him. His ready response: "Lieutenant, I'm short!"

Tuesday, August 8, 1972
DAY 91:

Dear Martha Anne,

You can probably guess I got my care (love) package today. It was really in the nick of time. You see the PX here is closed and the one at Da Nang was destroyed by a V.C. rocket attack. I think that old Bic pen had about one more letter left in it and that was all.

Today is exactly 3 months since I left home. I can remember when I was counting weeks, but now I count months. I can hardly wait until I start counting days. That is the last stage of a tour over here.

Pat McGarvey came back from leave today, so I can get a little more rest now. I spent this morning with the reaction force on the range and this afternoon building fighting positions on the perimeter. The defensive posture of this post is not very good. We need a lot of improvements and changes. The V.C. can see everything we have, so we need fake positions and fall back positions. Very few people take our position here seriously. I see so many things that need to be done but the majority of our officers only want to party and get drunk. I don't even want to serve in a M.I. aviation unit again. Pat McGarvey didn't even want a briefing on the enemy situation or anything. He only wanted to go to the party tonight. I really get disgusted here sometimes.

You are my hope, my life, my need, my desire, my everything. You keep me going. You give me hope. You make war bearable. You make me want to live forever. You are the most important person in my life. I don't know how I live without you. It seems impossible I have lasted three complete months. I love you more than ever before. I need you more each day.

I send you all my love forever. Your husband,
Joe

Wednesday, August 9, 1972
DAY 92:

This morning's mission was routine when it started on the flight line at four o'clock. Though midweek, it followed the pattern of my recent run of early Sunday morning missions. Once again Specialist Yarborough joined me as the observer, and after our preflight checks, we flew north to surveil four different mission points. The weather was clear today, and the coast was absent anti-aircraft fire—at least for me. Shortly after completing my fourth and final mission point, the air boss called me and asked me to assist another plane. I was in the vicinity of an Air Force O-2 Skymaster, which is a plane I know very little about. Apparently, I was the only plane near him that had any chance of flying slow enough to escort.

It didn't take long to find it limping its way back south. The O-2 has two propeller engines like my own OV-1 Mohawk, but instead of hanging from either wing, the Skymaster's engines are on the front and back of the fuselage. We call this type of plane a push me/pull me. It also has a horizontal stabilizer connecting the two booms at the rear of the aircraft, which gives the appearance of a giant spoiler without the sexy body and speed of a sports car to go with it. In fact, with both engines firing at full speed, it's obvious just looking at it that the O-2 could not reach anywhere close to the top speed of my Mohawk.

This Skymaster was wounded. The rear engine was totally shut down, so he was going to have to make it back to Da Nang on a single prop. His call sign was Outlaw 4-5, and I was able to reach him on the open frequency net. After getting cut off repeatedly in the first couple of minutes by other radio traffic, we convinced the air boss to shift us to a separate dedicated frequency. Outlaw 4-5 was a forward air controller, and he was observing troop movements and calling in fire when the ground fire became concentrated on him. He was fortunate to have only lost the rear engine, based upon the amount of fire he drew.

When we linked up, we were just under 100 miles from our bases back in Da Nang, over land in North Vietnam. The biggest threat there is 23-millimeter anti-aircraft fire, so it was not a comfortable position to be in. If Outlaw 4-5 had to ditch the plane and eject, I could call in precise coordinates for the evac choppers to find him, but I'm sure he was trying to avoid punching out in North Vietnam. Two problems were immediately evident with this escort mission. One, the Outlaw 4-5 was losing altitude at the rate of a hundred feet per minute. The single engine couldn't hold him at 10,000 feet, which is where he was when I found him. Two, his speed was 100 miles per hour. To stay with him, I put my landing gear down, released the air brakes on the fuselage, and set my flaps to 20 percent. That dragged me down closer to his speed but presented a new problem. I started to get the harsh beeping of my stall warning signal in my headset every half minute or so. At those incredibly slow speeds, I could stall and drop out of the sky like a rock.

Yarborough kept an eye on Outlaw 4-5 as I constantly maneuvered the plane to avoid a catastrophic stall. I began a pattern of circles around him which allowed me to fly a little faster and stay in his immediate area. Our bubble canopy cockpit gave us a 210-degree view around our Mohawk, and as long as Yarborough kept eye contact on Outlaw 4-5, I flew circles above and below his aircraft. For more than an hour, we kept up this flight pattern until we were on the brink of the Da Nang Air Base, and Outlaw 4-5 was under 3,000 feet in altitude.

Coming into the approach for the landing strip, Outlaw 4-5 thanked me and dropped with a nosedive to get down to the airstrip as quick as possible. I told Yarborough next to me "monkey see, monkey do" and proceeded to drop sharply down behind him, trading altitude for speed. I set my engines to full power and was well over 300 miles an hour when I got close to the airstrip and pulled up on the controls. As I gained a little altitude back and was smoking with speed, I executed a snap roll just past the Da Nang Air Base tower. Yarborough asked, "Sir, what was that for?" I just stated simply, "That was to let them know that the Army taught the Air Force how to fly." We cruised quickly over to Marble Mountain airfield in a matter of minutes and had our Mohawk on the ground before nine o'clock.

Shortly after lunch, I got word that the CO wanted to see me. When I arrived, he asked me, "How did you manage to get a commendation and a reprimand in the same phone call from the Air Force? What did you do over there?"

"Sir, I just showed them that the Army taught the Air Force how to fly and that I'm a shit hot Mohawk pilot."

"Damn, Joe, I don't know about you sometimes. At least you both got back in one piece."

Dear Martha Anne,

Today is the second day I have not received a letter from you. I got the care package yesterday but today was a blank. I guess the next time I get mail, I will get a bundle of letters. I love reading your letters.

When do you start school? I can't remember. You told me on the phone last week. You also said you were going to Theresa's wedding. I don't like the idea of you driving alone. I guess I'll just have to hope and pray you have a safe trip. Have the car serviced before you go. It may prevent any mechanical trouble. I wish someone else would make the trip with you or you fly there and have Lucy or somebody meet you in Atlanta. I guess I worry as much about you at home as you do about me being over here.

```
    I flew in with an Air Force plane this morning. The
Air Force plane had lost one engine so I flew along in
case the other engine quit. I followed him all the way
down until he landed. I guess the Air Force owes me
a favor. He was only flying about 85 to 90 knots. Our
Mohawk will fall out of the sky at that speed so I have
to be very careful. It added a little excitement to a
routine mission.
    I certainly do miss you. I can hardly wait till we
are together again. I want and need you so very much.
I have been up since 3:30 am and it's midnight or after
now so I will close with all my love.

                I love you completely. Your husband,
                                            Joe
```

Thursday, August 10, 1972
DAY 93:

Today, I had a great run to the Philco Ford direct support shop. I went to get parts with Mop before we promoted him, and instead of just parts, we got a whole five-ton truck. Mr. Moon informed me when I got there that they found this old truck in the back of their lot. Apparently, it had been sitting there at least six months awaiting parts. It was forgotten, and since I'd taken over the motor pool, I had no record of it being there either. The Koreans at the shop repaired it for us without prompting. These cigarette cartons are really paying dividends.

```
Dear Martha Anne,

    Today was another busy day. I worked in the morning
at the motor pool then flew during lunch and worked
late this afternoon at the motor pool. I finally got one
of my Spec-4s promoted to sergeant. We call him Mop.
Funny thing is all this promotion talk got started
after his hat blew out the window. The promotion will
```

help me and my motor sergeant greatly because the men can't believe we got Mop a promotion instead of a reprimand. The men in the motor pool think we walk on water now.

I got three letters from you, two from Lindler, and one from my father. I also got a package from my father with pens, paper, envelopes, Clorets, and soap in it. I feel like a small P.X. now. I probably have more stuff than anyone else in the company. I know I get more mail than anyone else. I certainly do enjoy it too. I don't know of anything that builds the morale better than mail.

I love you so very much. I don't want to wait until Christmas. I need to see you sooner. I'm afraid you may have trouble getting excused from night school. I guess you will miss prayer meeting on Wednesdays when you start. I didn't know until today that you were planning to go to night school. I don't think it is wise to try to teach and be a student at the same time. I fear for your health and safety. I don't want you at the Citadel at night or in downtown Charleston. I would much rather you had not worked at all this past summer and had gone to summer school. If you go to night school at the Citadel, it is against my wishes. Maybe you need to explain more about it to me. If another teacher from Goose Creek is going and you could travel together, I wouldn't mind so much.

I love you more today than ever before. I need you and want you very much. I'm amazed each day that I'm still alive without being with you. I was certain I would have perished by now. I'm feeling fine and I haven't been sick in several weeks.

Much, much love,
Joe

Friday, August 11, 1972
DAY 94:

Dear Martha Anne,

It is 6 p.m. and I thought I had better write you a
note before I went to fly. When I get back it will be late
and I have a busy day tomorrow. It seems that the days
are so busy now. I have somewhere to go or something
to do constantly. I didn't get any mail today, but I
didn't expect any either because I got six letters and
a package yesterday.

I guess everyone is expecting to hear from me. I
would like to write them, but I just don't have the time.
I'm going to try to answer my mail tomorrow night if I
can. The good part about staying busy is that days pass
by and I don't even get to mark them off my calendar.

Sometimes I feel so helpless here. I need you so
much yet you are so far away. I find myself daydreaming
about you and talking to myself. The only thing of
encouragement I can say is we have less than 9 months
to go. Who knows? Maybe we will all be out of Vietnam
by Christmas. I figure Nixon will try very hard to get
us out before the election or a large reduction of the
force that is left. I sure hope I get a drop but I can't
really expect one yet. I'm thinking about Germany after
here. What do you say about it? It may well be our only
chance to see Europe. I have always wanted to see it. We
could take my leave time and turn it into a European
holiday. Maybe Lindler and Freddie could come over if
Freddie is still working over there. This is food for
thought, but I would like to know your reaction to it.
You say you will go anywhere with me, but I would like
to plan this with you and not for you. I sure could use
a day or so just to talk to you. It just would make me
feel 100% better. I love you more each day.

Much love always. Your loving husband,
Joe

Last Infantry Unit: Combat GIs Heading Home

SAIGON (UPI)—The last American ground combat unit in Vietnam was deactivated today, the day after one of its companies returned from a four-day mission during which two men were wounded by booby traps . . . The unit, 3rd Battalion, 21st Infantry, with supporting artillery battery and medical detachment, guarded the big US aircraft and helicopter base at Da Nang. The battalion has 1,043 men. The deactivation was announced by a US command spokesman. He said most of the battalion's men will be going home in the next few days, but those with job specialties still needed in Vietnam and those with less than six months Vietnam service will stay . . . As of last week 44,600 American servicemen were left in South Vietnam. The figure does not include sailors in the US 7th Fleet off the Vietnamese coast or airmen stationed in Thailand and Guam flying missions over North and South Vietnam. The first American ground combat battalion landed in Vietnam March 8, 1965. It was the 3rd Battalion, 9th Marine Regiment, and its mission was to guard the base at Da Nang . . . At the height of the US involvement in 1968, the US Army and Marine Corps had 112 ground combat battalions fighting in Vietnam . . . "I feel like a 12-year-old kid waiting for Christmas," said Sgt. Larry Silver, 25, of Floral Park, N.Y. "I'm going home tomorrow." "It's a great feeling, knowing I won't have to come out here again," said Pfc. Rudy Flores, 23, of Arleta, Calif. "Why did they send us on a four-day mission," asked Spec-4 Gary Hoffman, 20, of Spokane, Wash., a member of Delta Company which went on the patrol. "After all these years, four days won't make much difference."

I arrived tonight for my mission block at ten o'clock, but I only got as far as the preflight checks before I discovered the autopilot was not functioning. I've had the autopilot go out on me before while I was on mission and there was no way that I was going to start a SLAR mission without it. It's impossible to hold the plane steady enough by hand controls to get usable imagery. I'm not risking my life up north for nothing. So the operations officer bumped me until eleven thirty, when a Mohawk was scheduled to return from its mission.

While training in the states, we often had Mohawks missing a radar altimeter or missing a TACAN navigational system. There would be a hole in the dash with a note or tag describing when the missing item was supposed to return from repair. The instructors always told us that when we got to Vietnam, the Mohawks will have all functioning equipment since the war zone is priority one for repair parts. The instructors obviously weren't accounting for flying at the end of the war. The aircraft maintenance supply chain was nearly as bad as the vehicle maintenance I struggled to overcome. Hardly a mission went by when I didn't have a VHF radio or an altimeter out and sometimes the INS navigational system—usually one or two instruments. But tonight, I wasn't going to fly SLAR without the autopilot.

The technical observer assigned to me for this mission was Spec-5 Daniel Richards. Not only had I never flown with him before, I'd never even seen him around the unit area.

"I just got back from Thailand," he said. "Been stationed there for the past two months."

That explained why I missed him on previous missions.

"You're packing some extra weight," I said, eying his middle.

"I've been staying in a Thai hotel eating Kobe steaks and big hotel meals," he said.

He was clearly more than 200 pounds, and I could have grounded him for the mission. But he said he really wanted to fly, which was refreshing to hear. Most guys over here are looking for ways to get out of doing things, so I appreciated his desire to fly and not get grounded. Against my better judgment, I consented. We passed the wait time in the operations center. I went over the mission sheet and got a little bit to eat. Richards talked to some of the enlisted soldiers in operations. It was the end of another long day. I didn't like the prospect of starting my mission well after midnight. That's what we do, though. We are the Nighthawks.

Saturday, August 12, 1972
DAY 95:

The substitute Mohawk was late and did not return until close to midnight from its mission. Spending a long day working in the motor pool followed by flying night missions is exhausting and killing time in the operations center had nearly lulled me to sleep. But this would be my 66th assigned flight reconnaissance mission in Vietnam, and I expected my body to respond. I had risen to the occasion many times before. We put on our ejection harnesses and survival vests before moving out to the flight line. I slipped my Bible in a front pocket along with my checkbook. Out of habit, I pulled at the sleeves and leg cuffs of my Nomex suit, which were a good two inches too short. It was pointless. I always felt like a school kid who had outgrown his clothes.

After the plane was refueled, Specialist Richards and I started our preflight checks. It's a challenge for me not to allow the checks to become too routine and overlook something crucial. Richards said he was ready to roll, so I taxied the plane to the navigational site to plug in the coordinates for our mission area and check the navigation equipment one more time. Finally, by one o'clock I was sitting in my Mohawk at the end of the runway conducting my final preflight checklist on this, the last day of the American ground war. All instruments were in the green. Once the tower cleared us for takeoff, we moved onto the active runway.

I gave the plane full power, and we began to roll down the airstrip. One last crosscheck revealed all my gauges in the green, and we accelerated rapidly. As we approached 100 knots of forward thrust, I rotated the nose gear off the runway. The silhouetted two humps of the Marble Mountains were just off in the distance as we began our climb into the hot night. Between 200 and 300 feet in the air, I heard then felt an explosion in the right side of the aircraft. I was sitting in the left side of the cockpit. Richards was eighteen inches to my right. He turned to me and calmly said, "Sir, we've been hit in the number two engine."

I leaned forward and looked past him to see the engine cowling missing, with blue and orange flames dancing out of both sides. The sight of the burning engine sent a jolt of adrenalin coursing through my veins, making the hairs on my body stand at attention. I got busy real fast.

I immediately shut down the damaged engine and feathered the propeller. I informed the tower that I'd been hit and was on fire and needed the runway cleared. The tower replied that the runway was still clear and asked if I needed any other assistance. I never answered.

Next, I reflexively shut down the fuel and hydraulics going to the burning engine and quickly pulled the cockpit fire handle. This released two 500-pound fire extinguishers onto the engine, but it didn't stop the flames. The fire-retardant chemical was set to be most effective when the engine cowling was still attached. With the cowling gone, the chemicals just sprayed uselessly into the night air.

The plane was banking hard right and about to roll over and invert in a death roll. I put full left aileron into the control stick and put my left foot against the floor with full left rudder, trying to cross control the dead engine. We had not been very high to begin with, and we were losing altitude fast. The aircraft slowly returned to a thirty-degree bank, and I looked back to see the runway lights over my right shoulder. We were too slow and losing speed. The full load of fuel was like an anchor. I put my hand on the release handle, about to jettison the fuel tanks, when I stopped and pulled back, realizing that the left-wing fuel tank would probably drop right down into our fuselage. The angle was too extreme. It would have been like firebombing our own plane.

The minimum altitude required for ejection was 200 feet. My digital altimeter said we were 105 feet off the ground and were dropping at such a rate that I knew we couldn't make it back to the runway. At ninety knots forward air speed, we also were below the safe threshold of 100 knots. Because we were so low and slow, this was a far from ideal ejection scenario.

When I was a student in flight school, the Army forced me to test the ejection seat. At only one third the power of an actual ejection, the training seat fired me sixty-five feet up a steel rail with such violent force that I decided then and there never to use my ejection seat unless I absolutely had to. At full power, I thought it would certainly break my back. At the 131st, I had to become an expert on the Martin-Baker ejection system, as I was required to teach classes on it to fellow pilots and observers. It was just another of the extra duties assigned to me by Major Smith. In an ideal situation, I would sit back in my seat and pull my arms and legs in tight while pulling the primary ejection handle above my head. In actuality, I was pulling the controls as hard as I possibly could to the left trying to keep the plane from rolling over into certain death, and I simply could not let go of the controls long enough to get in position. Given the position of my left arm and leg, I thought that they would be torn off immediately when the ejection seat fired me out of the cockpit.

I shouted to Richards, "Let's go! Eject! Eject!" We didn't have time to shed the canopy—that's why we had penetrators on the tops of our seats. I waited until I heard his seat charge explode, and then I reached for the secondary ejection handle between my legs and pulled. Less than ten seconds elapsed from the time the engine exploded to the moment I pulled the ejection handle.

I was knocked unconscious.

★ ★ ★

I awoke to the sound of a pistol discharging close by and what felt like a noose around my neck, cutting off my breath, intense heat consuming me. My parachute cords were wrapped around my neck. With my right hand, I went for my survival knife to cut away the cords. The knife resembled a miniature Marine Ka-Bar with a stacked leather handle, but it was missing from the sheath on my survival vest. I used my hand, wrangling the cords from my neck only to inhale hot air into my lungs and with it the detestable smell of burning chemicals and human flesh. The heat from the fire was melting my parachute, turning the nylon into molten liquid. It ran down my back, hissing and sizzling. I suddenly realized the burning flesh I was smelling was my own.

Rounds of ammo exploded in the fire, and I could hear four or five shots coming either from Specialist Richards's sidearm or possibly my own weapon, since my .38 pistol had also been torn away from my survival vest. When I looked at my left arm, dangerously close to the raging fire of the crash site, I had trouble focusing until I realized I had no vision in my right eye. With my good eye, I saw my arm was charred black and split open—the muscles moving inside. I rolled away from the direction of the fire and tried to stand. I took a couple of steps and stumbled to the ground. Just ahead of me was the safety of the perimeter fence at the end of the runway. I dragged my body toward it. Behind me, the wall of fire burned white hot and vivid orange. It sounded like the buzzing of a thousand bees trying to eat me alive. I could feel the adrenalin surge inside me as I dragged myself, trying to get away from the intense heat of that inferno.

I finally reached the perimeter knowing the only way to cross was to scale the cyclone fence and razor wire. I spread my fingers spider-like to climb the fence, but the razor wire fought back. Rolls of wire entangled my feet and legs, relentlessly pulling me back to the ground like a giant slinky. I tried again and again. Each time I grabbed the cyclone fencing, pieces of charred flesh ripped off me. My screams went unanswered. No one came to help. Caught in the wire, I laid down on the hard ground with my back to the searing heat of the crash site. I re-tucked the sleeves and pant legs of my flight suit back into my gloves and boots. Just weeks ago, as leader of the mobile reaction force, I had helped to re-construct and fortify that very same section of fencing and wire to keep the enemy out.

I pulled down my visor and prayed since I thought I was going to die right there in our own defensive perimeter. My prayer included the words, "Jesus, please help me. No one's going to come where I am." As I repeated the words, a calmness came over me.

I lay there at the base of our perimeter entanglements. With my flight helmet pressed to the ground, I struggled to gather oxygen as the scorching heat of the fire on the back of my body reminded me just how close I still was to the crash site. Finally, the first lieutenant who oversaw that section of the perimeter, spotted me. With wire cutters, he cut through the cyclone fencing and the wire entanglements, then pulled my body through the ragged opening and back into the base.

An ambulance arrived, and I was laid onto a stretcher at the end of the airfield. Our unit flight surgeon had a Greek name that was hard to pronounce and impossible to spell, so we referred to him in the unit simply as Dr. D. When he arrived, Dr. D proceeded to cut away my survival vest, flight suit, and every piece of clothing except my underwear. This wasn't an easy task since my flight helmet and nylon chin strap had melted to my head. Like a bandage being pulled from an open scab, he cut my chin strap and pulled it free from the flesh of my chin. Carefully, he then removed my wedding band and looped it to my dog tags. I was placed in the back of the ambulance with a clean white sheet draped over my body. They gave me morphine. As we made the fifteen-minute drive from the end of the runway to the adjacent 95th Evacuation Hospital at China Beach, I watched orange-red puddles of fluid bleed through the sheet.

★ ★ ★

In the wee morning hours of August 12th, an eye surgeon happened to be on duty at China Beach. I had many broken bones and burns over large portions of my body, but the most critical injury was my right eye. Torn from its socket at some point during the ejection—possibly when I penetrated the shattered glass canopy—I could not see from that eye. Since I was knocked unconscious for an unknown amount of time, the eye surgeon could only use a local anesthetic and not general. He was able to hold a conversation with me on the operating table, so he asked me a series of the standard questions like "Where are you from?" I grew tired and frustrated with the small talk, so I looked up at him with my left eye and asked, "What are you trying to do, Doc—keep me from going into shock?"

He laughed.

"Don't you think if I was going into shock, I'd already have been there by now?"

"Yeah, I guess so," he said. Then, he started to explain exactly what he was doing with my eye during the surgery. "I don't know if I'll be able to save the sight in your right eye."

"Yeah, I'll be able to see," I responded.

"How do you know that?"

"I've been talking to my other doctor."

"Who's that?"

"Jesus Christ."

"Well, if he's on the job, then you don't need me."

He placed the eye back in its socket and stitched up my face and eyelid with eighty-seven very small stitches. I found out afterward that he was the last eye surgeon left in Vietnam.

South Vietnamese Paratroop Unit Hit by Red Tanks

By Arthur Higbee, SAIGON (UPI)—North Vietnamese troops and tanks attacked a South Vietnamese paratroop company near Quang Tri city at dawn today and killed or wounded most of its men, military sources said. A company in the field usually totals about 120 men. In the air, about 120 US B52 bombers flew a record number of raids over North and South Vietnam in the past 24 hours . . . Seven Americans and seven South Vietnamese were killed today in two separate airplane accidents, one in Da Nang and one at Soc Trang in the Mekong Delta, the US command announced. The two accidents and a record number of B52 bomber flights underscored continuing US participation in the war, despite the disbanding on Friday of the last US infantry battalion in Vietnam. President Nguyen Van Thieu observed the occasion Friday of the disbanding of the battalion by remarking that the air war over North Vietnam never should have been halted. Thieu, in a brief radio broadcast, said, "I argued against the bombing halt in 1968. Now we see the results of that: 700 North Vietnamese tanks and 15 divisions concentrated against South Vietnam." A C130 transport aircraft crashed on takeoff from Soc Trang air base in the Mekong Delta, 90 miles southwest of Saigon, killing six Americans and seven Vietnamese, and injuring five Americans and an undetermined number of Vietnamese. **A US Army OV1 Mohawk observation plane crashed on takeoff from Da Nang, killing one crewmember and injuring the other.**

August 12-20, 1972—China Beach Hospital
DAYS 95-103:

A light flashed and the buzz-hum above me jerked me awake. I heard the sound of JP4 jet fuel igniting and braced myself for the wall of heat that would follow. I screamed, my voice ringing with terror as I tried to get up. Someone pushed me back and a woman's voice entered my ear, hushing me. The voice belonged to a nurse, her hands gently but firmly holding me down. I stared up at the tube of light above me as my head cleared. Housed in a four-foot-long box and mounted against the wall above my head, two fluorescent light tubes made a humming sound when turned on. There was no wall of fire in the room, just one in my head.

I'm trying to keep track of time, but with the morphine flowing in my veins and the Quonset hut construction of the hospital wards with their lack of windows, the days and nights run together. Rows of fluorescent tube lights under plastic concave covers illuminate the walking paths between the beds. Whenever the medical staff wants to take a closer look at us, they pull the chain on the light above the bed, casting a sickly glow and triggering a disquieting buzz.

After the eye surgery, they wheeled me on a gurney to the main ward for treatment and recovery. That's where I am now. It feels like I have been rolled back in time. The room appears like a scene from a World War II movie. The metal frame beds and the curtain partitions have not changed—just the patients. The nurses came to my bed and said they needed to clean me up. Because of the extreme heat, the hair on my head inside my flight helmet had melted together in clumps, so they shaved it clean with a pair of clippers.

I was wide awake for the transfer from the gurney to the hospital bed. Because of the extensive burns on my arms and legs, the bed sheets had to be overlayed with sterile pads. I have compression fractures in my C-5 and T-9 vertebrae. Two nurses attempted the transfer, but they quickly aborted the effort and got two more to help. But even with four personnel, it was a struggle. Every movement caused excruciating pain. They laid me flat on my back. I could feel the burn of the fluorescent light tubes in my one good eye. The smell of ammonia is pervasive.

Amazingly, my New Testament survived the crash in the breast pocket of my flight suit unscathed. I'm just not sure if the same can be said of my observer. Neither the doctors nor the nurses can tell me what happened to Specialist Richards. They say he's not at the hospital. Maybe he ejected clear of the burning wreckage of the crash site. He could have been quickly treated and returned to the unit to fly more missions, which I assume haven't stopped rolling. I have seen members of our unit get medical treatment for minor injuries in the past and get returned to duty quickly. I hope that's where he is, but none of the medical personnel can confirm it for me.

My body is constantly weeping fluids. I can't get enough to drink. I'm so incredibly thirsty. One of my nurses told me I went through eight units of blood over the past twenty-four hours. They are constantly changing the sterile pads lining my bed sheets. The fact that I have burns on both butt cheeks makes this process torturous. The pads stick to my ass like glue, and I can't help but scream when the nurses roll my fractured body to one side and then the other to rip out and replace the pads.

The IVs are not in my arms because of the burns. Instead, the nurses have them running through the tops of my feet. I can see the fluid bags hanging from an old metal stand at the foot of my bed and the network of lines hooked up to my feet like strings on a puppet. If I turn my head to the left, I can see a young enlisted soldier who is being treated for rifle wounds. His body has multiple entry and exit wounds, but he appears to be stable. Turning to the right, the situation is far more critical for a sergeant whose grenade fragment wounds tore eighty-plus openings all over his body. He is not conscious.

When the portable A/C unit kicks in, I cringe. Even in the dense tropical heat, I cannot get warm. Muscle spasms in my legs are causing knots the size of golf balls to rise up between my knees and groin. The pain is like nothing I've ever experienced. My nurse, Captain Smith, is trying desperately to help me. The spasms are causing more blood loss. I'm not sure I can keep this up. I'm not sure I'm going to make it.

The sergeant next to me died in the night.

When Nurse Smith came on duty today, she had her personal electric blanket with her. She's about my age, maybe late twenties, with brown hair and freckles. She carefully placed half-moon-shaped metal hoops over my bed, constructing a tent frame on which she draped sterile sheets. On top of the sheets, she placed her electric blanket and plugged it in. It didn't take long to feel the warmth, like an incubator. The effect on my body was powerful. The warmth calmed my lower body and the knots diminished. I feel like without Nurse Smith, I would not have survived the night.

This evening all the doctors and nurses—even those who were off-duty—began flooding into the ward. They analyzed patients quickly and prepared them for movement, whisking them away to the helipad outside to be airlifted to a base camp on Monkey Mountain. I thought for sure that our base was being overrun. It is an all-too-common occurrence at this late stage in the war to hear that the North Vietnamese are pushing us out of an area.

The frenzied activity level was like turning spotlights on a colony of cockroaches. Together with another warrant officer in critical condition, I was left behind to be moved last. The warrant officer was totally blind, having buried his face in his gun sights during a Cobra helicopter crash. My pain was so great that I just wanted to be left there alone on my bed, even if we were being overrun.

Four nurses came back for me. They attempted to transfer me to a stretcher. The sterile pads underneath me were soaked with fluids from my wounds, and in their haste to make the transfer, they lifted me by holding the sides of the saturated pads. These promptly ripped and separated down the middle. My broken body dropped between the edge of the bed and the waiting stretcher. In a panic, they grabbed my arms and legs to catch me before hitting the floor, and their clutches instantly tore out chunks of skin and flesh. The sudden start and stop of the drop caused indescribable pain to my broken back. I started screaming, begging them to kill me.

When they got my stretcher to the helipad, they loaded me onto the chopper but stopped short of taking off. Instead, some sort of all-clear message was passed around the helipad, and I was taken back into the hospital and returned to a bed.

★ ★ ★

Some of my men from the motor pool visited me today, including Dubose. I learned that we were being evacuated due to the threat of a tsunami. Some pilot offshore observed a large wave at sea and called it in as a tsunami approaching Da Nang. In reality, the big wave was moving away from the shoreline, so when the actual direction was confirmed, the evacuation was halted. As painful as my false alarm had been, what they relayed to me about the evacuation at the 131st was both comical and sad. Our pilots jumped into the fourteen available Mohawks, filling both seats in each plane with officer pilots, leaving the enlisted soldiers and most of the technical observers at the airfield to fend for themselves. My motor pool soldiers inflated rafts, donned life vests, and sat in them awaiting the giant wave. Others pulled surfboards from their hooches and boasted of catching a ride as it came in.

While there was some legitimate concern about getting the planes to a safer airfield, it really showed the chasm between the officers and the enlisted. When I signed up for military service, I so badly wanted to be an officer and a pilot, but at that moment, I was ashamed to be included as one.

My men left the ward to head back to the unit area, but Dubose stayed behind to tell me that Specialist Richards was dead.

"I thought I heard his pistol fire when I was down in the crash site. What happened?"

"We think he may have burned to death. His hands were over his face so we think he might have survived the ejection," Dubose reported.

I felt sick. We'd never flown together, and I had just met him a few hours before we took off. I desperately wanted to get us back to the runway, but I just didn't have the time or the altitude to do it.

★ ★ ★

My bladder isn't working. They inserted a catheter. So added to the bags of fluids going in is a bag for fluids coming out. Because the skin on my tongue and the roof of my mouth is raw and cracked from burns, I am unable to eat any solid foods.

They want me to try to get up and walk today. I have my sights set on walking to the water cooler. It's about forty feet from my bed, and my thirst is constant. Walking to the water cooler would be a reward. I think I'll drink it dry when I get there.

When they got me ready to walk, the nurses wrapped me in gauze bandages from both armpits to both wrists and from the tops of my thighs to my ankles, like a mummy. Any movement is torture, but when they sat me up on the side of the bed and hoisted me upright, I thought my legs were coming out of joint even as my burn sites stuck to the sterile pads on my bunk.

With assistance, I eased to my feet and began the long, slow shuffle over to the water cooler. I suppose that I was walking, even though I was being held on each side. My feet never really lifted from the floor but merely slid forward with the sound of fine-grained sandpaper. I pushed myself beyond what I thought I could take, keeping my sights on the goal. I finally got there. Never did a cup of water taste so good.

★ ★ ★

On what felt like my fourth day but it was hard to be sure, the crash scene investigators arrived. My bed was immediately flanked by three Army personnel in their jungle uniforms—two officers and an enlisted soldier. The soldier scrawled notes on a pad while the two officers alternated asking me questions. They wanted to know what happened, and I told him we were hit in the number two engine right after takeoff. I was trying to be honest and tell them exactly what I remembered.

"Are you certain you were shot down?" they asked.

"I can't swear to it because I didn't see the actual round fire."

"Did you see any ground fire?"

"No."

"Did you see any tracers?"

"No. It probably came from my rear. I heard it and felt the impact. Richards told me right when we were hit, and I looked over him to the right wing to see the cowling missing and the engine on fire."

"What happened next?"

"I notified the tower we'd been hit and asked them to clear the runway, and I immediately started my engine shutdown procedures. I feathered the prop. Cut the fuel and hydraulics going to the engine. Pulled the fire handle to release both the 500-pound fire extinguishers on the number two engine, but it did nothing to stop the flames."

"Why didn't you jettison your fuel tanks?"

"I had my hand on the handle to do just that but when I looked out the left side of the aircraft, I looked up at that left-wing fuel tank above me at such a sharp angle that I decided not to do it. I just knew that tank was going to drop right into our cockpit and set us on fire too."

"Did Specialist Richards eject first?"

"Yes, after I told him to eject, I waited until I heard his seat explode and then I pulled my ejection handle."

"Did you actually see him eject first?"

"No, I honestly didn't see it. I had my whole body pressed against the left side of the cockpit trying to keep the plane from flipping over. Full left rudder and full left aileron. I just heard his seat explode, and I assumed he had ejected. I pulled right after him."

"Your right eye was severely damaged. Why didn't you have your visor on?"

"Because we were flying at night and I can't see through it."

"Why didn't you use the clear visor instead of the tinted one?"

"We only have one tinted visor on our flight helmets. It's not like the Air Force helmets that have two."

They went on to ask me a few more questions, and I repeated some of the same details we'd already covered. It was frustrating for me. I performed a lot of different actions in just about ten seconds or less. These were the reactions I was trained to perform in the event of a blown engine on fire. I desperately wanted to get us back to the runway and land the plane, but at the angle we were banking and at such a low altitude, I didn't think there was any way to get us back. I made the decision to eject, but only one of us survived the ejections. The way they were asking questions made it feel more and more like they were blaming me for crashing the plane. I'm not even sure they believed we were hit by enemy fire.

★ ★ ★

Day five, or maybe it was still day four, was a turning point for me in the hospital. In the morning, my doctor, Major Bowman, stopped by for one of his routine checks, and I was lucid enough to engage him in conversation. Like me, he is thin and tall, but with thinning hair. He appears to be older, maybe in his late thirties. He is a blunt, straight talker who lacks the traditional bedside manner one might hope for in a doctor. The nurses here are so friendly and helpful, but the doctors simply are not. The doctors just seem overwhelmed with too many patients.

"When am I going to get released to go back to my unit?"

Major Bowman laughed and replied, "We've been waiting to see if you went home on a stretcher or in a body bag. We didn't think you were gonna make it."

"When will I be able to fly again?"

"I don't think you'll fly again. We're planning to send you to Texas once you're strong enough. You're going to the burn unit at Fort Sam Houston."

"So that means I'm going back to the States soon?" That reality was slow to set in.

"Yes, of course."

"When will I go?"

"I don't know. We've got to stabilize you before you can go."

"Can I get access to a phone to contact my family?"

"I'll see what the nurses can do."

I saw many injured soldiers get hospital treatment and then return to our unit. Despite my injuries, I actually thought I was going to be eventually returned to my unit. The doctor all but laughed at that.

The lone telephone in the ward was located at the nurse's desk station a good seventy-five feet away from where my bed rested. With a rhythmic clicking sound of the bed's wheels, a couple of corpsmen and a nurse pushed my old metal frame to the phone desk. I tried to place a call to my parent's house in South Carolina. I didn't want to upset Martha Anne, so I hoped to reach my father first. The phone was the standard MARS line, so I had to wait thirty minutes, holding the phone near my head while the HAM radio operator picked up the necessary signal. Eventually, I was connected to my family's home phone line in Charleston, but to add to the complexity, we had to say *over* at the end of each spoken line so the operator could flip a switch to allow the person in the States to speak. Finally, I heard my father's voice say, "This is Harry Tallon, and I accept the call."

I stated, "Get everyone off the phone except you, over."

"I'm the only one on the phone, over."

"I've been burned, and I'm going to Fort Sam Houston, Texas, over."

"What happened, over?"

"My plane was shot down, and I'm in the 95th Evacuation Hospital at China Beach. They are sending me to the burn unit, over."

Suddenly silence.

It became quickly apparent that our connection was lost. We

waited in vain for a few minutes hoping that the HAM radio operator would find a way to reconnect us. It never happened, so the nurses wheeled me back to my spot in the ward.

★ ★ ★

Other than Dubose and my men from the motor pool who visited frequently, no officers or leadership from my unit had come to visit me. It was known as the *One Thirty Worst* for a reason. After months of rumors, the unit was preparing to finally leave Marble Mountain Airfield to permanently relocate to the Da Nang Air Base, so I'm sure they were busy preparing planes and equipment for the relocation. Plus, my adherence to strict motor vehicle maintenance procedures had made me a bit of a pariah among the unit's officers. Apathy and self-preservation were the order of the day. So I was a bit surprised to see my commander Major Smith stride up to my bed this afternoon.

"How are you doing?" he inquired.

"I'm hanging in there, Major."

At my response, his eyes welled up. He reached up to wipe his eyes. There was a long pause before he spoke again.

"I thought you were dead. I didn't know who you were until you spoke."

"I'm not dead yet. I'm still here, I think."

"I was told you were killed. We reported you as killed in action, and we reported the observer as injured. So, I came here to visit him. I was gone to Saigon for a few days when you went down and just returned yesterday when they told me the pilot was killed and the observer was in the hospital."

Unbelievably, my CO didn't even know I was still alive. My face was covered in black crusty burn scabs, and all my hair was shaved off my head. He could only see my head as the sheet covered my entire body from the neck down. I thought again about my observer Daniel Richards, and I truly regretted not grounding him for being overweight. It was his first mission since returning from that long stay in Thailand, and we joked about his weight. The Martin-Baker ejection seat was rated for a maximum of 200 pounds, and he said he probably weighed at least 225. Maybe it would have made a difference, but at our low altitude, it might not have even mattered.

"Do you have a Purple Heart yet?"

"No, sir, I don't."

"Well, you'll be getting the Purple Heart and the Bronze Star."

"Sir, they're going to be sending me to the burn unit at Fort Sam Houston in Texas."

"They do excellent work there. They'll take care of you. What happened to take your plane down?"

"Richards said we were hit in the number two engine. I felt something hit the plane and an explosion, but I don't know for sure what hit us. I didn't see it."

Major Smith spoke a few more minutes about how the unit was planning to make its move from Marble Mountain to Da Nang. He said he would have to find another unit movement officer now that I'm going home. I had trouble keeping my eyes open and, right after he left, I slipped into a morphine slumber. But my sleep did not last long. A pair of MPs appeared at my bedside and riled me awake. They were in full regalia—from handcuffs to holstered pistols.

One of them looked at me and said, "Lieutenant, we are here to arrest you for sharing classified information."

"What are you talking about? What classified information?" I asked.

"Your plane being shot down is classified information."

"Who are we trying to keep that a secret from?"

Maybe the idea of attaching handcuffs to the charred flesh on either one of my forearms discouraged them or maybe it dawned on them just how insignificant of a security threat my broken body was, but they stormed out five minutes later as quickly as they appeared. I wished that this was some morphine-induced hallucination, but unfortunately, it was all too real. Every call to the States using the MARS line is monitored, and we all know that. I just never imagined that the downing of my Mohawk could in any way be sensitive, but at least I knew why my phone connection with my father had been abruptly cut off.

Just two days or several morphine-induced sleeps later, I had some special visitors. Still blind in my right eye, eating no solid foods, and suffering from no bowel movements for several days, it was not exactly the ideal condition I would have wanted to meet a Miss America winner. But nonetheless, Laurel Lea Schaefer from Ohio came to my bedside and just so happened to also be Miss America 1972.

Laurie Lea Schaefer
Miss America
1972

Coming over to Vietnam, I was hoping to get to see Bob Hope on his USO tour since my uncles had seen him during World War II. It just seemed like witnessing Bob Hope in person in a combat theater was a rite of passage for American soldiers. By August 1972, no one was really expecting to see Bob Hope return to Vietnam, as everyone was hoping to pull out soon. I was shocked when Laurel Lea Schaefer bent over and kissed me on my right cheek. I smelled of decaying, burnt flesh, and still, she kissed me. Later the next day, Miss South Carolina and Miss Louisiana returned to my bedside and left me a poster signed by all of the girls on the USO Miss America tour. It was personalized *to Lieutenant Joe Tallon.*

★ ★ ★

My nurse, Captain Smith, stopped by my bed this afternoon and told me I'll be leaving on a medevac flight tomorrow. It's hard to really know how long I've been in here, but the nurses say today is my ninth day.

Dubose stopped by once more to check on me. This time he came alone. He talked about the preparations the unit is undertaking to make the move to Da Nang. The fact that we now have operational vehicles is going to make moving much easier than it would have been. Dubose talked to one of his noncommissioned officer friends earlier in the weekend and learned that they are investigating the parachute rigging shop. When Dubose and others recovered Richards's body, they found him still in his jump seat. The seat never disengaged from his body as it's supposed to do during ejection. Apparently, the drogue chute didn't pull open the main chute as it's designed to do either. I still don't know why I survived the ejection, and he didn't.

Monday, August 21, 1972
DAY 104:

This morning I awoke to a frenzy of activity around my bed. To make the trip back to the States, the nurses packed the worst of my burn wounds with white antibiotic cream and wrapped my arms, legs, and a good portion of my chest in gauze bandages. I was through the roof in pain. They rolled me out on a gurney with wheels into the bright sunlight of the beach. Fortunately, a relatively smooth sidewalk led to the helipad because I could feel every bump. The engine was on and the rotors were turning on the medevac helicopter in the distance, so I could hear it long before I could see it.

As I got closer, I saw at least a dozen of my motor pool men lined up at the helipad like a bunch of schoolchildren. They came up and said goodbye and made jokes about getting on the *big silver bird back home* and heading to the *land of the giant PX*. When I got closer to the rotors and the end of the line of *misfits*, I raised up on my right elbow and looked Specialist Asbell directly in the eye and yelled "Short!" as loud as I could. His expression changed from a smile to dejection. The lieutenant who he constantly chided about how much time he had left in country was going home before him.

For the final stretch to the chopper, two corpsmen grabbed the handles on either end of my stretcher and lifted me off the gurney. Those olive drab canvas stretchers were made for short guys, and I hung off both ends. They loaded me in with the Cobra pilot warrant officer from my ward who was blinded in both eyes and suffering from a broken leg. Lying down in the chopper, I could no longer see my men lined up. I stared at the roof of the helicopter and squinted my eyes as we took off. The bright morning sun shined right into my face.

Joe at age six with his older sister, Lindler, at Woodlawn Avenue in North Charleston, SC

Joe's 1965 senior class photo at Chicora High School

Wedding day on July 2, 1971 at Holmes Avenue Baptist Church in North Charleston, SC

Joe's graduation from Rotary Wing School in 1971 at Fort Rucker, AL

Joe Tallon's official
promotion packet picture
for 1st Lieutenant

Taken in 1943, Joe's
father, Harry Tallon,
in US Navy uniform
during World War II

Joe seated in a
Bell UH-1 Huey
helicopter at
Fort Rucker

Joe testing the
Martin-Baker
ejection seat in
March 1972 at
Fort Rucker

Marble Mountain Army Airfield near Da Nang

Joe returning from an OV-1 Mohawk mission over North Vietnam with mission packet in hand

SSG Larry Dubose who served as motor sergeant

Group of motor pool 'misfits' with 1st Lieutenant Joe Tallon standing to the right

Joe seated in the cockpit of an OV-1 Mohawk with
technical observer Specialist Yarborough

Joe's call sign 'Spud
7' with the 131st
unit insignia of
Nighthawks

131st unit photo of
Specialist 5th Class
Daniel Richards
taken in Thailand

SP5 RICHARDS

Etching from West 1, Line 64, of Daniel M. Richards taken from
the Wall in Washington, DC

Joe with his beloved German shorthaired pointer Cocoa in Fayetteville, NC

Joe with his new Franchi 12-gauge shotgun standing in front of his Chevy stepside pickup in Fayetteville, NC

Joe with baby Matthew
on a Schwinn in
spring 1980 in
Summerville, SC

Joe outside the Charleston Southern University Lightsey Chapel in November 2008
after his Purple Heart award ceremony with sons Josh (left) and Matthew (right)

Sample handwritten letter from Joe to Martha Anne written after a completed mission late on the night of July 26-27, 1972

Dear Martha Anne,   26½ July 72

I'm so tired I can't see straight. I was scheduled for one mission and ended up with three tonight. I started my preflight at 6:15 p.m. I then got word not to take off until 9 p.m. I started my engines at 8:15 p.m. and started my runup checks. I took off at 9 p.m. and landed at 11:45. It would have been later, but I did a high speed dive to get back quicker. That is why it is tomorrow and I'm trying to write you a letter.

I love you very much but it's 1:30 a.m. and I'm beat. I worked all day in the motor pool. I got a letter from you today and it was great. I'll write you the night of the 27th

if I get back from flying in time. I'm going on a mission with Mike McClendon. I love you very much.

Much love
Always,
Joe

Formal photo taken after retirement from teaching

PART II

★ ★ ★

THE RECOVERY

Late August 1972

MY LONG TRIP back to the States finally ended two nights ago. We landed at Kelly Air Force Base, and I was transferred by ground ambulance across the city of San Antonio to Brooke Army Medical Center at Fort Sam Houston where the Army's burn unit is located. I wanted to report my horror story to someone in authority as soon as possible, but it took a day before I got a major to come to my bedside and listen to what happened to us in transit. I told him everything I could remember.

The chopper that picked me up at China Beach dropped me off at Da Nang Air Base just before an incoming rocket attack. I was rushed by stretcher to an airfield bunker where we waited until the all-clear horn sounded. Every bone in my body seemed to radiate pain as they ran me bouncing across that airfield. I wished they would have just left me on the runway to take my chances with the rockets.

When our C-9A medical evacuation plane touched down at Clark Air Force Base in the Philippines, we were loaded onto buses to be moved across the airfield and into the local hospital for the night. It was already getting dark when we landed. Laid on the back of that bus, I felt every bump and indentation in the pavement. I swear we crossed the same railroad track three or four times. By the time I was shuttled through triage areas, it was nearly midnight. I found myself in a two-person room with the injured warrant officer Cobra pilot who was at China Beach hospital with me.

A group of five male corpsmen appeared in our room. They wore light green surgical scrub gowns with no name tags and made it abundantly clear they resented the fact that our late arrival extended their shift. Having already been in transit for many hours, I made a simple request for a toothbrush to clean my teeth, and one of them responded, "If I was burnt up like you, I wouldn't be worrying about getting any cavities."

They started working on the warrant officer first. When his helicopter crashed, his face was driven into the gun sites, blinding him in both eyes. Like me, he had severe burns that required frequent attention. They began the painful process of cleaning his burns but used only a single gauze pad to do it. This was shocking. Back at China Beach hospital, nurses used thirty to fifty gauze pads for cleanings in a painstaking effort to avoid contamination. The warrant officer cried out in pain. He shrieked and writhed and begged them to stop. His screams in pain were unlike any I'd ever heard before. I pleaded for them to stop. The corpsmen showed no compassion.

My right eye was severely damaged, with eighty-seven stitches holding the brow and lid in place, but I saw more than I wanted to see as I turned my head to the left. I was wrapped up like a mummy in bandages and couldn't move my body. I couldn't figure out why they were treating him like that. I looked back up at the ceiling and fixated on the IV bag dripping fluids into my body. I cried for the warrant officer, and the tears streamed down my cheeks and pooled in my ears. If I had my .38 sidearm, I would have shot each and every one of them in the head. I was enraged. I expected this kind of treatment from the North Vietnamese if we were shot down and captured but not from our very own comrades. I never met a Vietnamese person while I was in country who I wanted to kill as badly as those corpsmen.

The warrant officer's leg was broken and not even set in a plaster cast, and they just dragged him from one bed to another without holding or securing his leg at all while he screamed in agony. All of this *treatment* was for the supposed purpose of creating a sterile environment and seemed to be orchestrated by the heavyset man they called Haymaker.

Next, they began to work on me. Using just one sterile pad, they rubbed the burned areas on my body like course-grain sandpaper. The pain was indescribable. For an hour afterward, my arms and legs were still convulsing in spasms from this painful process. They finally left our room and turned out the light.

At China Beach, I received morphine injections every two to four hours, but in transit, I lost track of the time and the injections. Hours later, I awoke and yelled for a nurse repeatedly. My screams grew louder and louder because my call button was nowhere to be found on my bed. Finally a nurse came to our room, and I forcefully complained about the treatment that we received from the corpsmen. It seemed like she was concerned about my story, but maybe she was just faking it. She then discovered that my IV line was disconnected, and the fluid had puddled and saturated my bed. Dehydration had already set in. I could not swallow, and even though I was in tremendous pain, I didn't have enough moisture in me to make tears. I'm certain those corpsmen pulled out my IV line on purpose.

The major here is skeptical of my tale and told me to wait a couple weeks and see if the treatment I'm receiving at Brooke is better than what we received in the Philippines.

★ ★ ★

I got the surprise of a lifetime at lunch today! Out of nowhere, Mama and Martha Anne appeared in my room. At first I thought I might be hallucinating, but when Martha Anne ran to me and kissed me, I knew she was as real as could be. I was worried about my appearance, but they assured me that I didn't look that bad. It's been almost two weeks since the crash, so the skin on my face is actually starting to heal.

Martha Anne looked beautiful in a blue pantsuit she made for herself. It had little half dollar sized spots of rainbow colors in the patterned material. Very stylish. But she looks great in anything (or nothing for that matter!). They drove all the way out here to San Antonio from Charleston in our Oldsmobile.

My left arm is wrapped in a sling and elevated above me since my fingers and arm are swollen and need to drain. My left leg is resting six inches higher than my right leg on an inclined fracture board. I've got bandages wrapped around my body, and I'm laid out on sterile pads because of the fluids seeping out of my burned butt. A sterile sheet is draped over a hoop frame covering the core of my body like a miniature Quonset hut. This little tent keeps me warm, as I am naked underneath except for the bandages.

Mama rubbed lotion on my feet and Martha Anne helped feed me my lunch today during their visit. They were only allowed to stay for ninety minutes, but they'll be back soon. They are both staying in the temporary lodging quarters for families of burn patients.

★ ★ ★

For the third morning in a row, I was taken to the Hubbard tank. Before they transferred me from my bed to a gurney, the nurse injected me with another morphine shot in my thigh. Boy, did I need it too. The tank is a stainless-steel tub that resembles a German iron cross. I'm told this will be part of my daily ritual. Because of the injuries to my neck and back, they place me on a metal-framed fracture board before submersion. The metal frame is suspended by four cables from the ceiling, and then they slowly lower me into the water. The tank is filled with warm, sterile water to soften the scabs, and the first few minutes are sheer bliss. The tank is the only place I can get truly warm and where my leg cramps and spasms subside. After a few pleasant minutes of soaking, the nurses begin the debridement, cutting and scraping off the decayed areas of flesh. Using scalpels, scissors, and shaving razors, they cut and scrape off the decay, exposing new raw flesh. It doesn't take long for the water in the tank to turn blood red.

Following the Hubbard tank treatment are the wet-to-dry wraps. I have to go through the removal and application of wraps three times a day. By the time the nurses are done covering the burns on my arm and legs, I look like a mummy. Thankfully, none are put on my back or butt. The bandages were intentionally wet going on and allowed to dry to the skin. While drying, I lay there in dreadful expectation because I know what's coming next. The removal of the dried wraps is extremely painful. Like the concept of getting waxed to remove unwanted hair, the nurses pull the dried bandages off, bringing with them chunks of scabs and partially healed flesh. The morphine does little to stave off the pain when those dry wraps are ripped off.

★ ★ ★

Staff Sergeant Murphy, who we often refer to as Murphy or just Murph, is already a favorite nurse of mine and many others in our ward. He only works nights, and I'm learning already through Martha Anne that the spouses refer to him as *the phantom* since they've heard so much about him but have never seen him. Murphy has a technique of seesawing the dried bandages back and forth before pulling them off. The other nurses just rip them off, but Murphy's method with wet-to-dry dressings is much less painful. Murphy is a stocky white guy with broad shoulders and great upper body strength, probably from lifting patients in and out of beds. He usually wears white scrubs when he makes his rounds, which adds to the phantom mythology. Tonight, we were talking while he pulled my bandages, and he said that it would be at least two months before I got out of my bed and started to walk again. The hospital here in San Antonio has done much more imaging on me than was done at China Beach finding small fractures in different areas from my ribs down my left leg. I told him that I would walk in two weeks. I set the date in my head. He laughed at the idea, so we made a $20 wager.

★ ★ ★

My dad and younger brother Roy made the drive from Charleston to Texas in a Buick Electra without stopping anywhere to spend the night. They were dog tired when they came in yesterday during visitation time. They told me that before leaving home, a family friend recommended my father turn the air breather upside down on that Buick to get better horsepower and better gas mileage. Instead, Roy reported that the car was terribly loud and still got passed by almost everything on the road when they went up a hill. Around one or two in the morning, they stopped at a motel and asked about getting a room. Daddy wanted to know if he could get a room for just three hours to sleep, but when they quoted him the price, he just said, "I just want to rent the room, I don't want to buy it." With that, they were back on the road. They didn't waste any time hunting for meals either. The whole ride was just crackers and water. Their only stops were to get gas and pee.

When they drove through southern Georgia and the Florida panhandle, the hurricane damage was still present from June when Agnes came through. Sand and debris littered the small towns, and boats were still strewn about the dry ground. Daylight was breaking by the time they entered Texas, and Daddy was so worn out from driving that Roy took the wheel in Texas. Daddy was restless and wondered why so many cars were zooming past them on the highway.

He said to Roy, "Son, if you don't speed up, they're gonna run us off the road."

Roy replied, "I'm doing eighty-five now!"

Once Daddy peeked over at the speedometer and saw that, he just pulled the cap down over his eyes and said, "If we wreck up, I hope it's so hard I don't wake up. I ain't looking anymore."

After getting at least twelve hours of straight sleep, they came back over to the ward today. Mama and Martha Anne were here too, so it was a packed house. Roy was still hungry from his crackers and water rations, so he went downstairs to get a Coca-Cola and some food out of the snack machines on the first floor. When he came back up the elevator, he got off at the wrong floor. I'm on the third, but he went to the one above us by accident. As he walked through that ward, he quickly realized his mistake. He said it was a much more silent floor, and it smelled worse. As he scanned left and right, he saw scenes from a horror movie. They were grown human beings no more than three feet long—no arms, no legs, no facial features. To him, it looked like chunks of meat laid out on beds. He told himself to keep his eyes straight forward and get out of there quickly. When he got back to my bed on the third floor, he nodded his head at me and said, "He gonna be all right. He gonna be just fine."

He told us that compared to what he just saw on the other floor, I was looking good. Real good. He tried to convince Daddy to go back up to the other floor with him to see what he had seen, but Daddy refused.

"No, I seen enough of that during World War II."

After just a short couple of days, Daddy and Roy hit the road back to Charleston so he could get back to work. Nobody knew his rural sales routes like Daddy did, and his customers would be looking for their Greenbax stamps.

★ ★ ★

When Mama and Martha Anne arrived for the lunch visit today, they brought three pieces of mail with them—two cards and a letter. With some encouragement from my family, our home church in Charleston started a letter writing campaign, so I'm looking forward to getting mail. Mama read them to me while I slowly ate some lunch. They came to visit me straight from a morning training class on skin grafting. Together with the other spouses and family support members in the guest housing, Mama and Martha Anne have been getting trained on our burn treatments by the Army medical staff. One lesson they apparently didn't absorb in today's training was the prohibition against kissing the patients. Martha Anne was bent over my bedside kissing me on the lips and face at the precise time the head nurse was walking through the ward. She's a no-nonsense lieutenant colonel, and she didn't even crack a hint of a smile when I suggested the kiss was a part of my treatment. Then she proceeded to reprimand Martha Anne for leaning over and touching me. The threat of dangerous infection is still very real.

★ ★ ★

I've grown tired of the patient in our ward who we call *Bob the Buddha*. I'm not the only one. He's short and round like a Buddha but with gray hair. He's keeping everyone awake at night with his whining, groaning, and moaning. Even though he has only first and second degree burns and requires no grafting, he still complains constantly and makes the most pathetic noises deep into the night. All of us in the ward are fighting through pain, but most of us are trying not to cause it for others. There is always some noise on the ward as the sounds of someone in agony are not blocked by the curtains. I've bitten numerous holes in my wool blanket clamping my teeth down in excruciating pain while trying not to make any loud noises. He's a civilian, and I wish they'd take him to another ward or another hospital. Anywhere but here.

Last night, a new young female lieutenant arrived on our ward. She's a dietician making the rounds to see if everyone's eating well. A couple of beds over from me is Sergeant Frank Skinner. When he saw the dietician, he started groaning and carrying on, which was odd for him.

"My ears. My ears," he kept saying. Sergeant Skinner is an Army cook with significant burns on his head and chest from a cook stove gas explosion. He rarely complains, but just then he was making enough noise to lure the young dietician to his bedside.

"Is there something I can do to help you?" she asked, a worried look on her face.

Skinner's hands were cupped over his ears. "They're missing!"

"What are missing?" she asked.

"My ears!" He took his hands off the sides of his head to reveal that his ears were in fact not there.

The dietician gasped. "What happened to them?"

He pointed at her feet. "Miss, you're standing on them."

Her gasp turned into a scream. Sure enough, at her feet were Skinner's artificial ears. The dietician wasted no time leaving the ward, and we didn't see her the rest of the night.

★ ★ ★

To get off the IVs, which are connected into the tops of my feet, I am required to consume at least 5,000 cc of fluid per day. This amounts to twenty-two small eight-ounce glasses of water. However, they monitor all the liquid I consume, so the tea at lunch and the milkshake at night before going to sleep all count toward the daily fluid intake. The nurses measure everything meticulously—what goes in and what comes out. The stainless-steel urinal they leave for us looks like a squatty flower vase tilted at an angle with a small hoop handle on top. When you place that cold steel contraption between your legs, it's hard to remember why you needed it in the first place. Today I used a cup left by my bedside to meticulously fill the urinal to the very top. Normally I can't get it that full moving it in and out of the bed. When Murphy made his rounds early at night, he snatched up that urinal in his typical fashion, which caused urine to splash out all over his arm. I found it much more amusing than he did as he claimed I ambushed him.

Yesterday was my thirteenth night in the burn ward—one day ahead of my wager with Murphy. I hadn't seen him yet, but I decided to make my move. The lights were dimmed for the night, and I used the quiet as the opportunity to embark on the journey out of the ward and down the corridor to the nurses' station. It was less than 100 feet away, but it might as well have been a country mile. It took long pain-filled minutes just to hang my legs over the side into position. Finally, I pushed myself to a stand. The pain immediately radiated from hip to toe. It felt as if my legs were being pulled from my hip sockets. I sat back down and waited until it subsided. The pain remained, but not so severe after a minute or two. I tried again to push myself to a stand. This time I was determined to make it across the ward.

I took my first step, which was not really a step but more of a slide. I slid the other foot out front. The bed was no longer close enough to prop me up. I pressed on, one foot in front of the other. It was like my feet were in clay blocks. I couldn't pick them up. I dragged them across the floor, one step, another slide. My worst burn wounds were seeping a rust-colored mixture of fluids and blood. Small puddles of pink-red fluid pooled on the floor at every step along the way. I was breathing hard by the time I got to the nurses' station. But I got there. I won the bet! Exhausted, I collapsed against the wall of their station. Murphy wasn't even there for me to collect my wager. The nurses were very upset that I got myself out of bed, and on top of that, I left a mess on the floor. Once they got me back to the bed, they had to change all my dressings immediately.

★ ★ ★

I didn't connect with Murphy last night on his shift. Maybe the urine bottle turned him away. Instead, this morning, I received a personal visit from my doctor, Major Warden. Like the nurses, he was very upset that I got out of my bed.

"Lieutenant, I'm going to have to give you a direct order to stay in bed. You can't be getting yourself out of the bed like that."

"I'm going to continue to walk," I said. "I don't want to become an invalid."

"I can have you court-martialed if you don't stay in the bed."

"Look around the ward. People who came in here as warriors are leaving as invalids because you are keeping them in their beds. I'm not going to let pain dictate what I'm going to do the rest of my life."

We stared at each other for a moment as he seemed to digest what I was saying while I was trying to not appear intimidated, which I certainly wasn't.

"Fine, when you get ready to jaunt around the hospital again, let my nurses know an hour in advance. They can put you in compression bandages, so you don't bleed all over the ward."

I'm paying the price now for the mess that grew into my burns during that long, painful transit back across the Pacific. The Hubbard tank has not cleaned all of the fungus and infection from my wound sites, so today they had to put me under for deeper debridement. When I asked what they'd use to put me out, they said it was ketamine. They told me to count to fifteen, but by the time I reached forty, the nurse said I could stop counting since it clearly wasn't effective. My doctors authorized another dose. I heard a fluttering in my ears that sounded like a covey of quail getting flushed and that was it. I don't have any idea how long I was out, but Martha Anne and Mama were sitting at my bedside when I came out of it. Or sort of came out of it. Apparently, the first thing I did was start to sell tobacco. I played the role of a fast-talking auctioneer for the American Tobacco Company. Those tobacco sales were part of my childhood experience, and back then, I actually wanted to be an auctioneer when I grew up.

Next, I transitioned to chanting in the style of a Buddhist monk. I have no background in the Buddhist faith other than what I briefly observed in small glimpses while living in Vietnam. Finally, I transitioned from chanting to hog calling. My Uncle Paul lived on the Caw Caw Swamp near Ravenel, South Carolina, and many times I helped him call the hogs out of the swamp for evening feeding. The hog call was obnoxiously loud. Embarrassed by my antics and loud noises on the ward, Martha Anne put her hand over my mouth and tried to calm me down. I actually bit down hard on her hand before finally coming to my senses.

When I realized again where I was, I noticed the feeling of something foreign on my arms and legs. Then I remembered what they told me before the procedure. My worst burn sites—the ones that would likely require grafting—were now lined with thick strips of pigskin. It has a surprisingly human look to it. I'm not sure if that is why I decided to call in the hogs from Caw Caw Swamp or not, but it did certainly make me think back to all the pork rinds I made with Daddy after we roasted whole hogs.

★ ★ ★

A lieutenant colonel stopped by this morning from the Inspector General's office to follow up on my report of abuse in the Philippines. I assured him that my treatment in the Philippines was nothing like the good treatment I've gotten here at the burn unit. Sure, I'm in pain every day, but the nurses here do a great job of trying to make me comfortable. The lieutenant colonel told me that the warrant officer corroborated my story about Haymaker and the other corpsmen. I pointed out that we haven't spoken about that night together at all since it happened. We've been on different floors. The floor he is on is for people in much worse shape than I am, which has helped me to stop feeling sorry for myself about my injuries. I sure hope that they punish those guys, but I have no confidence that they will. If I could have done more or if I could have gotten to a weapon, maybe I could have stopped them.

I've been given the opportunity to make my way around the ward in a wheelchair. I love it since this gets me out of bed and gives me a small measure of control. My left leg is still locked and has to be extended out straight on a brace when I get in the chair. Plus, my left wrist and left ankle are still recovering from the hairline impact fractures, which make it more difficult to move the wheelchair. Since they have my left wrist taped down securely in a hard, plastic brace, I only have use of the tips of my fingers to move the wheelchair. The nurses seem to prefer that I use the wheelchair until my body's ready to test the crutches.

Mama and Martha Anne left to drive home to South Carolina today. I've gotten so used to them being here over these past three weeks, it really has been a cherished part of my daily routine. They've been reading aloud the letters written to me from the church and the family back home. But now they're gone. I am left to the silence of my own thoughts. The morphine didn't seem to work as well today either.

★ ★ ★

It's been about a week and a half since Martha Anne left, and this week my quiet isolation ended in a spectacular way. First, Bob and Sandra Gardner arrived for a visit. They live out in Tyler, Texas, but it's still a long drive to San Antonio, so I was both surprised and happy to see them. We talked about that Thanksgiving we spent out on their family ranch in Winters. I teased Bob about only killing one quail that hunt and asked if he had been practicing. I'd love to go back after those ranch quail again once I get up out of this bed.

Next came my Uncle Paul Cobb who lives on a farm in Ravenel, South Carolina. He can't read, write, or even sign his own name, but he possesses an old-time farmer's wisdom. Many of my best childhood experiences were spent on his farm riding horses or calling his hogs out of the swamp. Uncle Paul was amused that I called his hogs under the influence of ketamine. His son Larry, who he often calls Bubba, is a mechanic for Delta Airlines and has access to free flights. Early yesterday morning, they flew from Charleston to Dallas before catching a hop flight to San Antonio. Uncle Paul said it's the first time he's been on a plane in his life. By the time the lunch visitation session began, he and Larry were sitting at the foot of my bed in the ward. He said he came to see in person just how bad my injuries are and to ensure that I receive excellent care. Satisfied that I was being treated well, they were gone by the close of the midday visitation and back on the farm in Ravenel that very same night in time to feed the hogs.

Today I also completed my first walk in the ward without a wheelchair since that first jaunt that made everyone so upset. My left leg is still stiff, but the fractures in my left wrist and ankle are healing up nicely. I did three full laps today up and down the length of the ward. It feels like slow-going to me, but the nurses are telling me that my progress is excellent.

Satisfied that the debridement has sufficiently cleaned my wound sites, Major Warden decided that today would be my turn to do grafting with my own skin. Thankfully, I was put out for the surgery, and even better, I was told upon waking up that they thought they had done enough to cover the areas that require grafts. Some people on the ward had to go through multiple rounds of grafting surgeries, and I would just as soon not do that. To make my skin donations stretch further, they ran them through a machine which cut a mesh pattern of diamonds allowing it to expand. That's about where the good news ended. When I awoke, the pain at my donor sites was worse than the burns. On the tops of my thighs, the doctors removed strips of skin about a foot long and four to six inches wide. They only took the top two layers of skin from donor sites since the third base layer contains the hair follicles and sweat glands. But that's more than enough if you ask me. It feels like a dagger being slowly twisted in my thigh muscles. It only hurts when my heart beats. The morphine takes a little bit of the edge off the pain but not much. Hopefully these grafts take to my skin and heal up well.

★ ★ ★

Without Martha Anne here, I'm losing track of the days, but I think I've been at Brooke for six weeks now. Of all the visitors who have surprised me in the burn ward in the past week or so, I was absolutely shocked today when Staff Sergeant Dubose came to visit midday. He just got home from Vietnam for some much-deserved leave and informed me of how rapidly things changed for the unit after I was airlifted out of China Beach. Within a few days, the 131st moved to Da Nang Air Base, ceasing operations at Marble Mountain. Just a couple weeks later at Da Nang, the unit deactivated in Vietnam, and many were sent home. Dubose got transferred to Fort Hood in Texas, which is perfect for him since he's a native Texan. Most of our men in the motor pool got their tickets punched to come stateside as well.

Dubose told me more about Daniel Richards and the crash. An investigation was initiated into the parachute rigger's shop because the seat never deployed correctly. His drogue parachute was wired in and never opened properly. Speculation was that the riggers were smoking dope and shooting heroine and didn't pack it up correctly, but the investigation was dropped when the unit moved off Marble Mountain. I wanted to know more about what the unit learned after looking at his ejection seat, but that's all Dubose knew about it. He left after lunch but promised to come back again soon. His father lives in the city of San Antonio and his grandfather owns a ranch outside of the city, so he's spending most of his leave nearby.

★ ★ ★

Sure enough, Dubose came back about ten days later. This time, the burn unit let him sign me out for a three-hour pass. It was an opportunity for me to get out of the hospital for the first time for some fresh air and test my mobility. The grafts have taken very well to my skin, and the weeping of fluids has slowed down considerably. Dubose drove me just outside of San Antonio to his grandfather's ranch. He told me we were going to join his family for a barbeque, but what we ate was not at all what I expected. First of all, it was beef and not pulled pork like we do barbeque in South Carolina. I'm used to cooking the whole hog, chopping the meat up into small, shredded pieces, and saving the skin to make fried pork rinds. Instead, this was a large slab of beef charred black on the outside but still pink in the middle. They cut it in slices and served it from the grill that way.

I had a great time meeting his family and hearing what it's like living in south-central Texas. I told them how much assistance Dubose had been to me in Vietnam. He practically carried me through the start of that motor pool job when I had no idea what to do about those vehicles. By the time I got back into the car bound for Brooke Medical Center, I was exhausted and needed a lot of help. That was more than I'd moved around in quite a long time, but I'm glad we got to do it. And I'm really glad Dubose made it home from Vietnam safely.

★ ★ ★

Morphine is the drug of choice in the burn unit. With severe burns, the itching is so intense that the urge to scratch feverishly is almost impossible to withstand. I watched a young civilian boy in the ward the other day scratch off his new skin grafts repeatedly. Even after the hospital staff put his arms in bed restraints, the boy's mother stealthily released him from the restraints during evening visitation which allowed him to commence scratching and destroying the grafts all over again.

Pain is ever-present, and I'm given morphine injections every two to four hours to manage it. At first, I got some relief, but it did not take long until I was begging for another shot even before a full three hours passed. The shots have become less effective over time as I have developed a tolerance to the morphine's effects. Sometimes the nurses come back quickly with the morphine syringe and sometimes there is a long delay after my request. One of my nurses looks a lot like my Great Aunt Anna who herself was a nurse. She died years ago, but I remember her well. I call the nurse Aunt Anna, and in return, she calls me nephew. Today after administering a morphine injection to me, she looked at me and said, "Nephew, I think you are getting too many of these shots."

"Do you think I'm becoming an addict?"

"You're already an addict."

"Well, take my chart and write on it not to give me any more morphine for pain."

"Are you sure you want to do that, nephew?"

"I don't want anything habit-forming for pain from this moment on. No matter how much I cry or beg for it, please don't let them change that order."

I'm already feeling the effects of my decision. The crawlers have invaded my bed and my body like thousands of imaginary bugs infesting the burned areas of skin. They seem to be eating my skin, and they are so much worse at night.

★ ★ ★

When Martha Anne returned earlier this week, she immediately saw the gains I had made since she was here the first time. Because the grafts are taking well to my skin, I don't have to go to the Hubbard tank any longer for debridement. The grafts are red and inflamed around the edges, but as long as I resist the urge to scratch them, I should be on my way to getting out of the burn unit before Christmas. I told Martha Anne that I'm allowed to be signed out now for short stretches, so today we decided to do a meal out. I wanted to show her how tough I am and how well I'm doing in rehab, so I left my crutches and just opted for the cane. When we emerged from the hospital entrance, she pointed out her temporary lodging less than a quarter mile down the road. I said I'd walk her there to get her purse before we went out. I didn't make it to the edge of the first parking lot before I had to sit down and get her to call us a taxi. Walking outside in the humid evening heat was nothing like my practice walking in the burn ward. My energy was sapped instantly. We did get out to the restaurant and had a great Mexican meal on the San Antonio River Walk.

★ ★ ★

I'd never even heard of convalescent leave before they offered it to me. To be able to be cleared for one, I had to prove that I could move around sufficiently. Even though I have been demonstrating for a couple weeks now the use of the cane in the ward, I still fall when I turn too quickly to the left. My left knee is stiff and weak and buckles under my weight. The orthopedics section fit me for two pairs of custom compression stockings. The stockings assist with my circulation in my lower extremities, and I'm supposed to wear them the entire thirty days I'm gone on convalescence. I've been here at the burn unit a couple days shy of a full two months. They tell me that I'm healing quickly, and I should be able to fly back to Charleston for leave in the next week or so.

Late October 1972

Martha Anne and I boarded a Delta flight together in San Antonio early this morning. The Boeing 737 had one aisle in the middle with two seats on one side and three on the other. We made our way slowly to our seats, and it wasn't long before the crew noticed the stiff condition of my left leg and moved us up to the front of the plane with more leg room. At six-foot-three and in the condition I was in, I really appreciated it. We changed planes in Atlanta, which took some time. I was just happy, but a little anxious, to be heading home. I'm not sure how I'll be received, coming back injured. I am not the conquering hero who helped to win the war that I so naively predicted on my way out in May. My first real test will be getting off the plane.

We had to walk down the portable boarding stairs to get to the airfield. As I emerged from the side of the plane, I saw a sizable group of family members gathered near the terminal entrance almost in the same spot we gathered in May to say goodbye. Because I still couldn't bend my left knee at all and my swollen left wrist was stiff and painful, I took a long time to get down the stairs. Like a giant spotlight, the airfield stairway highlighted the crippling effects of my injuries. I put my hand on Martha Anne's shoulder to steady my balance as we walked forward. Finally crossing almost 100 feet of tarmac to where my family was gathered, one comment stood out above all others. My Aunt Ruby stated matter-of-factly, "Oh look, he's a cripple." The wind seemed to suck out of my chest. I had worked so hard to be able to walk out of that plane without crutches or the use of a cane. All the joy and excitement and expectation that had built up within me before my arrival was gone in an instant. It was all I could do to hold back the tears. I was not returning as a warrior or as a hero but instead as a cripple. I wondered if that was what everyone was thinking but was too afraid or polite to say.

The doctors in Texas told me that the stiffness in my left knee joint would likely be permanent. So when Martha Anne and I arrived at our second floor apartment in North Charleston yesterday, I didn't even bother to ask the building manager to switch to a ground floor apartment. Instead, I viewed it as an opportunity for me to extend my rehab.

This morning between eight and nine when others were leaving for work, I walked out to the landing at the top of the stairs to begin a solitary ritual. There are two apartments on the second floor of our building and two apartments on the bottom floor separated by a single flight of stairs. Halfway up the stairs is a large flat landing where the stairs change direction. My left wrist was very stiff, and my left knee was totally locked when I started. But I was determined to keep walking on it to get movement again. It took me at least fifteen minutes to negotiate those stairs and get down to the bottom floor. I rested for a minute and then started working my way back up. After a couple of hours, my shirt was soaked to the waist with a mixture of sweat and tears. I fear that if I give in to the pain and quit walking, I'm going to lose the ability to move that left leg altogether, so my goal is to put in some time on these stairs every day.

Martha Anne and I decided to get out of our little apartment and head to one of our favorite places—the Blue Ridge Parkway near Asheville. It reminded us of the drives we took in northern Georgia above Rome when Martha Anne was still in school at Shorter. Many of the leaves had already fallen, so the peak fall foliage had come and gone, but the clear blue skies provided an unobstructed view of the vast expanse of tree-covered mountains. I've never liked crowds, and I've never liked a junky place where things are disorganized. With stands of tall trees as far into the distance as I could see from the parkway, the world seemed to be back in order for the first time in a long time. The chaos and crowds and general disarray in Vietnam have started to melt away for me up in the mountains. Plus, it seems like a world apart from the burn ward where we are confined to beds and listen to disturbing sounds of people in agony. The air here is fresh, crisp, and smells wonderful. My left side did get stiff as we rode around in the car, but we stopped frequently on the parkway and just enjoyed the portrait-worthy views. On our third day, we even drove to the top of Mount Mitchell where it was really cold, so we sat in a café drinking hot tea to warm my stiff joints. Martha Anne's company and the solitude of the parkway was exactly what I needed.

With only a week left of my convalescent leave, my branch headquarters called to let me know I have orders to relocate to Fort Bragg in Fayetteville, NC once my stint in the burn ward is over. Fayetteville is just three short hours away from my hometown of Charleston, so I am relieved to get reassigned there. While I was in Vietnam, I contemplated all kinds of exotic assignment locations, but now being close to home and family is the most important factor. That, and I'll be able to hunt and fish. I want to get serious about those activities when Martha Anne and I move to North Carolina, so I'm definitely going to need a new truck to do everything I want to do. As a traveling salesman, my Daddy has a loyal customer base across the state that he's come to know like the back of his hand. One of his loyal customers on John's Island just outside of Charleston had a six-cylinder 1966 Chevrolet step-side pickup in their lot for weeks. Pea green in color, the spare tire is mounted on the driver's side, and the bed is reinforced with a steel plate in the bottom, which is ideal for a custom dog box. The shop owner was asking for a thousand, but Daddy slowly pulled single hundred dollar bills out from his wallet and laid them dramatically one by one on the glass countertop before he stopped with five and then added a fifty to the stack. So for $550 cash, I've got a new bird hunting truck waiting for me back home when I get out of the hospital in San Antonio.

Late November 1972

When I arrived back on the burn ward a week ago, I noticed the horrible smell immediately when I entered the third floor. Being away for a month made me realize just how bad we smell on this floor. The aroma of decaying and burned flesh is so rank, I can no longer eat my meals in the ward. I take the elevator down two floors to the cafeteria. It's too many steps for me and just too painful to take the stairs. Yesterday I went over to the recreation room to try and give it a go at the pool table. For years in the garage behind our house, my brother Roy and I would shoot pool for hours. Yesterday, I played one game against a young soldier and barely finished. My back was killing me as I leaned over the table to line up my shots.

Earlier this morning, I reported to the Beach Pavilion building next door to see the orthopedic specialist. In the waiting room, I noticed a fellow painting the metal entry door. I told him he could go on a break, and I'd keep the brush limbered up for him. He took off down the hallway, and I commenced to painting the door royal blue. There was a glass rectangle window about two feet tall and eight inches wide, which I carefully cut around. Otherwise, it was just feathering out brush strokes on a flat door. That freshly painted door looked nice, and I just needed to know I can still do it. I'm looking forward to getting out of here in a couple of weeks and heading to my new life in North Carolina.

Early Spring 1973

Since arriving at Bragg just before Christmas, I've been working as an intelligence analyst for the 5th Special Forces Group, where I report to work in the S-2 office on the second floor of an old wooden barracks cut up into office spaces. Since I don't do the morning physical training with the unit, I don't report in until eight thirty or nine o'clock. Martha Anne has to drive me in, and sometimes one of our sergeants helps me up the two flights of stairs to my office. I wear a brace on my left ankle, and some days my left knee is much harder to bend than others.

Being in Vietnam made me miss what I loved most— Martha Anne, fishing, hunting, family and sweet-tasting homegrown butterbeans. While I was lying in my hospital bed at the burn unit in Texas, I plotted out the rows I would plant in my own garden—corn, okra, running green beans, tomatoes, and of course, butterbeans. My Daddy not only got the custom dog boxes built in the back of my green pickup truck before I returned from Texas, but he also acquired a trained German shorthaired pointer named Cocoa for me. Our Fayetteville duplex, with its very small yard, is no place to lay out a garden or keep a dog penned, so I'm going to have to get creative.

Last week, a very kind civilian woman at the brigade headquarters referred me to her father who owns some land. Mr. Albert Goins lives in a small, unpretentious house off Highway 87 north of Fayetteville in an area known locally as Spring Lake. Last Saturday morning, I drove out to his place to talk about borrowing a patch of land to make a garden. I like to get my seeds in the ground around Good Friday, so I need to hurry if I'm going to get planted this spring. He's already in his late seventies and retired from the rigors of full-time farming. For his family, he keeps a three-acre vegetable garden that he dutifully plants each growing season. When I arrived, he saw my truck pulling up the drive and met me in front of the house. Shaking his hand, I towered over him and his bent back. Plus, his balding and wrinkled head, leathery tanned skin and calloused hands with crooked fingers testify to the impact of a lifetime spent working the land. He owns a 100-acre parcel, but he keeps the vast majority of the land rented out in his old age. Shortly after I arrived, we hopped into the cab of his pickup truck and proceeded to his farmland another three miles up the road from where his house is located. We chatted about gardening on the short ride as he laid out his expectations.

"Joe, I've had people plant out here, but they done let the grass take over."

"I can assure you that I'll work the land as if it were my own. I'll keep the weeds out."

"I've got a piece of land back by the dog pens that I don't plant. I have trouble turning my tractor around in that corner back there. It's tight enough to raise a blister."

"Well, I don't have a tractor or any equipment to work the land, but I've got plenty of tools."

"I'll break it up as best I can with my tractor 'fore you get in there," he replied. "What're you looking to plant?"

"I want a few rows of running butter beans. Some Blue Lake bush beans. I imagine I'll try some okra and tomatoes, too."

"Well, whatever you plant, you've got to make sure that you don't touch that dogwood tree standing in the middle of the field. I promised Miss Williams next door that I wouldn't cut it down. She sure does love watching that ole' dogwood bloom each spring."

When we got out of his truck and walked into the field, the dogs in the pens nearby barked with deafening exuberance. Sure enough, that dogwood tree stood prominently in the back corner, and since we are approaching Easter, its leaves are already bright green with small blossoms starting to take shape on the branches. Mr. Goins recounted for me the years he had good harvests and bad harvests as well as his pet theories for why things broke one way or another. I mostly nodded and listened and tried to soak up any lessons he'd learned that might benefit my planting. It didn't look like much and the ground clearly hadn't been tilled in years, but I can already envision my garden in that little corner of the field.

This morning, I reported back to Womack hospital on Fort Bragg for my weekly injections. I did these appointments three times a week in January and February, but it's been reduced to twice a week for a couple weeks now in March. My primary doctor—Major North— administered the injections today. Around the edge of my skin grafts and on the back of my left shoulder where I never required a graft, I have keloid scar tissues, which look like raised red bubbles. As I sat in my underwear, Doctor North injected the needle straight into the keloid tissue perpendicular to the surface of my skin and then followed that up with two injections at forty-five-degree angles on either side. Each individual keloid area usually gets three injections of medication to control the incessant itching and to flatten the bubbly scars. Every visit I have between 80 and 125 injections, and while each individual needle stick is not that painful, I had a couple tears run down my cheek today after about forty-five minutes. We were done in just over an hour, and the best news I got today is that we can reduce the injection appointments to just once a week now. I am still supposed to attend Army physical therapy sessions twice a week on base.

★ ★ ★

The patch of land Mr. Goins loaned me resembles an elongated triangle with a squared off tip. On the large end, it measures 150 feet wide, but it tapers down to only thirty feet at the small end. As he promised, Mr. Goins ran his tractor and disc through my corner to break up the soil earlier this week. Even so, it is still littered with stumps varying in size from small softballs to fifteen-gallon washtubs. Clearly, it is a section of land that hasn't been planted very often. I pulled twenty-four of these stumps out by hand my first Saturday working the land before I decided to ask another local farmer to cut the land again with his mechanical mule.

Cocoa and I have quickly grown very fond of one another. I try to make time to spend with him on a regular basis. He takes direction well, and it took him less than a week to learn some hand signals and to stop crushing the quail in his jaws. At the 5th Special Forces Group Intelligence shop, we are working on contingency plans for possible invasions into Latin American countries in the hopes that we can avoid mistakes made in the Dominican Republic in the 1960s. My team, if you can call it a team, is focused on Cuba.

We get our materials around nine in the morning and work for a couple hours before they collect everything starting at eleven thirty, just before lunch break. We return at one and have our research materials available until they start mandatory collection around three thirty. All total, it's about a six-hour work-day split in the middle by a lunch break. After working so many eighteen-hour workdays in Vietnam, it feels like the Army owes me a few shorter ones. Since I'm required to turn in my classified material in the early afternoon, I have time in the evenings after work to visit Cocoa where he stays in a borrowed kennel. He gets so excited to see my green truck pull up each evening that he often runs full speed to jump into the rear bed by his dog box to let me know he wants to go on a hunt.

This afternoon as I drove home from work, I decided to take Cocoa for a quail hunt on a property down by the Little River. It's owned by a member of our church who gave us permission to hunt quail and rabbits there. When I arrived on the land, I hopped out of the driver's side to get Cocoa from the back. Before I went to him, I opened the passenger door of the truck and left it open. When I released Cocoa from his box, he tore out the back of the truck in a full sprint, like a dark brown, sixty-five-pound missile. He sprinted around the front bumper of my truck and turned the corner, hitting that open passenger door at full speed. I thought it might have killed him. Stunned on the ground for only a few seconds, he jumped right back up and was ready to hunt birds. My truck got the worst of it, as Cocoa left a sizable dent on the passenger side door. Cocoa and I had a successful hunt anyway, flushing a few coveys of birds and killing nine quail in total.

★ ★ ★

After five weeks of preparatory work and some seriously calloused hands, I was finally ready to plant. It's hard to believe that exactly one year ago this week, I arrived in Vietnam. In my exuberance, I sowed much more seed than I really needed. I planted five rows of butter beans, three rows of corn, three rows of peanuts, two rows of onions, two rows of Blue Lake green beans, a row of okra, a row of cucumbers, fifty tomato plants, and fifty cabbage plants. My uncles taught me to target Good Friday for planting, but with all the preparatory work, it is already mid-May and I've just gotten these seeds into the ground. I am mighty proud that my garden spot is pretty much free of weeds and stumps. With the seeds in the ground, I'm turning my attention to the weather, which is hot and getting hotter. The weather in central North Carolina is much different than Charleston and the Lowcountry of South Carolina. Here, it's hotter and dryer. I don't think it has rained a drop yet this month.

I asked the neighbor about tapping into his water supply, but they get their water from a well, and there is legitimate concern that it might run dry. I'm not about to let my first full-sized garden succumb to a lack of water. Plan B appeared to me this week in the form of fifty-five-gallon drums that I acquired from outside the stockade at Fort Bragg. Painted bright yellow with the lids cut off at one end, they are used on post as trash barrels. The post commander has decided to get rid of them, even though they are only slightly rusty and mostly free of holes. I've never been one to throw away something for which I can find a good use.

On Thursday after work, I removed Cocoa's dog box and placed four of those drums in the back of my pickup, then used the hose at the duplex and filled the drums six inches shy of the top so water wouldn't slosh around. My body still isn't right, so there was no way I was going to even attempt to pick up those drums full of water. Instead, when I reached the garden plot, I ran a hose from them over to a series of watering buckets and started the flow like I was operating a siphon. Watering the rows by hand took a full two hours.

★ ★ ★

We are in the midst of a prolonged dry spell. In the four weeks since I planted, I don't think we have had a drop of rain. With my small watering cans, I am not soaking the rows but just giving it enough water to keep the rows alive. It's not getting wet enough to melt the 10-10-10 fertilizer pellets that I spread, so I returned last week to the local farmer's exchange for a gallon of liquid fertilizer, which I added to my watering drums. Since planting, I have watered it twice every week and even a third if I could find the time.

The old dogwood tree standing in the middle of the garden was a real nuisance to me when I first started working the land. I had to divert my rows around the base of it, and the root system spread out in all directions much farther than one would imagine for a tree of such small stature. I didn't dare cut the root ends off that dogwood and invite the wrath of Mr. Goins and his elderly neighbor Miss Williams. Today, I decided to make an ally out of the dogwood. Using some scrap two-by-eights, I constructed a simple wooden bench with just a single crossbeam for support. The tree has held its foliage even in the early summer heat, and it provides the only shade in the middle of the field. It's very easy for me to get overheated since the skin grafts on my arms and legs don't sweat. After an hour working in the garden, I can look down at my arms and see the sweat beaded up around the edges of the grafts. For the first time today, I sat down on my bench underneath the shade of the dogwood with a cool drink of water. I even sang a few of the songs I'm learning with Martha Anne in the church choir while I sat and watched my garden grow.

This morning I drove in to work at the unit and heard immediately of two captains who received RIF letters in the 519th Military Intelligence Battalion. RIF stands for *reduction in force*. They too have medical profiles like mine. I got a message to report to the Headquarters and Headquarters Company (HHC) of the battalion to see the company commander. He provided me with a memorandum dated May 31, 1973, with the subject line, *Release from Active Duty*. I didn't need to read the two pages to know what it was all about. Signed by a two-star general, the Army basically thanked me for my service and told me I have ninety days left. I'm also hearing that every officer from my year group with a reserve commission received a RIF notice. I don't know how many that is, but it's probably in the thousands. A captain told me this afternoon that I won't be seeing him anymore around the base. He got a letter as well, and he's not coming back to work during the next ninety days. He's starting to look for a job right away. I cannot believe this is happening to me. I've been working really hard on my rehab trying to get back to full duty. I might not be able to jump with the airborne or fly Mohawks, but there is a lot I can still do in the Army. By the time I got home, I was so upset that I handed the letter to Martha Anne and told her I don't want to talk about it.

★ ★ ★

The six weeks of drought finally broke! It rained several days in a row, and especially hard in the evenings. This is ideal for my garden and the growth is happening before my very eyes. The cabbages came in first. This week, I picked fifty-four lush green heads. There is no way just the two of us can eat all of that, so Martha Anne and I began giving away cabbage to everyone we knew. At church last Sunday, friends returned to their cars after the main service and found a cabbage or two on the front seat. We gave heads of cabbage to neighbors and even random people in the grocery store parking lot.

I encountered another problem this week with the rapid growth. I was forced to get bigger stakes for our loaded tomato plants and the running butter beans because the wooden ones are breaking from the weight. I am getting a dozen big red tomatoes apiece, with some as big as softballs. Overwhelmed by the harvest, we purchased an upright freezer just to store our frozen vegetables. Plus, we have our blue porcelain pot and Ball mason jars for an aggressive canning operation.

★ ★ ★

Today I went in for another weekly follow-up appointment and keloid treatment with Doctor North. I showed him a copy of the RIF letter I received at the end of May, and he was really angry about it. He told me that they cannot do that to me because I'm still undergoing treatment, and he will have me transferred from the 519th Military Intelligence Battalion to a medical holding company while I'm having active treatments. I'd already made up my mind to appeal the RIF and fight to stay in the Army, so I am really appreciative of Major North's willingness to help me.

★ ★ ★

Of my entire bountiful garden, it is the okra that boggles the brain. My one row of okra has caught the attention of Mr. Goins and many a passerby on the highway. Every stalk is more than a dozen feet tall, and many of them reach as high as sixteen feet. The center stalks exceed six inches in diameter. The plants have protruding limbs that produce multiple okra pods, so it is commonplace for me to get two to three dozen pods off each okra plant during the pickings. And I have to pick it every third day or the okra gets too tough to eat. To avoid using a stepladder, I bend the okra stalks over double to reach the pods at the top. Since that corner of the Goins farm used to be a hog pen, I have planted on top of a bonanza of rich, manure-filled soil. That rich soil combined with the liquid fertilizer and rain is the holy trinity that made it take off.

Late November 1973 to Spring 1974

Now that the weather has turned cold again, quail season is open. Quail hunting entails quite a bit of walking, and I am using these hunts as therapy for my still-recovering legs. I'm almost a full fifteen months removed from the crash, and my left wrist and left leg in particular remain very stiff. I prefer to do my exercise out in the woods with Cocoa, as opposed to any of the indoor fitness facilities at the post. The pain of walking through the woods can be severe, but the energy and enthusiasm that Cocoa brings to each hunt motivates me to keep going. We walked for an hour this weekend and did not find any quail. Then suddenly, I heard a quail flush on my left side. I twisted that direction to draw a bead on the bird, planted my left foot wrong, and fell into a deep ditch, unable to get up. My back and leg were in serious pain. Initially, Cocoa left to go find more birds because he was so excited to be on the hunt. But when I didn't follow behind him to shoot the birds he was pointing, he made his way back to me in that ditch. He licked my face and actually tried to push me out with his snout. Finally, I wrapped a handkerchief around the barrel of my shotgun to keep the dirt out and propped up myself up on the makeshift crutch. Using my gun as a temporary leg, I limped back to my pickup with Cocoa at my side the whole time. I stopped at the first convenience store I could find while driving home and bought a bottle of Tylenol. I took ten pills, put Cocoa in his pen, then headed to the hospital. They gave me muscle relaxer injections in my back and sent me home with some more pills. I've been laid up in the bed for two days, but I'm sure glad I had Cocoa with me in the woods.

★   ★   ★

It's been a month since my hunting injury, and Martha Anne and I moved out of the duplex apartment in Spring Lake to our own single-level house near the College Lakes area of Fayetteville. This house already has a cement-floored dog pen in the backyard that allows me to keep Cocoa close by. Next to this new subdivision is a 200-acre farm, and before we closed on the house, I sought out the owner about using his land. I asked, "Could I have permission to run my dog on your place for exercise?"

"What kind of dog is it?"

"He's a German shorthaired bird dog."

"Well, we've got three coveys of birds on the place and you can hunt them if you like. I usually run people off my place because they never ask permission to hunt."

"Well, if you're okay with it, I'll park my green Chevy pickup by your house or barn so you'll know it's me that's hunting if I arrive when you're away or working in the fields."

"That's fine with me."

So, just like that, Cocoa and I have a place to hunt and run each and every day after work. Even if it is just thirty or forty-five minutes, I'll try to get Cocoa out in the evenings.

My primary job for the Army the past few months has me tasked as part of a mobile training team that ensures reserve intelligence units are ready to deploy. A lot of reserve units have been penciling in their readiness, so we are required to do substantial retraining when we inspect the units and find deficiencies. One of my colleagues on the mobile team—Captain Dan Day— just drafted a letter of support for my RIF appeal packet detailing the good work that I'm doing. My role is to teach how to set up and run a secure technical operations center (TOC). We bring with us simulated problems for the units to negotiate using real world intelligence to make them as realistic as possible. The mobile team has taken me far afield to places like Atlanta, Orlando, and San Diego.

★ ★ ★

I got an official notification letter in the mail today from the Army. I'm going to be promoted to captain later this year. It's been almost a full year exactly since I received my ninety-day RIF notification to force me out of the service. This is remarkable. I might be the only officer on a RIF status that is getting promoted. Major North is helping me, and I'm fighting to stay in. He has me on medical hold status while we continue my treatments, and I continue to go to work regularly and stay busy with these mobile training teams.

October 1974

My left shoulder has been bothering me quite a bit, and the rehabilitation is not making the progress we have hoped. Major North had me admitted to the base hospital yesterday so I can see some orthopedic specialists. After just three days there, I was loaded onto a Huey for a medevac flight to Walter Reed Medical Center in DC. It certainly wasn't on my account that we got a helicopter transport but more likely because the 82nd Airborne Division command sergeant major also required transport to Walter Reed. When I arrived, a doctor came to evaluate my shoulder and my medical records. The next day, a group of doctors inspected me and began to draw elaborate black lines on the skin of my left shoulder. On my third day, a group of students arrived in my room, and a pair of doctors read to them details about my case as if I weren't even in the room. Apparently, this is a teaching hospital. The stated objective of the surgery was to remove keloid tissue from the shoulder and repair some of the damaged ligaments. Now two full years removed from the crash, I've lost count of the number of times I've gone under the knife for surgical repairs.

After the students left my room and one of the lead doctors returned, I said, "I haven't signed a release or anything for this surgery."

"No, you're in the Army. You don't need to do a release."

"What if I don't approve of it?"

"We'll operate on you until we get you fixed. You're like a piece of equipment to repair."

"How many operations am I going to need on this shoulder?"

"I don't know. We'll see how this one goes."

That made me nervous when he said that. In fact, I was more nervous than any time I remember in Vietnam. These doctors seem to be more than happy to cut on me until they feel like they have it right. I hate doing the rehab after these surgeries, and I'm really starting to question how many more of these procedures I can tolerate.

October 12, 1974

The orderlies came to my room today just after noon and helped me work my way into my dress green uniform. It was not easy and quite painful. The surgery was only four days ago and left me with 138 stitches in my left shoulder. Since then, my left arm has been taped to my chest. But today, I got dressed for a field trip to the White House. With more than a dozen other ambulatory Walter Reed patients and their dependents, we loaded onto a bus for the drive to the White House. Betty Ford requested our attendance for an afternoon social event, which was scheduled to be her first public appearance since her mastectomy surgery for breast cancer. She knew what it felt like to be stuck in a hospital for days, so she specifically requested us— wounded Vietnam veterans—to share the afternoon with her.

Betty Ford standing on the balcony

I didn't have any family with me, but I did have a small Kodak instamatic camera that my friend Captain Dan Day let me borrow. He happened to be in town and stopped by the hospital yesterday to visit, and when I told him I'd been invited to the White House, Dan came back to my room with the instamatic camera, three flash cubes and a roll of film.

Our driver parked the bus in the looping drive on the

White House grounds about seventy-five yards from the entrance. It wasn't easy for me, but I walked to the entryway without the use of a cane. Other patients in our party used crutches or canes, but we all eventually made it there. We could hear the Marine Corps band playing boisterously on the portico one level above us. As we walked indoors, I removed my overseas cap, folded it flat and looped it over my belt at my waist.

First Lady Betty Ford personally greeted us, welcoming us as her special guests. She wore a red cocktail dress, a gold necklace, bracelets, and what looked like a very nice watch. I thought she looked pretty healthy considering she was battling breast cancer.

To our right along the wall was a long table with snacks and refreshments. People milled about, getting food and drink. I pulled out the camera to capture a picture of the bald eagle presidential seal on the carpet just outside of the room where we stood. I wanted to get a photo before our tour started and everyone moved to stand on the seal. Lining up a steady shot with just my right arm was not simple, but I did my best alignment and fired off the first photograph. The flash cube rotated and emitted a bright light. As soon as I brought my arm down, a man in his twenties wearing a suit was standing in front of me. He took the camera away and said, "You are not authorized to take pictures in this area." Just as quickly as he arrived, he was gone with Dan Day's instamatic camera.

I turned to walk back over to the table with refreshments when Betty Ford approached me directly. Standing in front of me, she asked, "Lieutenant, what's the problem?"

"They said I wasn't able to take pictures in this area and confiscated my camera."

"We'll see the hell about that!"

She stormed off down a corridor to another end of the room. Because of my height, I could still see above the crowd as she strode to the far side of the room where a suited man was posted outside a door. The door opened, and after a brief moment, another man emerged from the small room with my camera. Betty Ford then walked directly back to me flanked by a nice-looking young woman who must be her assistant.

"All you have to do, Lieutenant, is point at what you want a picture of. She'll take the picture for you." With that, she nodded at the young lady next to her. "Thank you so much ma'am," is all I could think to say in response.

As we toured the White House during the afternoon, I eagerly pointed out things to shoot. No more trying to steady the camera with just one hand. The only problem was that my flash cubes and one roll of film ran out long before the tour ended.

December 12, 1974

At the 519th Military Intelligence Battalion headquarters today, I was promoted to captain. Martha Anne came on post to pin the captain bars on my lapel. Despite the promotion, my appeals of the RIF notification are not going anywhere, and it appears the only reason I'm still in the Army is because of my medical hold status.

December 30, 1974

Because I have been on a medical hold status, the Army is required to conduct a medical review board to evaluate my physical condition and make recommendations according to their findings. I feel like I'm in a good place. Along with my promotion to captain, some of my intelligence work on Latin America last year earned me the Army Commendation Medal. My body is damaged, but my mind is working fine. I feel like I'm contributing to the mission.

This past Monday on the last workday of the year, my medical board convened at Fort Bragg. It consisted of five doctors— one of whom was my doctor, Major North. I originally thought it was going to be an open hearing where I would be allowed to give testimony regarding my treatment, my condition, and my efforts to return to full active duty. Instead, I wasn't called to be present or testify on my own behalf. It was a closed hearing. The board issued its findings to me this morning, stating that I was unfit for military duty and should be retired on 70 to 80 percent disability immediately. Even though these findings are just a recommendation, it feels definitive to me— like a knockout punch in the twelfth round. The Army that I have served with all my heart, mind, and body is in the process of getting rid of me. First the RIF notice and now the medical board.

March 6, 1975

When I arrived at Fort Gordon in Augusta this Thursday morning, I was met by a JAG officer just thirty minutes before the hearing who said he had been through many medical board hearings before. As a judge advocate general, his role was to legally represent me in the proceeding. Neither my doctors from Fort Bragg nor my doctor from Walter Reed were in attendance to testify about my condition. Based on his experience with other cases, the JAG officer outlined the makeup of the board and said that I should receive about 70 to 80 percent disability retirement. This seemed fair to me since I could still do some limited work, so I was ready to go in the room to accept my inevitable forced retirement and move on.

We were in an old wooden building that was once a WWII-era hospital converted into office space. The hearing room was a small, dimly lit twenty-by-fifteen-foot box. Inside that old room, the panel of five officers was seated at a long table opposite the door. I only had about fifteen minutes with them. They asked and I answered questions about the work I was doing for the Army since Vietnam. They asked and I showed them my burn scars on my arms and legs. After that brief appearance, the JAG officer and I waited outside for half an hour to allow them to complete their decision. We returned to get the verdict, and the infantry colonel in charge of the panel summarized it best. Colonel Sullivan looked at me and said, "You were able to walk into this room, and you can walk out of the Army." He told me that I would be separated from the Army with 0 percent disability and therefore no retirement stipend or compensation. In disbelief, I couldn't speak. My JAG lawyer tried to get the panel to look at my medical jacket one more time with the reports from the medical board at Bragg. The colonel was not interested and seemed to be in a hurry. In less than two minutes, we had our decision, and I was on my way out of Fort Gordon and out of the Army.

May 1975

The JAG lawyer assured me that we could appeal the findings, which he thought were biased. But everywhere I turned for help on Bragg, I heard the Fort Gordon board findings repeated back to me as conclusive. I went to my company commander to get the appeals paperwork signed, and he was not at all moved by my pleas for assistance. He just sat back in his office chair and puffed on his cigar while blowing smoke rings toward the ceiling. He signed the appeal, and then he reminded me that he wasn't worried at all about the RIF because, unlike me, he had a regular Army commission. I still had the direct phone line to my old Military Intelligence branch manager Canfield. He was now a lieutenant colonel working at the Pentagon. Since he recruited me out of OCS to the MI branch to fly Mohawks, he had taken care of me numerous times. He told me he had to abide by the findings of the board. When I asked him which one— the Bragg or Gordon board, he simply said the final one. My appeal was rejected this week, and I learned that I was the last officer from my year group with a reserve commission still on active duty.

Large military bases like Fort Bragg are commanded by high-ranking generals, but the people who actually run the installation are sergeants, warrant officers, and Department of the Army (DA) civilians. A warrant officer in charge of the personnel section at the 519th MI Battalion felt that I should be put out of the Army as soon as possible, so I was called last week to the S-1 shop at the battalion headquarters and given a set of out-processing forms. He gave me a short five-day time window to turn in my gear and clear the post. Once I completed the requisite trips to the various office sections getting the necessary stamps proving that I did not owe any money or equipment, I reported to a corps-level personnel battalion for final review. It was the last day of May at three o'clock in the afternoon. I was received by a lieutenant named Timothy Tilsen. Since it was getting late in the afternoon on a Friday and his staff had knocked off early at one, Tilsen told me to come back on Monday to finish out-processing.

After the weekend, I reported back this morning at nine in uniform to complete the process. Lieutenant Tilsen gave me a final DD Form 214 official discharge paper with Friday's date as my last one in the Army.

I asked, "Wait a minute. I'm here today on your orders. Why is this dated last week?"

"The forms were already typed, and I didn't want to change them. You can either accept them or go to the IG."

I was pretty fed up with the personnel section at that point, so I took my DD Form 214 and left the office. By marking the official DD Form 214 with a Friday end date, I would lose the three days of pay— Saturday through Monday— and a fourth day of accrued leave. I was not in a mood to concede anything to the Army at that point. I went straight to the 18th Airborne Corps headquarters to see a case officer in the inspector general's office— a lieutenant colonel. I explained to him that the Army was putting me out, but I was ordered to return after the weekend to finish the clearing process. He looked at my papers and called the officer in charge of all personnel matters. I only heard one side of the phone conversation as he explained my situation. He said, "You're going to have to pay him for that extra duty day" followed by a pause and then, "Hell, yes, he's still here and he's sitting in my office right now in full uniform." When I returned to my personnel section this afternoon, Tilsen was in a much more accommodating mood. He made sure all my new amended paperwork reflects my new final day in the Army — June 2, 1975.

As I drove out of Fort Bragg today, I was stuck in a line of traffic. We were diverted into one lane due to road construction, so I had to sit and wait a while. It was just announced earlier in May that Fort Bragg had initiated a $14 million contract to repave all the streets on base. To me, it's a clear signal. Asphalt is more important than people.

September 1975

Major North's office called me today. It's been three months since they put me out of the Army. They wanted to know why I was not reporting for my medical treatments these past ninety days. I told them that it's because I have been put off of active duty. After a pause, Major North himself came on the line.

"Joe, that's not possible. You are assigned to the medical holding company, and your old unit has no authority to put you off of active duty," he said emphatically.

"Well, they sure put me out on June second. I've got a DD 214 and a DD 215 to prove it."

"As your doctor, I have to sign the release in order for you to exit the medical holding company and active duty."

He said I could file suit and request a return to active duty. I am truly fed up with the Army. People who said they would help me have not done so, and I don't feel like the stress of continuing a battle that already seems lost. Plus, I decided to use my GI Bill benefits this fall and have started a Master of Business Administration (MBA) program at the University of South Carolina in Columbia. I've been making the three-hour drive from Fayetteville to Columbia every Monday and staying with my cousin Elaine and her husband during the week for classes, returning home on Fridays. I'm thinking of going into the financial services industry doing some estate planning when I get done with this MBA program.

February 1976

Last week, I hunted with Cocoa in Bishopville, South Carolina near my uncle's place. It was an unusually cold day, even for early February, and a light misty rain started to fall while we were out on the hunt. The hair on Cocoa's back did something I'd never seen on him before or on any dog. The hair drew up in knots and arranged itself in corn rows. I saw the skin in between, and it looked like the skin was turning purple. Seeing that, I was afraid he might have pneumonia or something. We got him back to the truck and took him over to my uncle's house to get him warmed up.

Once back home in Fayetteville, I was able to take him to a veterinarian. The vet ran a battery of blood tests and confirmed Cocoa has heart worms, which are a problem for dogs in South Carolina. I couldn't imagine not giving Cocoa the treatment. I love him so much. So despite the fact that our only income is $800 a month from Martha Anne's teaching salary and a small GI Bill stipend, I agreed to pay for the $1,200 treatment. Cocoa stayed overnight for it.

I'm having my own internal issues too at the same time Cocoa is sick. During February, I found myself leaving class more and more frequently to pass blood in the bathroom. I even did a full colonoscopy at the hospital, which revealed no obvious causes for the cramping and bleeding. Meanwhile, every weekend when I returned home after classes, I found Cocoa to be a little worse off than when I left him on Monday. Last week, I had my worst episode yet. When I left my class to pass blood, I passed out on the floor of the bathroom. That resulted in me being transported by ambulance to the VA Medical Center in Columbia. Still no clear diagnosis—just presumed to be stomach ulcers. So I made the decision to withdraw from the MBA program this semester. I hope to re-enroll at a later date, but I want to rest and spend time with Cocoa.

★ ★ ★

It's been six weeks since the heart worm treatment, and I feel like I've made a terrible mistake. Cocoa is a shell of his former self. He has never recovered fully from the treatments. We are not hunting at all. The vet told me the treatments killed the heart worms, but those dead worms had to work their way out of the heart and many of them found their way into his lungs. He got to the point where he couldn't walk across the backyard without foaming at the mouth like he had rabies. His breathing became labored. He didn't eat properly, so for the past couple of weeks, I've been holding him in my lap and feeding him Dinty Moore's beef stew from the palm of my hand. It is one of his favorite meals, and I hoped it would help him get stronger and better. Earlier this week, he totally refused to eat and wouldn't even lift his head. I took him to the vet again, and he suggested that we put him down because there's nothing more he could do for him. We don't know his exact age, but the vet estimates him to be nine or ten years old. Then the vet told me he didn't expect Cocoa to survive the heart worm treatments at his age which really made me upset. Why didn't he tell me that before we did the treatment? At least I had a dog and not a ghost when I took him in there the first time.

Yesterday, I took him out to the farm near our house where we have hunted together so many times. My intent was to shoot him. I carried him out across the field and laid him down by the base of a big cherry tree. I then raised the barrel of my .22 caliber rifle and drew a bead on him only to pull right at the last second and shoot the tree beside him. I am an expert shot, but I missed badly. Tears streamed down my face, and I was shaking. With the methodical precision and slow pace of a military funeral gun salute, I fired six rounds over a period of a few minutes. It is a single-shot rifle, so I had to take the time after each shot to re-load my rifle. None of my shots hit Cocoa. I just couldn't do it. So instead, I left him there tied to the tree while I ran home to get him his water bowl and some food.

When I returned about a half hour later, Cocoa was dead. Slumped in a heap at the base of that cherry tree, he died alone without me. It felt like a part of me died, too. I already had my spade shovel out there from the first trip into the field, so I worked the soil just clear of the root structure to dig him a nice rectangular grave. I buried Cocoa there with no other marker than that big cherry tree pockmarked with my rifle shots.

June 1976

It's been almost exactly a year since I was forced out of the active Army. Today, I received a call from a major named Ted Mosh at the First US Army Intelligence School at Fort Bragg.

"Captain Tallon, we'd like to have you come to Bragg in the summer to teach a course to our incoming class of officers. We heard you did an outstanding job as an instructor here before, and we'd like to get you back. Are you interested?"

"No."

He continued, "First lieutenants and captains serving as staff intel officers are coming to the class. You can be a reserve officer and do your summer duty here at our school. We'll give you reserve points so you can make a good retirement year."

"No sir, I'm not really interested."

"You were highly recommended by the 18th Airborne Corps and the 5th Special Forces Group. You're an intel officer with combat experience, which is always a great value to our curriculum. They said you'd be an excellent instructor."

"I appreciate the offer, but no thanks."

"We'll pay you full per diem and local mileage as well. What do you think?"

"Uh, no. I'm planning to move back to Charleston this summer."

"Well, in addition to per diem, we'll give you full pay and allowances while you're working. You can live on our dime in the Appartel in Fayetteville or Carolina Trace or at home and we'll pay your mileage as well."

I paused for a moment to digest what he was saying. When I wanted to stay in active duty, the Army booted me out. Now the Reserves are eager to recruit me. It seemed like the more I resisted the more he offered. I couldn't help myself.

"Okay, Major," I said. "I'll give it a try this summer."

★ ★ ★

In these first two weeks of summer, the officers at the Fort Bragg Intel School have been checking me out as an instructor as much as I've been checking out this new opportunity. When I was on active duty, I viewed the reserve soldiers as part-timers who weren't serious professionals. Their general appearance looked sloppy to me. Wrinkled uniforms that did not fit properly seemed to match their lackadaisical attitudes. However, the reserve instructors working at the intel school have changed my perception rather quickly. Most of the reservists teaching at the school this summer are college professors or high school teachers during the normal academic year. So, I quickly learned the craft from these men, as I only had to teach a couple of fifty-minute blocks in these initial orientation weeks. The schedule afforded me time to observe the other instructors. I learned the most from Mac Miller, who is a University of Florida professor. He seems to be able to bring any subject to life, and he is happy to share some of his teaching strategies with me. Plus, we have assistant instructors for every course who pull requested materials from the library and help prepare handouts for us. We have an archive of existing lesson plans, too. I enjoyed the two weeks more than I thought I would. Sure enough, they invited me back for the next summer of 1977 when I'd likely be teaching four to five weeks in May and June depending upon the enrollment numbers. I'm back in the Army again, albeit the reserves this time.

January 1977

Last weekend, I took part in a big New Year's Eve deer hunt near Summerville on a tract of land owned by the Boy Scouts. With more than 3,400 acres on the Ashley River, there was plenty of great forest land for the deer to roam. It was the last full day of the hunting season, and the Boy Scouts authorized a controlled hunt with state game wardens present to monitor. My father-in-law works closely with the Boy Scouts, and he was our connection for me, my Daddy, and

Roy getting an invitation. For nearly a year now, I have been working closely with him selling Kansas City Life Insurance products. Earlier this month, I spent a week in Kansas City for training, and it was twenty below zero. I nearly froze my tail off, so I was happy to be back home for the holidays. My father-in-law doesn't like to hunt, but he sure does like to talk. So he came out—not to shoot deer, but to shoot the bull, as he likes to say.

At sunrise on Saturday morning, the air was clear and cold and just above freezing when we began the hunt, which was really us waiting for deer to run through our sector. By two in the afternoon, the shooting was quiet, and the hunt was called off by the game wardens. For the day, there were forty-two deer killed, evenly split between bucks and does. All of the deer were brought to one of the Boy Scout campground areas to be dressed. The temperature was not much higher than forty degrees, so it was like working in a meat locker. The recently killed deer steamed, especially when we opened them up. With that many deer to clean, there was plenty of work to do, and the men divided up the labor rather quickly. About twenty or so hunters worked directly on the deer while some left to gather the dogs, and others started digging deep holes with post-hole diggers to bury the guts. Others just stood on the periphery and talked about the hunt or rotated in when the gutters got tired. Since I killed two of the deer myself, I jumped right in with my knife.

We had plenty of meat to go around; every hunter could take a half a deer if they wanted. I took the meat from the buck I shot, which was the most deer meat I'd ever taken home from a hunt before. It wasn't until after darkness set in that we finished all the skinning. Having started the day well before sunrise, it was exhausting, but my body did not feel the full impact of the exertion until I put my skinning knife away. We were selecting and dividing up the deer halves when the smell of the entire site started to overpower me. Some of the hunters had started a wood fire in one of the camp's fire pits. The smell was eerily similar to the burning human flesh that I had encountered in the Blood Square of Da Nang. I closed my eyes, and I could actually see the Vietnamese women and children walking toward my truck with such desperate looks in their eyes. The smell quickly became nauseating, and I just wanted to take my deer home and get washed clean.

January 1979

Last year, my cousin Larry Cobb's half-brother Junior Cobb made $15,000 in ten days of shrimping. That's a lot of money, and we are definitely looking for a strategy to make some money. If an eighth-grade dropout like Junior could do it, Larry and I definitely thought we could. My cousin Larry was known by his family and friends in high school as Bubba, and the name seems to fit his persona well. He's thick and stocky with strong hands and a strong back—at least it was before he broke it. That's another thing we have in common. We both broke our backs resulting in disability ratings. My broken back was from crashing *in* a plane, but his came after crashing *off* a plane. While working for Delta Airlines in Charleston, a high-pressure refueling hose suddenly disconnected and knocked him off the plane's wing. He took an early retirement buy-out from Delta and began collecting disability. My appeal of the Army's initial 0 percent rating yielded a 30 percent determination and a small monthly VA stipend of $220, which I am working on appealing yet again.

The biggest impediment for us entering the shrimping business was the fact that neither one of us had a boat. One of the benefits of living in a coastal community like Charleston is that there are plenty of old boats around, so it didn't take us long to find one we could afford. In February, we paid $1,500 for an old twenty-four-foot Lone Star boat on Sullivan's Island that has been used for commercial crabbing. It's seen better days, but it has an operational four-cylinder Chevy II inboard engine. It needs a lot of work to get it ready for the opening of the shrimp season.

Bubba, who goes by Larry now that he's older, has done all of the welding on the boat, and since I have some experience in carpentry, I've done most of the woodwork. We purchased a hydraulic winch and designed an A-frame system to haul and lift the main net. While we got most of the modifications on the boat done ourselves, we had no expertise with the essential tools of the trade. So, we went to an old shrimper in Mount Pleasant and hired him to make our net, wooden doors, bridle, and tickler chain. To be legal, we also obtained a license to land and sell as well as a commercial captain's license. It has taken us twice the time we expected and the better part of three months to get the boat rigged and ready for the season.

May 1979

Opening day of the early roe shrimp season arrived today, and we were ready—at least we thought so. We were convinced that the reports of winter shrimp kill were surely overstated even though it was one of the coldest winters on record. We pushed out from the dock in Toler's Cove and headed toward Charleston harbor ready to haul in an abundant mess of shrimp. I thrust the throttle wide open, but, even so, the boat didn't break ten knots loaded down as it was with so much gear. I sarcastically named her the *Blue Bullet*.

Outside the harbor jetties, we dropped our net just off the Morris Island beach, the first barrier island south of Charleston. To locals with a boat, the uninhabited island is a haven for camping, shell collecting, and fishing. The southern end is marked by a tall, brick, red and white striped decommissioned lighthouse built in 1876. We are able to pull close to the beach without worrying about swimmers, and all we have to do is avoid running aground or getting our net hung up in the rocks. We have an advantage because our boat is much smaller than most shrimpers. On our first drag, it was a challenge to get the net and all the gear out, but we did it. Or, more accurately, the hydraulic winch did it. The gear includes two large wooden doors that help spread open the net and a hundred feet of heavy tickler chain. That's a lot of weight—too much to manhandle, especially given our compromised bodies.

Each pull should get in a full ninety-minute drag, but it was hard to resist pulling it up early to see what kind of catch we had. We held out, though. After ninety minutes, we tackled the hard work of getting the net back onto the stern deck so we could dump the contents into the sorting trough. With great anticipation, we pulled up the loaded net. Captured within was a mess of jellyballs, translucent with purple edges and the size of grapefruits and cantaloupes. There were hundreds of them. Added to that was a mix of crabs—horseshoe, blue, spider, stone, and speckled—more crabs than I'd ever seen in one place. Into the fluttering flurry of sea life were thick strands of seaweed and random sea trash. We had just about everything come out of that net but shrimp.

We made four pulls today, and it was exhausting work. When we returned to Toler's Cove to tie up the boat, we had a five-gallon bucket with three inches of ocean water covering the bottom. Swimming around inside were exactly fourteen shrimp. The get-rich-quick shrimp bonanza we expected did not land on our deck this morning.

Back at the cove, its namesake, Mr. Toler, was standing there watching us dock the *Blue Bullet*. He was a long-time shrimper himself, a salty old sea captain with leathery skin and gray stubble on his face. He's at the cove almost every day wearing his faded blue captain's hat with the scrambled egg-style braiding on the bill.

He peered into the bucket, and without removing the cigarette from the corner of his mouth, pointed a gnarly finger in the bucket.

"You've got two hoppers, a cotton shrimp, some grass shrimp, and some hardbacks, but no white shrimp," he said.

"What's a white shrimp?" I asked.

"That's your money shrimp. If you ain't catching da white roe shrimp, you might as well stay home. What you got here is only good for bait. You got about enough to catch dinner for one of you."

★   ★   ★

I don't know if old man Toler likes us or if he just feels sorry for us, but he sketched out a map to show us the *hangs* where all the old shipwrecks and snags are submerged off the shore of Morris Island so we can avoid tearing up our nets and gear while we are dragging. Our luck is about to change. I can feel it.

After two weeks of steady effort with low results, we cut back to twice a week until the shrimp start running. Plus, I'm still teaching a few weeks each summer at Fort Bragg for my reserve commitment. With fuel at thirty-five to forty cents a gallon, we'll sell anything we can find a buyer for. We peddle blue crabs and conchs to seafood markets in the poorer sections of Charleston. We even sell the sand dollars that get caught in our nets to local arts and crafts stores. We typically sell four to six bushels of blue crabs a day plus a five-gallon bucket of live conchs. It's been a couple of weeks, and we've managed to cover expenses with a whopping daily profit of about $1.25. Hardly sufficient with our first baby due any day now. It took us well into June before putting 100 pounds of shrimp or more on the boat became commonplace for us, but this bounty presented a new problem. Independent and not tied up to a company dock, we had to find our own markets to sell the catch. We had six or seven seafood markets and a few Chinese restaurants that we called upon to unload the catch in the afternoons. When these markets weren't enough, I sold to my friends, family, and neighbors. In a short period of time, I amassed a list of 110 customers who were buying in bulk for their freezers. With a scale hung on the corner of the tailgate and our pickup truck loaded with forty-eight-quart coolers, we became a mobile seafood market. Old Bubba Cobb might match his brother Junior's bounty after all.

June 20, 1979

We arrived early at Trident Hospital as scheduled. Martha Anne was still not experiencing labor when we left our house this morning, even though her due date was more than two weeks ago. But Dr. Putney said no matter what, today is the day. When we got to our room, Martha Anne changed into a hospital gown and they broke her water and started an IV with the drug Pitocin to induce labor. There was very little amniotic fluid remaining, which caused a little concern for our nursing staff, but we sat there playing rummy with an old deck of cards for hours. They came in and checked every hour or two, but for the first eight hours, nothing much happened. Then around four in the afternoon, things started to get painful for Martha Anne. I held her hand as she squeezed her fingernails deep into my palms. At some point in the more intense hours, a nurse told us our parents had arrived and were in the waiting room. Dr. Putney came in to check more regularly, but Martha Anne's labor was not progressing. After another four or five hours of labor, Martha Anne was exhausted and there was little of the precious amniotic fluid remaining. Dr. Putney recommended she go into surgery for a caesarean. Even when I underwent emergency surgery after being shot down, I was never as fearful as I was in that moment with my wife and unborn child at risk.

Just after nine o'clock, a nurse found me, my folks, and Martha Anne's parents in the waiting room. Martha Anne and the baby came through like champs. We have a boy! On our way to the nursery, we saw a nurse wheeling a bassinet down the hallway. Inside, was our baby—all eight pounds, nine ounces of him, a full head of dark hair sticking out around the edges of a soft blue cap!

"He's definitely got your round Tallon head, Joe," my Daddy laughed.

We weren't allowed to touch him yet, so instead had to content ourselves with pressing our noses against the glass window of the nursery. I was tickled beyond belief and started singing a song I made up on the spot.

"That's my boy, that's my baby boy. That's my bundle of joy."

I could hardly wait to see Martha Anne to share our happiness. But she was another full hour in the recovery room before they finally let us see her. What a day of surging emotions: excitement, fear, worry, and now joy.

★　★　★

On the third day in the hospital, the old lady from the Dorchester County office was getting quite put out with us for not having selected a name yet. She'd been coming in twice a day asking us, and they weren't going to let us take the baby home until we had a name chosen for the documents. It seemed like every name we came up with drew an objection from one of our parents or from Martha Anne. On the fourth day, we were watching television in Martha Anne's hospital room and *Gunsmoke* came on. We heard Festus call out for Matt Dillon. We looked at each other at the same moment—Matthew! Neither of us could find anything wrong with the name. We paired it with Alexander, a family name on my side, so his initials spell out M.A.T.

August 1979

Our shrimp catches have been getting bigger this month. A little after noon today, we were trawling our usual stretch of beach along Morris Island down near the southern end with the lighthouse. Long ago, the ocean eroded away the end of the island, leaving the tall lighthouse isolated in the waves. The white paint is fading a bit and the fencing around the base is rotting away, but the lighthouse stands defiantly like a sentry. Dark storm clouds stacked up on the horizon north of us. All of the bigger shrimp boats had it on their radar, and the radio chatter among them all said the storm would move inland to James Island and miss us out on the ocean, so we kept trawling.

Around one in the afternoon, the large and violent thunderstorm approached quickly. We could see waterspouts—eerily intense tornados over water. They connected to the dark low-hanging clouds that were moving directly in our direction as fast as the adrenalin surged inside our veins. We knew we had to get the doors and nets in the boat as quickly as possible. We had a makeshift canvas roof constructed to give ourselves some shade, and the wind began whipping the canvas so hard it threatened to rip apart. Together we wrestled that canvas down before the wind got it. That normally simple task took more than fifteen critical minutes in the developing gale. We struggled to get all the gear on board, even as we chugged along slowly with the net out. The drag from the net was bogging us down— the only way to get any forward speed to get us to the relative safety of the harbor meant we had to get that net back on board. We worked frantically, the wind and waves growing in strength. The seas offshore were reported at twelve to fourteen feet, and waves inshore were cresting above the gunwales when we finally got that net on the boat. As we pushed closer and closer to the breakers rolling onto the Morris Island beach, we were in less than ten feet of water. If we hit bottom, it could crack the hull and sink the boat.

The direction we wanted to travel was parallel down the beach and back toward the harbor opening, but that was off the port side and not an option. It seems we only had one choice and that was to turn the boat into the teeth of the storm and head out to the ocean. The rain and seawater sprayed over the windshield with such force that I had to duck my face down to keep water from pouring into my nostrils. Larry kept yelling up at me to turn the wheel. I already had the steering wheel fully turned right until it clicked stop, but the *Blue Bullet* wasn't turning. The storm swells coming in from the ocean threatened to turn the boat sharply parallel to the beach at any moment, and if that happened, the waves would cause the boat to roll and capsize. We were at full throttle and seemed to be going nowhere.

The old bilge pump happened to fail last week, a stroke of good fortune as it turns out. On Friday, we spent a half day installing a new pump. As much water as was coming into the boat, I was hopeful we had a fighting chance of staying ahead of it. It was a relief to look back over my shoulder at the stern and see a stream of water shooting out like a firehose. The new bilge line was pumping like a champ. Without it we would have sunk by now.

Suddenly, a particularly large wave slapped the bow of the boat, and I was jolted out of the captain's chair so hard it knocked the wind out of me, but I kept my grip on the steering wheel. I yelled back for Larry to come help me steer. He just yelled back at me to turn right. With each successive wave testing the limits of the boat, Larry's yells grew higher and higher in pitch, achieving notes that I'd never heard from him before. I felt him fastening life jackets to my legs, and I yelled, "Are you trying to save my feet?"

He yelled back, "No, I'm just trying to make it easier to find your body when we sink!"

I looked down and saw that he fastened a life preserver around each of my legs since I couldn't release the wheel long enough to get one over my shoulders. Minutes passed like hours, and we held our breath each time a wave clobbered the boat, many of them breaking and crashing over the bow. We worked our way back down the coastline, slowly, making short left turns during the troughs in between the violent swells. Exhausted, we entered the harbor through the Dynamite Hole opening at the south end of the jetties.

The rock jetties provided enough breakwater to stymie the large ocean swells, so I finally was able to loosen my death grip on the wheel. Near Fort Sumter, we came upon a yellow seventeen-foot boat with five older men huddled under the small canvas top fastened with snaps to the boat's windshield. The boat's engine had quit on them in the storm and they dropped anchor in the harbor hoping to ride it out. We hitched on to their front cleats and towed them back to Toler's Cove with us. When they got back to the marina and tied up their boat, all five of them got out and kissed the dock. One of them handed me the keys to the boat.

"You can have the boat," he said. "We ain't coming back."

It felt like we had just dodged a bullet in the *Blue Bullet*. I told my cousin that I can't buy enough insurance to get me back out on that boat again.

I retired from the shrimping business today.

★　★　★

Just two short weeks into my shrimping retirement, my cousin came over to the house very excited. He wanted me to go to Coburg Creek with him to look at a boat. I agreed to go take a look with him, but I made it clear that I wasn't going to be heading out on it. We arrived to find a 1966 Luhr's thirty-two-foot sports fisherman boat for sale by the original owner. The *Bridget* is her name. Despite all my assertions that I was just looking and not going out on another boat with my cousin, I found myself that very afternoon out on the water for a test drive with the owner. For a boat that size, the $10,000 asking price is actually pretty affordable. Plus, it has a lot of advantages over the *Blue Bullet*. It has a six-cylinder engine that provides greater horsepower and would be able to pull two nets in tandem rather than just one. It sits much higher up from the water line, a good four to five feet from the water's surface to the gunnels. It contains both an enclosed cabin and a flying bridge to steer and operate the boat. It is set up for sport fishing, but there is a lot to like about it. Much to my own surprise, I committed $5,000 this very week as my share in the purchase of the boat. I have agreed to go back out in that boat if we don't lose sight of land.

★ ★ ★

"Holy crap! A yacht shrimper!" That was the call that came over the radio from a salty local shrimper named Junior Magwood. The radio was abuzz with commentary from other shrimpers as we put our nets out behind the *Bridget* for the first time. They speculated that we would only be shrimping long enough to fill our freezers and then be done. We just didn't look the part of committed lifers in a boat that still looked too much like a recreational vessel. It is the tail end of the season because it took us a full six weeks to convert the *Bridget* from a sportfishing boat to a shrimper. With the mild temperatures in South Carolina, it's not a problem to keep shrimping well into fall. We used the lessons learned earlier in the season on the *Blue Bullet* to immediately begin putting large numbers of late season white shrimp on the deck.

It hasn't been the bonanza that Junior experienced last season, but the new boat is working well. I've enrolled in a master's in educational leadership program since I don't know how sustainable life as a shrimper will be now that I have a son at home. Since I head to the Citadel for night classes up to four times a week, my schedule is rough. I'm usually up at three thirty to be at the docks before five. After shrimping until two thirty or so, we have to refuel the boat and sell off the catch. Then I have just enough time to shower and grab a quick bite to eat before driving downtown to campus for night classes.

April 1980

It was nice to shut it down over the winter with the long hours of shrimping and schooling taking a toll on me but preparing the *Bridget* this spring has meant more hard work. Today, I drove over to the boat from Summerville with Matthew in his car seat and wedged into the jump seat of my new Datsun king cab pickup. I traded my yellow two-door Datsun pickup for this 1980 king cab so I could have more room for the baby. Martha Anne is teaching again this year at the high school, so I'm helping out with childcare any day that I can.

Matthew is an early walker at nine months. I figured he could toddle around the boat deck while we worked. As I pulled into the

Toler's Cove Marina this morning, I smelled the acrid aroma of baby spit-up. I realized Matthew must have gotten car sick riding sideways on the king cab jump seat. When I pulled him out of the truck, Old Man Toler came over to greet me, and seeing that I had a messy problem on my hands, he said, "Looks like you might-a fed that boy a little too much, Joe."

The ever-helpful Mr. Toler took Matthew's striped collared shirt and little blue shorts over to his own shrimp boat—a seventy-two-foot behemoth trawler with a full-sized kitchen and laundry on board. While Matthew's clothes washed on the old shrimp boat, he toddled around the deck of the *Bridget* barefoot in just a diaper, exploring and poking his fingers into every nook and cranny.

PART III

* * *

THE QUEST

Author's note: This final section is a first-person account written solely by Matthew A. Tallon.

MY FINAL ARMY job before leaving Germany was as an adjutant for the battalion staff. One of my critical duties was to ensure that the soldiers in the battalion received their earned awards in a timely manner. In this capacity, I reviewed legions of citations and often was the officer reading the citations to deserving troops. That the threads of my life organized themselves in a way that put me in this position with this responsibility seemed more than coincidental. I knew only glancingly of my dad's story. I knew he was shot down on the last day of our country's involvement in the ground war. I knew of his injuries, wounds that have plagued him every day of his life since that day. I knew he had not been awarded the Purple Heart—but I didn't know why.

After his retirement from teaching high school, my dad became very active in his local Disabled American Veterans (DAV) chapter in Summerville, South Carolina, where he raised money to help veterans get access to treatment at local VA hospitals. He proved to be quite good at it, using his sales skills honed over several years of selling life insurance policies with his father-in-law Joe Francese. By 2005, the commander of the local chapter wanted to help my dad pursue an appeal for his Purple Heart medal. The DAV had active contacts with veterans' advocates.

At the same time, my dad was taking his dad Harry to a seemingly endless parade of medical appointments, dealing with the effects of congestive heart failure. Often, his appointments were at the VA hospital in Charleston, the same place my dad volunteered time with the DAV. A smoker for decades, Harry told anyone who would listen that he would have taken much better care of himself had he known he was going to live so long. He promised my dad, "I'm not going to die until I see you get that Purple Heart."

Harry tapped his long-time acquaintanceship with local US Representative Henry Brown to make the appeal for his son's Purple Heart. "If anybody can do something for you, Joe, it's Henry Brown." Henry and Harry worked together at Piggly Wiggly Carolina Company for years—Harry on the road selling Greenbax stamps and Henry in the office supervising an early punch card version of computer tracking. In the course of a typical work week, they didn't see each other too often, but they got to know one another on dove hunts in the fall season. Joe's meeting with the congressman's representatives (Henry wasn't present) didn't yield a breakthrough because the military had no records of the crash, but Henry's assistant, Earl Copeland, did say an appeal could be filed with witness statements.

According to Army Regulation 600-8-22: "The Purple Heart is awarded in the name of the president of the United States to any member of an armed force or any civilian national of the United States who, while serving under competent authority in any capacity with one of the US Armed Services after 5 April 1917, has been wounded or killed, or who has died or may hereafter die after being wounded."

Service members cannot be recommended for the Purple Heart like they are for other medals. A Purple Heart is an entitlement reserved for those wounded in the line of duty under enemy fire.

The key issue that commanders must take into consideration is the degree to which the enemy caused the injury. Examples of injuries or wounds which clearly do not qualify for award of the Purple Heart: "Accidents, to include explosive, aircraft, vehicular, and other accidental wounding not related to or caused by enemy action."

When I looked up the official information about Daniel Richards, the deadly crash was categorized in the military record as *non-hostile*. And that was the crux of the matter. The Army didn't recognize the Mohawk flown by my dad that day was shot down by enemy fire.

For his part, my dad never wavered in his conviction that his OV-1 Mohawk went down in the early hours of the morning of

August 12, 1972, because of enemy fire. The final words of Daniel Richards were seared in his memory: "Sir, we've been hit in the number two engine."

My dad figured the surface-to-air missile that brought down his plane was probably a shoulder-fired SA-7 Grail, which had become popular with the North Vietnamese and Viet Cong by that late point in the war.

Computers may have transformed American life in the past half century, but my dad has never embraced them, so I took up an online search to help him track down witnesses. With him working through his channels, and me working through mine, we immersed ourselves in the quest. I helped to locate my dad's former motor sergeant, Larry Dubose, and his former commander Roger Smith. Phone conversations between those men and my dad ensued.

In 2007, a packet of information containing witness statements and medical records was hand-delivered by my cousin, Tim Bootle, who had a high-level security clearance to the White House Veterans Affairs (VA) liaison. No single phone call or email or in-person conversation necessarily moved the needle, but over a period of many months, the information eventually got into the hands of people who could make a difference. My dad fed the belly of the bureaucracy with paperwork requests. Forms would get filed and then get lost. He would file them again. That's one of the first lessons I learned in the Army—make copies of everything and assume the bureaucracy is going to lose the first copy of any submission.

A couple months after the materials handoff, the VA liaison at the White House asked my dad to sign an affidavit authorizing a lawyer from the AMVETS (American Veterans) organization to represent him at the hearing. He was happy to authorize a pro bono lawyer to be his advocate. The DAV had helped him to get his appeal this far, and now another veterans' organization was taking up the fight.

The AMVETS representative told him that he thought his written testimony detailing what happened in the cockpit was strong. He said that his account was consistent with the way others described how an aircraft behaved when a missile strike occurred immediately after takeoff.

Ultimately, though, the ruling would depend upon the five-judge panel at the US Court of Appeals for the Armed Forces. The AMVETS rep assured him that his written statement was sufficient, that being at the hearing in person was not necessary. My dad was relieved he did not need to make the trip to DC. He was still full of skepticism that this process would yield anything.

On June 30, 2008, a small parcel was delivered by the US Postal Service to his home in Summerville. My dad carried the package inside and sat in his recliner. It was a few long minutes before he took out his pocketknife, cut the adhesive seal, and opened the box.

My dad repacked the box and got in his car and drove the ten miles to his father's house. Harry was seated in his favorite chair in a corner of his darkened den.

Wordlessly, my dad placed the package on Harry's lap. Harry opened the shipping box. Inside was a blue soft-leather presentation case with *United States of America* embossed in gold leaf. The medal inside the case was cool and smooth to the touch, the edges in the shape of a heart. Harry ran his fingertip over the silhouette of George Washington. My grandfather, normally full of witty words and one-liners, said nothing. He stared at the medal.

"Turn it over, Daddy," my dad said.

Harry turned it over. Engraved on the back of the medal in capital letters was his son's name. Harry beat back tears.

"You can go ahead and die now, old man," my dad said.

"No, I ain't ready to go yet," he replied.

A month later I got the call while I was driving a moving truck through Connecticut, transporting the last of my household goods to Boston. Harry was dead.

★ ★ ★

On a warm autumn day in November, I arrived, along with my family, at my dad's alma mater, now known as Charleston Southern University (CSU). It was a Wednesday, and the student body was gathered for the weekly chapel service. Harry had been dead for a little over three months by that point.

My brother Josh and I both wore our green class A uniforms. Mine had the Indianhead patch of the 2nd Infantry Division on the left shoulder—my last unit in Korea. Josh's uniform had the famous double AA patch of the 82nd Airborne Division on both the left and right shoulders, signifying his combat deployment to Iraq with the 3rd Brigade in 2005. My dad wore his green class A uniform as well, complete with military intelligence insignia on the lapels and the silver oak leaf rank of lieutenant colonel on the epaulets. Despite being unceremoniously sent out of the Army in 1975, my dad had found a way to have a successful career in the reserves, serving for many years as an instructor at Fort Bragg but then transitioning into some interesting summer assignments at the Pentagon and in Heidelberg. In a funny twist, he ended his military career in 1996 working as the intelligence officer for the 315th Airlift Wing at Charleston Air Force Base, a place he once imagined himself serving as a pilot. We joined our parents in the front row of Lightsey Chapel while a cluster of close friends and family filled the next two rows. A few members of the CSU Air Force ROTC were present and in uniform.

The event had been organized by Rick Brewer, the vice president of student affairs and athletics. After a brief introduction, he called my dad, Josh, and me to the seats on the stage next to the podium. The head of the ROTC detachment read the official citations, and Josh and I alternated pinning the medals on my dad's chest. I attached the Air Medal and the Cross of Gallantry. Josh, as a combat veteran himself, went last, pinning on the Purple Heart. The act of saluting my dad on that stage reminded me of my commissioning ceremony years prior when he read me the oath of office on the day before my graduation from Duke. That was the first time I saluted him when wearing my uniform, and the Purple Heart ceremony would likely be the last.

Holding a sheaf of papers in his hands, my dad walked to the dark wood podium, a wooden cross nailed to it. He turned to face the chapel full of people. At first when he didn't speak, I thought he might be choked up. I caught my brother's eye, and we exchanged apprehensive looks. My dad was looking at the audience. He cleared his throat and finally started speaking, his voice strong and steady.

"There has never been a popular war. The War of 1812 was Mr. Madison's War; the Civil War was Mr. Lincoln's War; and the First World War was Mr. Wilson's War. In each of those wars, citizens were called out to serve. When I was called by my nation to serve, I had a choice to make, and I decided to stand in the gap and serve my country. You are going to face moments in your life when you have to stand for something."

I'd heard similar sentiments from him before, but it was different seeing him address an auditorium packed with college students. Like so many of his generation, the Vietnam War presented an ethical dilemma for my dad. I'd recently learned about the story of his visit to Dr. Carpenter, his religious studies professor, when he ameliorated my dad's internal conflict about being a Christian and going to war.

When my dad finished speaking, Josh and I exited the stage with him and returned to our seats on floor level. Everything went smoothly. In less than fifteen minutes my dad's hard-won recognition had been accomplished. The Purple Heart hung on the panel of medals and ribbons on his left breast. Harry wasn't there to see it in person, but my granny Bertha was there. We all sat quietly through the remaining forty-five minutes of the chapel service. Afterwards, our group of about forty friends and family met upstairs in the Gold Room for a reception. We had on display my dad's Nomex flight suit along with some of his other Vietnam memorabilia, like a Mohawk pilot's party uniform and his misfit headband. The display also included a few framed photographs from 1972 showing him standing with other pilots alongside Mohawks. In the center of the table was a large Publix sheet cake with a Purple Heart medal artfully frosted on top. My dad once again thanked the invited guests for joining us.

★   ★   ★

Growing up, I didn't know what caused the injuries to his body or the scars on his arms and legs, but even as a very young kid, I knew something really bad must have happened to my dad. I saw it each time he got out of the shower and methodically applied Vaseline intensive care lotion to the grafted areas of scarred skin left mottled and hairless. I saw it in the calm non-reaction he once had when he leaned a weed eater against the gutter of our house and the string whipped ferociously against the grafted skin on his shin leaving multiple red welts in the numb nerveless skin. I saw it when he occasionally pulled up from a task, straightened his lower back, and quietly winced in pain. We spent a lot of time together working in the yard, and long before I was ever allowed to push the real lawnmower myself, I had my own Fisher Price corn popper toy mower, which I pushed around the lawn a few steps behind my dad as he cut the grass. I loved the smell then and still love the smell today of a freshly cut lawn. As much as the yard work was simply required of me, whether it was picking up pinecones or magnolia blossoms or weeds, I think I also wanted to please my dad and do the tasks well. When I wasn't quite six years old, I tried to help him lift a lawnmower out of the back of his Datsun pickup. My job was to hold the front of the mower by the tops of the front wheels, and as I bent down to place the wheels on the driveway, my dad suddenly let go of the backend causing both the mower and him to crash to the pavement. I immediately thought I had done something wrong. He screamed out in pain. A neighbor came running from two houses down, and we somehow got him inside to his bedroom.

When the ambulance came to retrieve him, the paramedics couldn't fit him through his bedroom door on the fracture board, so firemen were called in to remove the bedroom windows. My mom, my brother Josh, and I watched as firemen slid him out the rectangular hole which used to be windows on two fire ladders that served as slide guides. Josh was not quite three years old yet but observing the scene he asked my mom, "Is daddy dead?" He wasn't dead at all, but he was the tall and strong one in the family, the one who made sure all the doors were locked in the house at night and who reached things for my mom on the highest shelves and sharpened the kitchen knives and lit the kerosene heater. He was the one who pushed the boat off the trailer to go fishing and the one who cut and split the logs for the fireplace. Yet it wasn't a chainsaw that felled the tall live oak of our family but an old lawnmower and a bad back for which I really didn't understand the cause. In the self-centered world of a five-year-old, I thought that I was the cause and that I had made him hurt bad enough to go to the hospital. I didn't know the back problems started in Vietnam on the same night they deactivated the last remaining battalion of American combat troops at the tail end of a drip, drip, drip fighting faucet that the country had been slowly and painfully trying to cut off for years. I didn't know about the Mohawk or the night of the crash or the Martin-Baker ejection seat or even the presence of a man named Daniel Richards.

It must not have been long after this appearance of physical fragility in my dad that I learned he was an Army officer in the Vietnam War. It was an immense source of pride for me to say my dad fought in a war, even though I understood precious little of what he did. At some point along the way, I learned he was a pilot, but it didn't stop me from wondering if he had killed anyone while he was there. I had seen him literally hold life in the palms of his hands—not human life—but life, nonetheless.

We did have one pet during childhood—a goldfish. I actually went through three or four different goldfish before I finally figured out how to keep one alive. I used the special drops to make the tap water safe for the fish, but there never seemed to be anything too special about those dechlorination drops. Each new pet goldfish always died pretty quickly. So, at the urging and advice of my parents, I devised a new technique. I captured rainwater in five-gallon buckets strategically placed in my backyard, after which I painstakingly strained the collected rainwater from the buckets into empty plastic gallon milk jugs using paper towels and a plastic funnel. Sometimes green algae caught in the paper towels, but if I bottled the water soon enough after a rainstorm, it didn't have too much funky stuff in it.

As soon as I started using the new rainwater collection system, my luck changed after I came home from school one day with a goldfish in a glass mason jar. We named him Rocky since he had a habit of picking up the rainbow-colored rocks in the bottom of his bowl, rolling them around in his little mouth, and then spitting them back out again. I kept Rocky in a wide circular but flat glass bowl on top of our television set. The set was one of those large, heavy Zenith sets from the mid-70s that looked like a piece of wooden furniture as much as it looked like a television. We didn't have to worry about it getting stolen since it would have taken four grown men to carry it out of the house. The large wooden top of the Zenith had a VCR, some family photo frames, and plenty of open space where I placed my fishbowl atop a white lace doily. Rocky was my only pet, and it was my responsibility to keep him fed and to keep his bowl clean.

Rocky was a pretty resilient goldfish. He developed a sore on the left side of his body near his tail that looked like an erupted wart, but it didn't seem to faze him. I placed a ceramic street sign in his rock bed, and he didn't seem to mind that either. Rocky didn't seem to care that I often stretched it a week or so past when I should have cleaned out his bowl before I finally washed it out thoroughly and gave him some fresh strained rainwater. After my dad caught his eleven-and-a-half-pound trophy largemouth bass in 1987, Rocky could stare up above his Zenith platform and see the giant bass mounted to a piece of driftwood flanked by lily pads. Even having a monster fish looking down on him from the wall above didn't seem to faze him.

Then, after three years of Rocky enjoying a solitary goldfish life in his round realm of rainwater, we left for a short overnight trip. We weren't supposed to be gone more than two days and a single night, so I put a little extra food in Rocky's bowl before we left and didn't think too much more about it. When we returned late at night the second day, we were all looking to get to bed quickly. It was after eleven, and we'd been in the car for a really long time. The lights were off in our den when we passed through, and none of us thought to check on Rocky as we passed by in the dark. I brushed my teeth and put on my pajamas before I remembered to go back and see if I should feed Rocky a little bit more food before bed. When I turned on a den lamp and looked at the top of the Zenith, I immediately saw that Rocky's bowl was totally abandoned. I panicked a bit, and I couldn't find him anywhere. I looked all around the top of the television, and he was nowhere to be found. I did see that there were some yellowish gold stains on the white doily so it looked to me like he must have jumped from the bowl. I had some tears forming in my eyes, and even though I couldn't find Rocky anywhere, I thought he might be behind the giant television or on the floor underneath it. My mom came in to check on me and found me lying on my stomach searching on the floor. She saw how upset I was at the loss of Rocky and went to the back of our house to get my dad. When they came in with a flashlight, they found Rocky pretty quickly tucked behind the VCR in the mess of cables that ran through a wooden circle cut in the back of the Zenith. I carefully picked him up, and his body was dry and stiff. He felt a lot lighter than I remembered him to be. We had no way to know how long it was since he jumped from the bowl, but it had to have been a while. Both he and the white lace fabric of the doily was dry.

My dad took Rocky from my hand and dropped him into the fishbowl, and I watched as he placed Rocky in between his thumb, his forefinger, and middle finger and circulated him round and round the bowl. "What are you doing?" I asked. "I'm running some water over his gills," came his response. Minutes passed by slowly, and he continually massaged the fish with his fingers as he circumnavigated the bowl. I wondered how long he was going to try this, but I just sat silently and stared. I felt sick that I hadn't put something over the top of the bowl while we were gone. Maybe a piece of Saran wrap would have done the trick. Five, six, seven minutes went by, and my dad leaned his left elbow against the top of our Zenith as he continued to circulate Rocky with his right hand. We were all tired from the road trip, and I wondered how long he was going to keep this up. I felt like I was going through the stages of grief while I watched him. Then after maybe nine minutes that seemed like a full hour, he said he felt the pectoral fins twitching. We all looked closely. My dad stopped moving Rocky and sure enough, the fins on the side of the body twitched. He let Rocky go and slowly the body tipped over and sank listlessly to the bed of rainbow rocks in the base of the bowl, and what scant hope I had for Rocky went down with him. My dad picked him up again and continued the slow massaging ritual of rounding the bowl. I could swear I saw Rocky's lips move. Then his tail. This second time when my dad released Rocky, he flicked his tail fin and pectoral fins a couple times. I couldn't believe what we were seeing! Rocky was showing clear signs of life. His body then tipped over again and fell broadside on the rainbow rocks. My dad resumed the ritual, and we all stared in silent disbelief as Rocky started to twitch and kick more frequently in his fingers. He let Rocky go a third time, and this time, Rocky kept his body upright. He clearly had some life back in him. His fins moved and his tail twitched. We had a chance! Only now, he swam backwards as he moved slowly around the bowl in reverse. All three of us just stood there in stunned silence around the giant Zenith staring in awe at Rocky swimming backwards in his bowl. He stayed in reverse for the next three weeks until one day he just starting swimming forward again. After that, he lived another three years before he finally died of what I suspect was old age.

When I saw my dad bring Rocky back to life that night, I had no idea he had his own pets which he loved dearly and lost tragically in both childhood and adulthood. I didn't know that he watched a Studebaker run over Mitzy in the street right in front of him, and I didn't know that he fed Cocoa Dinty Moore beef stew from the palm of his hand as the heartworms tore away his insides and his will to live. I certainly didn't know the pain it caused him to lose those dogs. The same man who killed doves in his bare hands and gutted and cleaned all the many fish we caught together also possessed a deep well of tender love for his own pet animals. He did for me with Rocky what he couldn't do for Cocoa.

★ ★ ★

In the fall of 2011, my dad was invited to a college football game at his alma mater. Even though the Baptist College at Charleston rebranded itself as Charleston Southern University in 1991, it was the addition of a football team that solidified its legitimacy as an institution of higher learning in the South. CSU president Jairy Hunter invited him to watch a home game one Saturday afternoon. Up in the president's box with soundproofed windows, it was very difficult to follow the action of the game. People milled about talking, slapping backs, shaking hands, and eating catered food—seemingly more of a social event than a sports competition.

My dad, however, was more interested in the game, in which the Buccaneers were going head-to-head against the Stony Brook University Seawolves. He'd never heard of Stony Brook, but by halftime, he decided to take the elevator down to field level for a better view of the game. That decision is what landed him on an elevator at the very moment that US Congressman Tim Scott was riding it, too. Congressman Scott was a CSU alumnus as well—the class of 1988. My dad recognized him immediately and wasted no time.

"I'm Colonel Joe Tallon. I helped to get you elected." My dad reached out his right hand to shake the unsuspecting hand of the congressman, and he did not let it go for the duration of their brief conversation.

"I don't know if you remember, Mr. Scott, but I did the Pledge of Allegiance at a prayer breakfast event during your campaign last fall. I was in uniform at the time."

"Oh, yeah, certainly I remember you. Thank you for doing that."

"I supported the campaign to help you get elected and now I need help from a fellow Buccaneer."

"Thank you for your support, Joe. What can I do for you?"

"I've tried to get this accomplished for many years before with several other politicians, including your predecessor, and none of them have gotten it done. A tremendous wrong needs to be made right. After thirty-six years, I was finally awarded a Purple Heart, but my observer,

Daniel Richards, still hasn't received his. We were shot down together near Da Nang, Vietnam, and he was sitting right beside me in the same plane but died in the wreckage. Daniel's never been awarded the Purple Heart, and it's just not right."

"You're absolutely right. This sounds like something we need to get fixed. It will be taken care of. I will do it." At that, my dad released the hold on the congressman's right hand.

Congressman Scott then turned to his aide, who was the only other person in the elevator, and asked him to take down my dad's contact information. My dad gave him one of his retired business cards, and in less than two minutes, the elevator conversation was over. That was a Saturday afternoon. On Monday morning at eight thirty, my dad was a little surprised to get a phone call from Roger Yongue, Congressman Scott's aide. He requested the sworn statements and medical paperwork used to get my dad's Purple Heart. My dad happily provided the documentation that very day. Later that same week, Mr. Yongue called back asking him for a cover letter as Daniel's aircraft commander. Within twenty-four hours, my dad took the signed and notarized cover letter to the congressman's local office.

Over the next seven months, Roger Yongue kept him informed of progress as he ushered the paperwork through the bureaucracy. Eventually Mr. Yongue called my dad on an afternoon in May 2012 with a great deal of excitement in his voice. It was done. Daniel Richards's Purple Heart was approved.

My dad received in the mail from the congressman's office a copy of the official orders awarding the Purple Heart to Daniel Richards. Reading that document in his hands, he began to think about his final mission for the Army as being complete. The satisfaction of seeing a copy of the official paperwork was short-lived, however. He knew from past communication with the Army that he would have to be the one to locate Daniel's next of kin, and he had no idea how to get started on that search.

It had been forty years since the plane went down, and my dad had faint hope that Daniel's parents might still be alive. We knew that Daniel had a wife when he was killed at the age of twenty-three, but we did not know if he had any children before leaving for Vietnam. I joined the effort to search for Daniel's next of kin with my mom. We knew his birth date and social security number but little else beyond that. Our search began on the internet, which informed us that Detroit was Daniel's hometown of record. My mom activated a paid membership on Ancestry.com, and with access to its database, entitled *US, Vietnam War Military Casualties, 1956-1998*, she downloaded a report:

Name: Daniel Martin Richards
Birth Date: 21 Jun 1949
Death Date: 12 Aug 1972
Gender: Male
Race: Caucasian (White)
Home City: Detroit
Home State: Michigan
Religion: Roman Catholic
Marital Status: Married
Citizen Status: US
Death Date: 12 Aug 1972
Casualty Country: Republic of Vietnam (South Vietnam)
Casualty Type: Non-Hostile—Died of Other Causes
Casualty Reason: Aircraft Loss/Crash Not at Sea
Casualty Air: Fixed Wing Air Casualty—Non-Aircrew
Body Status: Body Recovered
Service Branch: Department of the Army
Component: Regular (RA, USN, USAF, USMC, USCG)
Military Grade: Specialist Fifth Class
Pay Grade: Specialist Fifth Class (US Army)
Province: Military Region 1—Quang Nam
Data Source: Combat Area Casualties Current File

I bristled when I read the line *Casualty Type: Non-Hostile—Died of Other Causes.*

In February 2013, I found a couple of online tributes to Daniel Richards on Vietnam Memorial websites. The posts showed that Daniel graduated from an all-boys Catholic high school in Detroit called Notre Dame, and he played football there. A photograph showed Daniel wearing a University of Wyoming football uniform, and this was news to us since we didn't know he had attended college before Vietnam. The names Ed Sera and Jim Mandl were attached to the postings. I tried to reach out to them through the websites but got no response. Both the posts were older, and the sites didn't seem to get much active traffic.

By April, my mom decided to use what little we learned online to launch a letter writing campaign. She drafted *To Whom It May Concern* letters to Daniel's Notre Dame high school alumni association, the local Detroit DAV chapter, the Saint Veronica's Catholic Church parish, the cemetery where he was buried, and the funeral home that handled his funeral. With a clutch of letters dated April 1, 2013, she drove to the main post office in the town of Summerville and entered its oyster tabby covered walls to mail the letters. Days passed, then weeks. We thought the correspondence was going to go unanswered. But then on the 17th of April, an email arrived in my mom's inbox:

> **We have received your letter, and I'd like to do everything I can to help. I know that Daniel is buried here next to his mother Arline. When Arline died in 1999, her next of kin was Leonard Herdzik. I am assuming that he was her brother. He has the same address as her. I would like to mail a copy of your letter to him to see if he is [1] still alive and [2] the uncle of Daniel. Please let me know, and I will mail the copy to Leonard ASAP.**
>
> *Lisa L. Curtis*
> *Office Manager*
> *Mount Olivet/Mount Elliott Cemetery*

This was the potential breakthrough we had been hoping for. Finally, we had a credible link to a next of kin. My mom immediately replied to Lisa Curtis encouraging her to send the letter forward to Leonard Herdzik. Lisa Curtis called the next day and missed speaking with my dad directly because he was off at the farmer's supply store purchasing seed and fertilizer. It was the spring planting season, and after forty years, he still got excited to mark out neatly lined rows in the freshly tilled soil to sow the seeds for a new garden. Ms. Curtis told my mom that Leonard "Len" Herdzik is a first cousin of Daniel Richards, and he was living in the state of Alabama. This same cousin had come to Detroit to organize the funeral for Daniel's mother. Ms. Curtis told my mom that she would call him first to see if he would be willing to talk to us before giving out his name and contact information.

Not long after Lisa Curtis's email, another arrived in my mom's inbox. This one was from Jim Mandl Jr. I recognized his name right off from the posting on the Vietnam War memorial site, though the Jim Mandl who wrote the online post turned out to be his father. The senior Mandl graduated from the same all-boys Catholic school Notre Dame in Detroit the year before Daniel Richards. Jim Mandl Jr. graduated many years later in 1990.

Hi Martha,

I received your letter today. I am going to do everything that I can to help you find the family of Daniel Richards. No promises, but I think if anyone can find them, I think we can. I will keep you posted. Thank you for writing to us.

Jim Mandl '90 NDHS
President, Notre Dame Alumni Association

Two more weeks passed, and my parents were concerned they'd hit an impasse with Len Herdzik. But then, Lisa Curtis called. She said Daniel's cousin Len was a Marine, and he remembered Daniel very well. She said he would be happy to speak with my parents. As she relayed this over the phone, Ms. Curtis began to cry. My mom and dad had tears in their eyes as they listened to her explain it. Finally we had located someone who truly knew Daniel.

When my dad hung up the phone that day, his initial excitement turned tepid. What would he say to Len Herdzik? Would Mr. Herdzik blame him for Daniel's death? My dad blamed himself, so why wouldn't the family blame him as well? He wondered if he could make Mr. Herdzik understand how hard he tried to get the plane back onto the airfield. He could explain that as the officer who gave classes on the Martin-Baker ejection system, he knew how dangerous it was to eject from an aircraft even in ideal speed and altitude conditions much less so slow and so close to the ground. It was exhausting my dad just contemplating the phone call. He went outside to till and water his garden, and he waited until the next day to make the call.

He picked up the phone mid-morning and dialed Len Herdzik's number. My mom took notes of the phone conversation.

"Mr. Herdzik, this is Lieutenant Colonel Joe Tallon. Lisa Curtis from Detroit referred me to you. How are you doing?"

"Good."

"I was the pilot on that last mission in Vietnam when Daniel was killed. It's taken over forty years, but I've finally gotten Daniel's Purple Heart approved."

"Thank you for your call. I heard from the funeral home in Detroit that you might be reaching out. Danny's mother was my godmother, and the family never got much information from the Army after it happened. They told us that it was an accident. We knew he had been burned, and it was a closed casket funeral. We didn't even know he had been in an airplane when it happened. We assumed it was in a plane crash, but we got very little official information. What really happened?"

"Our plane was hit by a missile in the engine on the right wing just after takeoff. We both ejected. I waited until Daniel's ejection seat charge went off before I pulled my handle. My parachute opened close to the ground. Daniel's did not open. I was knocked unconscious the moment that I ejected, so I ended up in China Beach hospital for nine days before getting shipped back to the States. The hospital staff wouldn't tell me anything when I asked about Daniel. It was days before men from my unit came to visit me and told me he was killed. I can't explain why I survived the ejection and he didn't."

"Danny was a big boy, a football player. Did his size have anything to do with the chute not opening?"

"The recommended weight limits on the seat were two hundred pounds. He'd been stationed in Thailand for a while and living in a hotel eating their food. He looked pretty heavy to me, so I questioned his weight before the takeoff. He told me he was two twenty to two thirty but losing the weight since he was back in the unit. He really wanted to go on the mission, so I didn't ground him. It could have been a contributing factor, but we were just really close to the ground at the time of ejection."

"When his mother passed away years ago, I got all of Danny's medals. Each year since then on August 12th, I take out the medals and do a little memorial service of my own."

"You're exactly who I've been looking for. I've wanted to find Daniel's next of kin who would care most about this Purple Heart. I'm so glad we've found you. I'm not sure what else you want to know. I can tell you his last words. After impact, he said, 'Sir, we've been hit in the number two engine.' To my knowledge, that's the last thing he ever said. I tried to get the Mohawk turned around and get back to the runway. I just couldn't do it, so I ordered the ejection."

Len Herdzik didn't speak. My dad remained quiet. The silence on the other end made him ache. Finally, my dad broke the silence and asked, "Are you still there?"

"This is just too much for me at one time. Please don't share this with the rest of the family. You're telling me stuff I've never heard before. I need to think about this a little while. I need a little more time."

They agreed to end the phone call and talk more when he was ready. My dad's eyes stung with tears of sadness and pent up anger. When I called him the next day to find out how the call went, I could hear the strain in his voice.

"Why did the Army withhold this information from the family? Who were they hiding this information from?" he said. "We knew we were shot down. Our unit on the ground knew we were shot down. The people who shot us down knew that they got us. What was the big secret?"

I had no answers.

"Well go ahead and put together that ceremony for the family like you talked about earlier to try and make it right for them," I said.

At first, my parents wanted to do a ceremony in the Herdzik's hometown in Alabama, but after exchanging a few phone calls with the Herdzik family, they mutually decided to have a Purple Heart ceremony on November 2, 2013, in the town of Summerville. My dad picked that Saturday because it fit into Senator Tim Scott's schedule. He was a busy new senator. The governor, Nikki Haley, had appointed Tim Scott to fill the open senate seat vacated by Jim DeMint, who left in late 2012 for the Heritage Foundation. When Tim Scott filled the seat in January 2013, he became the first Black American to represent a Southern state in the US Senate since Reconstruction. Later in May

2013, a special election was held for the congressional seat recently vacated by Tim Scott. Much to my dad's chagrin, the seat was won by the disgraced former South Carolina Governor Mark Sanford, who infamously had an affair with an Argentinian woman and tried to cover it up with a story of hiking on the Appalachian Trail.

About a month prior to the event, I called my dad to see how the preparations were going.

"We've got a nice room reserved at the old hospital building in downtown Summerville. It's in the county council meeting room. Tim Scott is scheduled to be there to hand out the Purple Heart and make some comments. Then we're gonna do lunch afterward at Oscar's right across the street."

"That sounds good. You guys love Oscar's."

"You know what—last week I got a call from Mark Sanford's office. They found the certificate and the Purple Heart medal when they were moving in so they called me about what to do with it."

"Well, what did you tell 'em?"

"I said to send it to Senator Scott's office, and I gave them Roger Yongue's name and number. They asked me if Mark Sanford should do the presentation. I told them no because Tim Scott has already put it on his schedule to do it. Then they said, 'Our office did all the work, so why shouldn't we do it?' I told them again that I reached out personally to Tim Scott about this, and he and Roger Yongue initiated this process for Daniel. The Senator's already got it on his schedule, so I don't know what the problem was with Sanford's people."

"Did you ask if the Congressman might be off hiking the Appalachian Trail on the day of the ceremony?"

"Ha, I guess I should have. Who knows if he'd actually show up or not."

"Who were you talking to?"

"I don't know. Some staffer. I didn't get his name."

★ ★ ★

On the Monday evening just days before the Saturday ceremony, my dad called me back.

"You will not believe the phone call I had today," my dad said, fury in his voice. "It was from Roger Yongue. I called him early last week to make sure he received the medal and the certificate from Sanford's office. He said he hadn't seen or heard anything from them yet. So he said he'd check on it with Sanford's people and get back to me. Then this afternoon he calls me back. Roger tells me that they don't have it."

"Who doesn't have it?"

"Sanford's office. Scott's office. Neither one of them has it! They shredded the damn thing! Can you believe that?"

"Who shredded it?"

"Somebody in Sanford's office. Roger Yongue wouldn't give me a name. I asked him for a name. I practically begged him for a name. He wouldn't say or didn't know. I was ready to go down there right now. Somebody needs to get killed for that. There's just no excuse for that. I cannot believe anyone would shred a Purple Heart certificate."

"What about the medal?"

"I guess they shredded that too. I don't even know how you shred a medal. Who in the world would even think to do something like that?"

I was floored. "What are you gonna do?"

"I have a copy of the official orders. I just don't have the official certificate. Roger's going to have to reorder that printed again and send it directly to the Herdzik family. I told him I'd take care of the medal. I can go over to the air base and buy one. I'm just so sick when I think about it. I better not find out who destroyed Daniel's award."

"Well, I can make a copy of your certificate and just read that. Except for the name, it should read exactly like Daniel's."

My mom and dad had worked and worried through the details of the ceremony. The program my mom created had a silhouette of the Purple Heart medal in the center. I had a copy of it in hand on my flight from Boston to Charleston, and I marveled at the simple beauty of the medal. I regretted that my wife and two sons weren't with me, but a baby and a toddler in the mix would have added an unnecessary layer of complication.

I was listed as the master of ceremonies. Before I opened the proceeding, however, a prayer, the Pledge of Allegiance and the National Anthem would come first. I was to introduce Jim Mandl Jr., the president of the Notre Dame High School Alumni Association. He was making the trip from the Detroit area to participate in the ceremony. I was looking forward to meeting him and hearing what he had to say about Daniel Richards. My flight landed on the afternoon before the event the next morning, so we had some time to game plan for the ceremony one last time.

My dad was so angry earlier in the week because of the shredding incident I was a little afraid to ask him about the status of the Purple Heart medal when I arrived. Turns out that he'd gone to the Charleston Air Force Base and purchased a Purple Heart medal from the exchange. Then he went to a local jeweler to have it engraved. Unlike the distinguished-looking blue soft-leather presentation case the Army sent my dad, the medal he purchased at the base exchange came in a cheap-looking blue plastic box.

"This is the case my medal came in," he said. "Seems right his family should have it."

I carefully pulled the medal out of the leather case. On the back, it read "FOR MILITARY MERIT SPC-5 Daniel M. Richards, 12 AUG 72" in neatly cut engraved letters. The jeweler had done a good job.

"He didn't even charge me for the engraving," my dad said.

As composed as my dad usually was, I could see the stress in his face. I was worried about him—his manner was off. He talked fast and then he would drop into silence. As we rehearsed the ceremony the day before, I realized there were times he didn't hear me or my mom. We would repeat ourselves and he would respond like it was the first time he'd heard it.

The two years it took to secure the medal for Daniel Richards and to track down his family had allowed him to channel his energy in a focused and positive way. But now that the culmination of the effort was upon him, I could see it was doing the opposite of what he intended. It was not bringing closure, but rather opening a wound of guilt that brought back his second guessing. There were many places to lay blame—the parachute riggers who may or may not have been too doped up to pack the gear properly, the Vietcong who fired the surface-to-air missile that brought them down, President Nixon and the policymakers for still having them there long after they promised to end the war, the weight that Daniel himself was carrying.

He blamed himself for not getting the plane back down on the runway. He blamed himself for not grounding Daniel before the flight. He just could not answer why he survived and Daniel Richards did not. He was anxious about the ceremony, but the prospect of meeting Daniel's next of kin—the Herdzik family of Alabama—

daunted him. He didn't know how they would receive him or this entire ceremony. He seriously questioned whether or not he should have turned this award presentation into a public event of any kind.

My dad was scheduled to make his comments in the middle of the program in a segment my mom labeled *The Last Mission*. I asked him if he wanted to review his presentation with my mom and me. I was not prepared for his response.

"I don't have anything ready. Not word one." He got up from the kitchen table where we were working and went to his recliner and sat down. "Just write whatever you want me to say."

My dad had begun the writing of this book by then. He had already written in detail about the August 12th crash. My mom and I dug in, culling the manuscript for the right words. We worked together on it the rest of the night, and I continued working and reworking it into the late-night hours. By morning, I had produced a detailed but concise description of the crash and the words to help him through.

As the master of ceremonies, my role was to maintain the momentum of the event. After Jim Mandl's speaking portion, I was scheduled to read a brief history of the Purple Heart medal followed by my dad's narrative of the night of the final mission. Once that was done, the last speaking part was reserved for Senator Tim Scott to commend the medal to the Herdzik family. I had conducted many award ceremonies over the years but never one so close to home. I knew how it was to run, and it was my job to run it well.

We arrived early Saturday morning to meet retired Air Force Colonel Jim Shumard, who had prepared some of the video montages to be used during the ceremony. Fortunately, a tech support member of the county council staff was on hand to help test and connect the audio visual. Jim Mandl Jr. came in shortly after us, and we greeted him with a handshake. He tested his files too—he had a lot of digital photos for his presentation. I really looked forward to Jim's part of the program since I only knew Daniel through my dad, which means I only knew Daniel's last two-plus hours on this earth. I knew precious little of what he was like before that final mission.

The Herdzik family arrived about fifteen minutes before our start time, and it was Paul and Fran Herdzik—the cousins of Daniel Richards and the brother and sister of Len Herdzik. Len, the man with whom my dad spent the most time speaking on the phone, could not make the trip out from Alabama. My dad was disappointed not to be able to see Len in person.

Just minutes before the ceremony was to start, two of Scott's constituent services representatives arrived to let us know that Senator Scott would not be present at the event. We had been tipped off the day before that the Senator's schedule might change at the last minute.

"Thank you for letting us know," my dad said. He was polite, but I could read the disappointment in his face.

We got under way with the prayer from a local county councilor, Larry Hargett, followed by my brother leading us in the Pledge of Allegiance, hand over heart. Then came a rendition of the National Anthem piped in through the room's audio-visual system in conjunction with a rousing *hooah* collection of patriotic photos assembled by Colonel Shumard. It set the stage for the event—more celebratory than solemn. As I walked up to the podium to assume my duties, I glanced at my dad. He absolutely loves formality, and we'd just hit a ceremonial trifecta to set the tone. What I couldn't tell was how the Herdzik family was responding.

I called Jim Mandl Jr. to the podium to make his presentation, and the ceremony zeroed in on its proper focal point—Daniel Richards, class of 1967. Jim had some photos displayed as part of his presentation, several of Daniel in football uniforms. In short order, Jim Mandl Jr. described the Notre Dame Wall of Fame, in which Dan, as he was known to his classmates, was prominently displayed. He was good enough to earn multiple offers to play collegiate football.

Jim (class of 1990) and his father (class of 1966) took the initiative to rescue the wall of fame plaques among other keepsakes when the school closed its doors permanently in 2005. In the subsequent decade, they systematically returned each of those plaques to those who earned them, except for the Dan Richards recognition, which stayed at Jim's house due to the unsolved mystery of the next of kin.

"Being a part of the Notre Dame family is a special brotherhood. Dan Richards may be gone, but like Notre Dame High School, he will never be forgotten by his Notre Dame family." The Herdziks then came up front to receive the wall of fame plaque from Jim Mandl Jr. as well as a Notre Dame varsity football letter.

I glanced at my dad before calling him to the podium. He wore his Army green class A dress uniform with all its medals and polished regalia. He sat straight-backed. I invited him up, and he appeared perfectly calm as he approached. He reached into his coat pocket and pulled out the two-page script my mom and I had prepared for him, but he opened off script.

"Those of you who know me know I'm a man of few words." That made everyone in the room who knew my dad laugh. He is a man of many words. Many, many words.

He started out by following the script and reading what was written on the page. It described the events of August 12, 1972, with acute detail. At one point, I could hear his throat closing up. He stopped talking. There was a long pause and I thought I would have to jump up and finish for him. I counted to three. Just as I started to make my move, my dad continued on. Then it happened again. Another long, uncomfortable pause. I readied again to jump to the rescue. But instead he stepped away from the prepared speech and told the story of the crash from memory. He stared above the heads of everyone seated in the room as if he were watching a movie projection on the back wall.

When he got to the part about Daniel's last words, *Sir, we've been hit in the number two engine,* everyone in the room was silent. My dad directed his attention to the Herdzik family. His voice was steady. "Even though Daniel and I had met just three hours earlier, we became blood brothers that night because we shed our blood on the same ground."

I returned to the podium, moving slowly, giving people time.

The last of the program was the awarding of the Purple Heart itself. The two constituent representatives from Senator Scott's office—Brian Goff and A.D. Jordan—came forward. Before issuing the award, they surprised us with a recognition certificate of their own. They apologized for the senator's absence and read aloud from a framed citation.

"This is to certify that a request was made and a flag was flown over the United States Capitol in honor of Daniel M. Richards, who made the ultimate sacrifice in service to our country. It is signed United States Senator, Tim Scott, South Carolina."

Then I requested Paul and Fran Herdzik to step forward. I called *attention to orders* and read the official Purple Heart citation.

"This is to certify that the president of the United States of America has awarded the Purple Heart, established by George Washington,

Newburgh, New York, 1782, to Specialist 5th Class, Daniel M. Richards, United States Army, for wounds received in action in the Quang Nam Province, Republic of Vietnam—12 August 1972. Signed on the 8th day of May 2012, by John M. McHugh, Secretary of the Army."

The Herdziks received the engraved medal in the blue soft-leather presentation case.

To complete the ceremony, my brother Josh came to the podium and recited a poem by Kelly Strong, "Freedom Is Not Free."

> *I thought, how many men like him*
> *Had fallen through the years?*
> *How many died on foreign soil?*
> *How many mothers' tears?*
> *How many Pilots' planes shot down?*
> *How many foxholes were soldiers' graves?*
> *No, Freedom is not free.*

The program closed with a tribute video to Daniel Richards showing pictures of him in Vietnam, ending with "Taps" played on an old brass bugle by Kisa Mayo, a member of the Summerville Baptist Church and a former member of the Summerville High School marching band. On the last sonorous note—"all is well, safely rest, God is nigh . . . "—I looked at my dad. He was standing at attention and holding a crisp salute.

Once everyone relocated to the Oscar's Restaurant across the street, the Herdziks shared stories of the man they knew as Danny. He had a love of fast cars, especially his 1968 Corvette. He was a talented football player and had multiple scholarship offers. He chose Wyoming, but he left after one year when he fatefully decided to return to Michigan to enroll in college closer to home. But before that happened, he was drafted into the Army. While on R and R, he got married. Six months later he was killed. The two families exchanged some friendly banter about the Crimson Tide and the South Carolina Gamecocks before the Herdzik family departed to make the drive home to Alabama.

★ ★ ★

Ever since I learned as a kid that the burn scars I saw on my dad were related to a plane crash, I've wondered. My dad certainly has some measure of survivor's guilt. I don't know what to call what I have. Given everything that transpired in 1972, I realize how unlikely it is that I was even born. Of the letters my dad wrote to my mom every day during his 104 days in Vietnam, there was this excerpt from one written on June 20, 1972, from Marble Mountain.

> Until now you have never said you wanted to have my baby. Maybe it is pride or something, but a man wants a son to carry his name. We have not seriously talked about children yet. I think we should have our children while I'm still in the Army, but we can wait. I don't want any children until we are both completely ready for them. It is a lot of responsibility and I want to be ready. I think this time alone will mature both of us a great deal.

I was born exactly seven years to the day after he penned that letter. It felt like something more than just a random coincidence when I read this letter for the first time forty-three years after it was written.

I don't know how one goes about measuring a hero. Growing up, my dad was my hero long before I knew anything about his experiences in Vietnam. He was larger than life to me. It seemed like there wasn't anything he didn't know how to do, or if he didn't, couldn't figure out. He had the answers to questions that I hadn't even thought to ask. We didn't embark on this narrative project together as an act of hero worship. We thought my dad had a unique story to tell, and we wanted to capture it as honestly as we could while his memory was still sharp.

Today, other than him, no one knows more about his Vietnam War experience than me. I still cannot tell you what it means to be a hero, especially in a war like Vietnam. My dad viewed men like Larry Dring and Duke Cunningham as heroes, not himself. My dad certainly had a naïve set of expectations when he got on the plane in Charleston to go to Vietnam. He was a righteous cowboy pilot ready to win a war. Some people view just surviving a war, especially the bitter end of an unpopular war, as heroic.

In my own life, I've studied both the Vietnam War and war in general quite intensely. I became an Army officer, and I taught high school history—both just like my dad. Maybe a large part of my life choices has been an effort to better understand him and who I am because of it. I didn't recognize the twenty-five-year-old man whose voice I read in those letters to my mom. He was different then. I certainly didn't think of my dad as someone who would have a crisis of conscience about the morality of warfare and seek out his professor for counsel. The man I know talks about killing and violence in such a nonchalant manner that it is unsettling to folks within his social sphere.

War changes people. I don't know if it unlocks something deeply repressed within or if it imprints something new on the psyche of its participants. What I know is the man I knew growing up was harder-edged, less forgiving, and more judgmental than the young man who wrote those letters. But also his enduring capacity to love his family through countless acts of kindness and to serve his church and veterans community with humility prove that a strong thread of positive optimism has remained in his heart these many decades after Vietnam could have totally broken him.

What I also know, though, is the quest to secure the Purple Heart for Daniel Richards that led to the ceremony that he made happen was one of my dad's finest moments. That was truly heroic action. For my dad, that was his end of mission.

ACKNOWLEDGMENTS

TO MARTHA ANNE, who holds the distinction of being both wife and mother and original English teacher to the authors of this book and who deserves the most credit for this story having a happy ending. Without her love and support, Joe's post-war recovery is not as successful, and Matthew's use of the English language falls short. Additionally, Martha Anne has the distinction of sending both a husband to war in Vietnam and a son to wars in Iraq and Afghanistan. She paid her dues in full long ago and has laid a few more generous deposits into an abundant account of sacrifice to see this book project to fruition.

To Susan Kammeraad-Campbell, editor-in-chief of Joggling Board Press and the first professional editor and publisher to believe in this project. You saw power and potential in our narrative and pushed us to add the letters and to go deeper. Thank you for believing in us and this story. We are eternally grateful.

To Becky Hilliker, editor at Köehler Books, for your expert eye for the details and the heart of our story. You know well the thrills and travails of being married to a military pilot, and you brought your passion for our story to each editorial decision. Also special thanks to the team at Köehler Books who believed in our project and worked hard to bring it to fruition: John Koehler, Joe Coccaro, and Kellie Emery.

To Staff Sergeant Hodge, Joe's Drill Instructor, who turned him into a soldier.

To all of Joe's flight instructors at Fort Wolters, Fort Rucker, Fort Stewart, and Fort Huachuca, who taught him how to fly both helicopters and fixed wing aircraft.

To Staff Sergeant Larry Dubose, Joe's motor sergeant and comrade in Vietnam, for his expertise in the motor pool and his skill as a chess partner.

To all the medical personnel who contributed to Joe's healing, starting with the famous but still underrated medical staff at China Beach 95th Evacuation Hospital to the medical staff at Brooke Army Medical Center at Fort Sam Houston and then critical follow-up surgeries and procedures at both Womack Army Medical Center at Fort Bragg and Walter Reed Medical Center.

To Captain Larry Dring, 5th Special Forces and recipient of six Purple Hearts and two Silver Stars from Vietnam, for his inspirational friendship and assistance with disability claims.

To Larry Richards, warrant officer and fellow burn patient, whose humor helped Joe endure treatments at Brooke Army Medical Center.

To Jimmy Edwards, Joe's hunting and fishing buddy in Fayetteville, whose support helped him to recovery in body and soul.

To the Herdzik family of Alabama, Len and Fran and Paul, for your warm embrace of Joe Tallon and your willingness to drive to South Carolina to share in a ceremony to honor your beloved cousin Danny. To Jim Mandl Jr. and the Notre Dame Alumni Association for caring to remember Daniel Richards enough to save his memorabilia and bring it to his family to honor his memory. To Lisa Curtis for connecting the families to help make right in 2013 what remained of what went wrong in 1972.

To those who helped Joe acquire a Purple Heart and the Purple Heart for Daniel Richards: US Congressman Henry Brown and his staff, particularly Earl Copeland, for their advice; and US Senator Tim Scott and his staff, particularly Roger Yongue, for their follow-through.

To Joe's sister, Lindler Tallon Bootle and her family: Lindler, for her proofreading and honesty; Joe's brother-in-law, Freddie Bootle, for encouraging Joe to stick out OCS; to their son Tim Bootle, for hand-carrying Joe's Purple Heart appeals packet to the White House staff; and to Martha Bootle for providing her photography skills.

To Joe's devoted friend, Commander Jack Olson, an encourager, a DAV co-volunteer, and a fishing buddy who knows how to keep fishing spots secret.

To the many authors who have read earlier drafts of this manuscript and have provided their input and inspiration: first to Greg Harris and Sandy Kaye, writing instructors at Harvard who shaped the first bits of this project in its infancy; to Christina Thompson, author and Harvard instructor for your wisdom and guidance; to Scott Kaple, consummate teacher and lover of the written word; to Stuart Albright, respected teacher, coach, and author with a keen eye for detail; to Matt Weber, beloved author and joyful loving spirit; to David Tannenwald, author and journalist of the highest order; to George Daughan, wise author who loves military history and loves our story; to Harry Castleman, friend and fellow fighter for conservation lands, for your helpful feedback on the manuscript; and to Kate Theriault and Ann Hardt Williams, classmates and authors who encouraged the earliest drafts to get better.

To Howard Yoon, an exceptional literary agent who took the time to read our manuscript and offer valuable advice.

To Sara Lawrence-Lightfoot, a beloved teacher and chronicler of the human condition, whose poignant portraits inspire generations, we appreciate your support for our project.

To H.R. McMaster, a general officer whose military career we admire and whose book on the Vietnam War inspired us, we appreciate your belief in our project very early on.

To Lieutenant Colonel Josh Tallon, a loyal son and loving brother to the authors and a family hero of multiple overseas deployments, we appreciate your love and support as well as that of your wife, Kristen, and your wonderful children.

Lastly, we finish where we began these plaudits: with insufficient accolades to a spouse. To Dr. Lindsay Alison Tallon, loving and supportive wife to Matthew, who has endured the decade-plus grind that brought this book project to fruition in countless hours of a missing partner sequestered away with the manuscript. Having birthed three sons and completed your own PhD during the course of this past decade, no measure of gratitude is sufficient to thank you for your steadfast love and support.

NOTES

Chapter Two: Standby

Staff Writers, "Adm. Rembrandt Robinson, 47; Commanded Flotilla in Vietnam," *The New York Times*, May 10, 1972, https://www.nytimes.com/1972/05/10/archives/adm-rembrandt-robinson-47-commanded-flotilla-in-vietnam.html.

Chapter Three: Leaving for Saigon

John Darnton, "Antiwar Protests Erupt Across US," *The New York Times*, May 10, 1972, https://www.nytimes.com/1972/05/10/archives/antiwar-protests-erupt-across-us-columbia-rally-ends-again-in-clash.html.

Robert B. Rigg, *How to Stay Alive in Vietnam: What it Takes to Survive in this Different Kind of War* (Harrisburg: Stackpole Books, 1966), 9-10.

Map 20: Easter Offensive March-May 1972, "The US Army in Vietnam from Tet to the Final Withdrawal, 1968-1975," in *American Military History Volume II: The United States Army in a Global Era, 1917-2003*, ed. Richard W. Stewart (Washington, DC: United States Army Center of Military History, 2005), 361, Accessible at https://history.army.mil/books/AMH-V2/AMH%20V2/chapter11.htm.

Chapter Four: In Country

Day 1:

Associated Press, "Before Deadline: 5 Ships Leave Mined Harbor," *Charleston Evening Post*, May 11, 1972.

United Press International, "Antiwar Protests Spreading," *Charleston Evening Post*, May 11, 1972.

Day 6:

DA NANG JULY 1970: Strip map drawn by Terry Cochran in 2008 on www.boomernet.com and used with his permission.

United Press International, "Wallace Shot, Badly Wounded, Spinal Damage Feared," *The News and Courier*, May 16, 1972.

Day 7:

"US Marines Land at Da Nang: This Day in History March 8, 1965," History.com Editors, accessed November 15, 2020, https://www. history.com/this-day-in-history/u-s-marines-land-at-da-nang

Day 13:

United Press International, "Nixon, Brezhnev Talk Privately," *The News and Courier*, May 23, 1972.

Associated Press, "US Planes Renew Bombing in North," *The News and Courier*, May 23, 1972.

Day 17:

Associated Press, "Offensive Missiles Frozen: Nixon Signs Arms Curb Pact," *The News and Courier*, May 27, 1972.

United Press International, "Communist Tanks Attack Kontum," *The News and Courier*, May 27, 1972.

Day 28:

Mike Feinsilber of UPI, "McGovern Wins in Four States," *Charleston Evening Post*, June 7, 1972.

United Press International, "US Planes Attack Hanoi Power Plant," *Charleston Evening Post*, June 7, 1972.

Associated Press, "US Rejects Demand to Return to Talks," *Charleston Evening Post*, June 7, 1972.

Day 30:

Associated Press, "B52s Hit Enemy Depots," *The News and Courier*, June 9, 1972.

AP Photo by Nick Ut used with permission from the Associated Press.

Day 31:

Peter Arnett and Horst Faas, AP Writers, "Vann: A Soldier's Soldier," *Charleston Evening Post*, June 10, 1972.

Day 32:

Carl D. Robinson, AP Writer, "Kim Phuc Recuperates in Hospital," *The News and Courier*, June 11, 1972.

Associated Press, "US to Shift Vietnam Units," *The News and Courier*, June 11, 1972.

Associated Press, "Churches' Board to Question US Role in War," *The News and Courier*, June 11, 1972.

Day 34:

Jack Leland, "Newest City is Chartered; Council Meets Thursday," *Charleston Evening Post*, June 13, 1972.

United Press International, "Reds Fire on Refugees," *Charleston Evening Post*, June 13, 1972.

Day 38:

United Press International, "US Jets Fly 340 Strikes Over North," *The News and Courier*, June 17, 1972.

Day 39:

Alfred E. Lewis, "5 Held in Plot to Bug Democrats' Office Here," *The Washington Post*, June 18, 1972, https://www.washingtonpost.com/wp-dyn/content/article/2002/05/31/AR2005111001227.html.

Day 41:

United Press International, "Hurricane Agnes Hurls Tornadoes into Florida: 13 Dead, 20 More Missing," *The News and Courier*, June 20, 1972.

Day 50:

Associated Press, "Nixon Slows Vietnam Pullout Rate," *The News and Courier*, June 29, 1972.

Associated Press, "Weyand Made Commander of US Forces," *The News and Courier*, June 29, 1972.

Day 52:

Arthur Higbee of UPI, "US Planes Soften Up Red Defense," *Charleston Evening Post*, July 1, 1972.

Day 59:

United Press International, "Two US F4 Phantom Jets Downed Near Chinese Border," *Charleston Evening Post*, July 8, 1972.

Day 63:

Associated Press, "Title Match Adjourned with Fischer in Trouble," *The News and Courier*, July 12, 1972.

Day 65:

United Press International, "Woman is Selected Democratic Chairman," *Charleston Evening Post*, July 14, 1972.

Associated Press, "Actress Denounces Bombing of Dikes," *Charleston Evening Post*, July 14, 1972.

Day 71:

Texts of Jane Fonda Broadcasts to US Servicemen: Committee on Internal Security, US House of Representatives, eds., *Hearings Regarding H.R. 16742: Restraints on Travel to Hostile Areas before the Committee on Internal Security in the Ninety-Second Congress, Second Session* (Washington DC: US Government Printing Office, 1972), https://archive.org/details/hearingsregardin1972unit/page/n3/mode/2up.

Day 84:

Carl Bernstein and Bob Woodward, "Bug Suspect Got Campaign Funds," *The Washington Post*, August 1, 1972, https://www.washingtonpost.com/wp-srv/national/longterm/watergate/articles/080172-1.htm.

Associated Press, "Kissinger Holds Another Secret Meet," *The News and Courier*, August 2, 1972.

Day 94:

United Press International, "Last Infantry Unit: Combat GIs Heading Home," *Charleston Evening Post*, August 11, 1972.

Day 95:

Arthur Higbee of UPI, "South Vietnamese Paratroop Unit Hit By Red Tanks," *Charleston Evening Post*, August 12, 1972.

Days 95-103:

Photo of Miss America 1972 provided by Mrs. Laurel Lea Schaefer Bozoukoff and used with the permission of The Miss America Organization.

Part III

Excerpt from poem entitled "Freedom is Not Free" is used with permission of author Kelly Strong, copyright 1981, kellystrong@aol.com.

CPSIA information can be obtained
at www.ICGtesting.com
Printed in the USA
LVHW031323240621
691050LV00006B/404

9 781646 632558